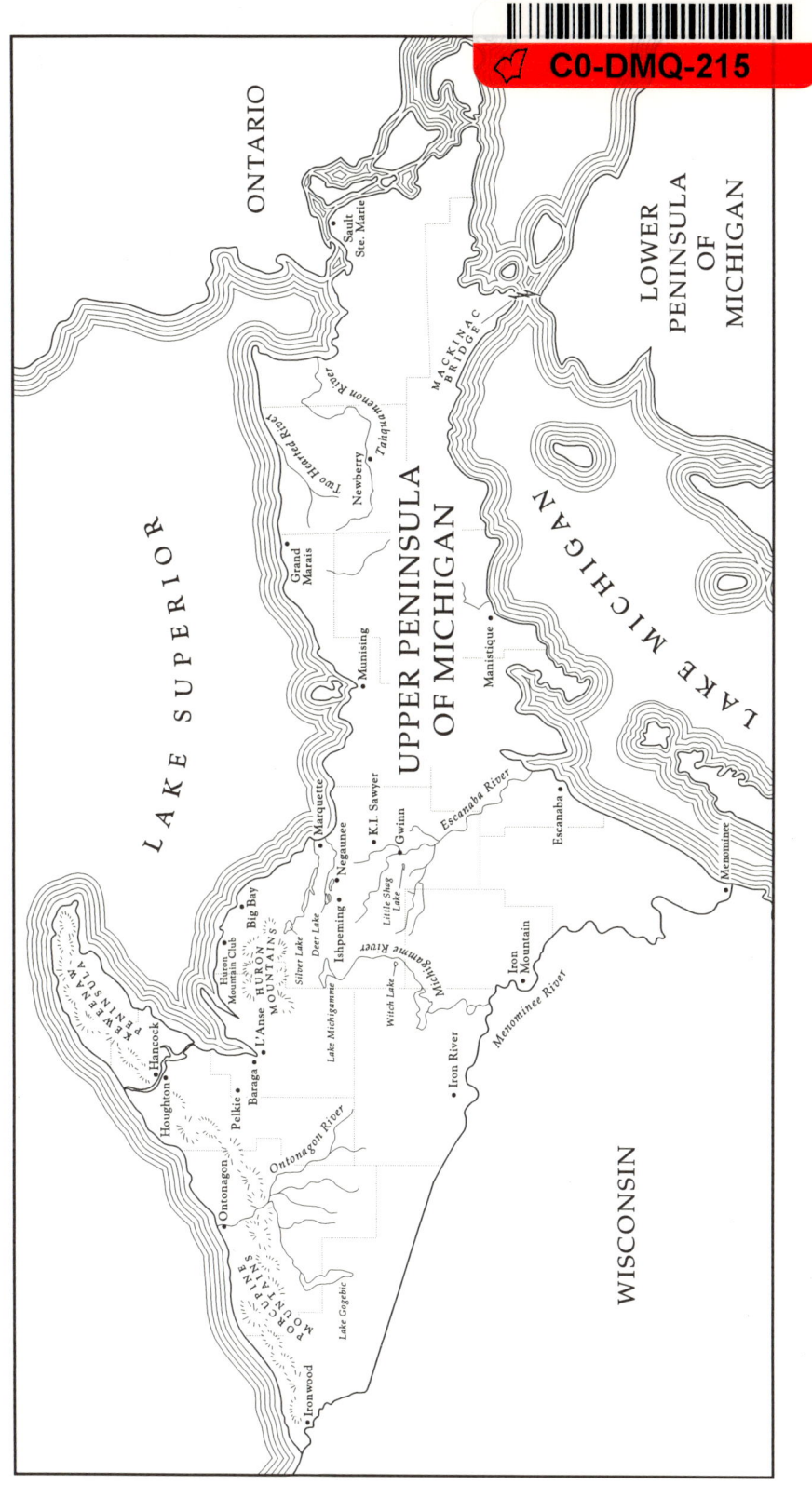

A Sense of Place
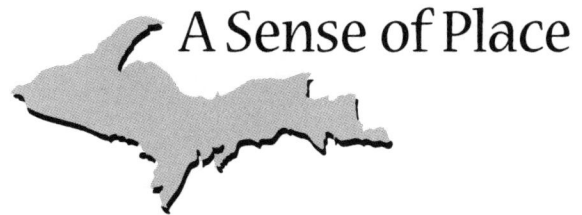
Michigan's Upper Peninsula

William and Margery Vandament

A Sense of Place
Michigan's Upper Peninsula

❧

Essays in Honor of
William and Margery Vandament

Russell M. Magnaghi
and
Michael T. Marsden
Editors

A publication of
Northern Michigan University Press
in conjunction with
The Center for Upper Peninsula Studies

Marquette
1997

PROPERTY OF
BAKER COLLEGE
Owosso Campus

A Sense of Place: Michigan's Upper Peninsula
Essays in Honor of William and Margery Vandament

© *NORTHERN MICHIGAN UNIVERSITY PRESS*
1401 Presque Isle Avenue
Marquette, Michigan 49855
1997

Library of Congress Cataloguing
Published 1997
Editors: Russell M.Magnaghi and Michael T. Marsden

Cloth cover: ISBN 0-918616-20-4
Paper cover: ISBN 0-918616-21-2

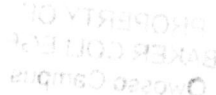

TABLE OF CONTENTS

Acknowledgments i

Preface
   Harold Enarson iii

Introduction
   Russell M. Magnaghi and Michael T. Marsden v

Culture
   The First Yoopers: The Archæological Evidence
      Marla Buckmaster 1
   Cultural Tracks: Finnish Americans in the Upper Peninsula
      Michael Loukinen 15
   Iron Mining and Immigrants: Negaunee and Ishpeming
      Judith DeMark 35

History
   Pre-Statehood Perceptions of Michigan's Upper Peninsula
      Russell Magnaghi 45
   UP Statehood Efforts Span Many Decades
      James L. Carter 77

Economy
   Crucial Crossroads: The Economy at Century's End
      Harry Guenther 89
   K. I. Sawyer: Wm. Vandament & Lake Superior Jobs Coalition
      James Collins and John Marshall 101

Foodways
   Foodways of the Upper Peninsula
      Russell M. Magnaghi 109
   The Cornish Pasty: Its History and Lore
      Russell M. Magnaghi 119

Literature
   Anatomy of a Murder
      Leonard Heldreth 135
   The Story
      John VandeZande 151
   Three Poems
      Philip Legler 154

Environment
   Living Farther North: A Year's Cycle
      Lillian Marks Heldreth 161
   Fly Fishing in the Upper Peninsula
      Earl Hilton 169
   Upper Peninsula Summer Camps
      Jon Saari 177

Research Collections
   The Losey Collection of Inuit & First Nations Art
      Eileen Roberts 197
   The Voelker Papers: Anatomy of a Collection
      Heather Sorensen and Gayle Martinson 213

Education
   Education for the 21st Century
      Glenn Seaborg 229

TABLE OF CONTENTS (Continued)

William & Margery Vandament
Introduction of Pres. Vandament on December 14, 1996
Robert "Buzz" Berube 241
Commencement Address, December 14, 1996
William Vandament 243
The Wit and Wisdom of William E. Vandament 251
Chronology of William E. Vandament's Career 253
The Peripatetic Life of Margery Vandament
Madonna Marsden 257
Contributors 263

TABLES
Finnish Americans by UP Counties 16
Education of Third Generation Finnish Americans 27
Canadian-US Trade 92
Sault Ste Marie International Bridge Traffic 93
Distances between selected US & Canadian Cities 93
Economic Strengths and Weaknesses of the UP 95

ILLUSTRATIONS
William and Margery Vandament .... frontispiece
Scottsbluff Points 4
Scottsbluff-Related Points 4
Eden Points 6
Side-Notched Points 6
Agate Basin and Hell Gap Points 8
The State of Superior 76
Statehood Poster of the 1970s 84
Peter White Punch 108
Pasty Time: Underground miners 118
Open Wide: The World's Largest Pasty 129
John Voelker at Work 134
Little Shag Lake 186
Saari Camp and Niemi Camp 189
Ash Basket and Corn Husk Dancer 199
Birch Bark Container and Tamarack Goose Decoy 200
Moosehide Gloves and Scrimshaw Owl 203
Shaman Dancer and Bear Mask 204
Voelker Display at Superior Dome 212
Voelker Law Office 215
Peterson Case Principals 218
Anatomy of a Murder Premiere 220
Abandoned Log Camp: Setting for *Danny and the Boys* 223
Nobel Laureate Glenn T. Seaborg 228
William E. Vandament 240
William and Margery Vandament, 1964 252
William and Margery Vandament and daughters, 1962 256
William and Margery Vandament, 1997 commencement 269

Acknowledgments

This publication was underwritten by the Board of Control of Northern Michigan University. With respect and gratitude, the editors thank the following board members who served during William E. Vandament's term of office:

Samuel S. Benedict★	Scott L. Holman★
Robert O. Berube★	Hugh E. Jarvis
Sandra B. Bruce	Barbara B. Labadie★
Mary L. Campbell★	Samuel Logan, Jr.
Richard J. Celello	Ellwood A. Mattson★
Daniel G. DeVos★	Ellen G. Schreuder
Leo F. Egan	Gilbert L. Ziegler★
Edward F. Havlik	

★member at time of publication

Special thanks to Karen Wallingford, Steve Hirst, and Madonna Marsden for their careful reading of the text.

Thanks to Eric Christiansen, John Kolehmainen, Anton Maki, and Dan Maki for information and assistance provided to Michael Loukinen for his article on Finnish Americans.

The material for Jim Carter's article on Upper Peninsula statehood comes from his book *Superior: A State for the North Country*. published in Marquette by Pilot Press in 1980.

Thanks to Marquette's resident food expert, Don Curto, for the insights offered to Russ Magnaghi for his Foodways piece.

In addition to contributing her own article on First Yoopers in this volume, Marla Buckmaster graciously allowed Eileen Roberts use of the Anthropology Lab's photographic studio to illustrate her piece on the Losey Collection.

The editors thank the Marquette County Historical Society, Marquette residents who shared their personal knowledge of events, Elizabeth Delene and Mrs. John D. Voelker for their comments—and the late John D. Voelker himself—for the background they made available to Leonard Heldreth for his article on *Anatomy of a Murder*.

The editors are indebted to *Marquette Monthly* for the parts of Lillian Heldreth's "Living Farther North" which which appeared previously in that magazine and for Madonna Marsden's "Peripatetic Life of Margery Vandament."

"The Wit and Wisdom of William E. Vandament" is excerpted from "Primer For Academic Administrators," published in *Change* (January/February 1989)

i

PREFACE

William E. (Bill) Vandament, late-blooming Yooper, will treasure these faculty essays commemorating his service to Northern Michigan University. After agreeing to serve a year as Interim President, Bill was implored to stay and now retires with honor after six years of service. In the twenty years that I have known Bill and his wife Marge—first at Ohio State where he served splendidly as my Vice President for Finance, later at New York University and the California State University System, and most recently at this University—never have I seen Bill and Marge so happy and fulfilled in their work as they have been at Marquette.

Very soon Bill came to like and appreciate the University—its students, faculty, staff, trustees—and the people of the Upper Peninsula. Accustomed, though not reconciled to working with large bureaucratic systems, Bill rejoiced (most of the time) in having his own show.

The Upper Peninsula, remote in the mental maps of most Americans and even of many Michiganders, became a source of surprise and pleasure to the Vandaments. This marvelously eclectic volume continues their voyage of discovery to a place which was almost part of Canada, which was almost a state, which rejoices in long cold winters, which prizes the legacy of its Finnish and Swedish forebears, which celebrates fly-fishing with the informed criticism that the Spanish afford bull-fighting, and which counts the pasty as its very own culinary treasure.

An aside: I was introduced to the tasty pasty by several NMU trustees when I hitched a plane ride to Detroit after giving a commencement talk in the wooden cathedral. They stopped to buy a sack of hot pasties to eat on the plane. Unfortunately, we had no spoons and these pasties were juicy. Styrofoam cups when broken create a moderately satisfactory spoon. Be proud of your improvising trustees.

In our years together at Ohio State, Bill became my trusted confidant and wise adviser on matters beyond finance. He was invariably my "point man" in explaining the need for tuition increases to skeptical student leaders. He was masterful in using plain English and homely examples to present highly complex financial data to our Board of Trustees and to legislative committees. His integrity bred trust; his candor inspired belief. In presentations to students, trustees, and the university senate, Bill was sophisticated about the human condition but never cynical. These attributes, I am sure, served him well at NMU.

In his "Primer for Academic Administrators" (*Change*, January–February 1989), he noted, "An important appointment or decision too easily gained will not endure. They'll eventually understand what you've done." Along with the other seventy-four aphorisms, this one invites reflection. It was, in a sense, an admonition to himself. Disciplined in analysis, affable, unflappable under fire, master of the gentle arts of persuasion, Bill was aware that guile in selling a decision risks a backfire. It was an option he rejected. Integrity, he knew, offers the only zone of safety for an administrator.

Respecting scholarship, he was realistic about individual scholars and about the faculty, noting in the Primer, "The faculty's customary role is to bury change, not to praise it."

He adds, "Nothing of significance should ever be done for the first time."

He also offers this observation: "With respect to general education, failure is an orphan. General education is an orphan. It follows: general education is a failure."

Eschewing grand schemes for academic reform, he recognized that the faculty owns the curriculum. It is theirs to improve, necessarily piecemeal, with encouragement and prodding from the President.

A psychologist by training, he was a self-taught expert on finance. Author of the excellent *Managing Money in Higher Education* (Jossey-Bass, 1989), he notes in the Primer, "There are more ways to steal from the university than your controller can imagine."

He further observes, "Overspending is not considered a serious transgression by many deans and the faculty they represent."

Finally he reminds us, "In a college or university all you have to work with is people."

Bill Vandament relished the job. And why not? Where else could a man of modest ability on the trumpet command, albeit briefly, captive audiences. Bill and Marge will be remembered as a team that, loving the university and the Upper Peninsula, served both well. This volume is part of their larger reward: knowledge of a job well done.

Harold L. Enarson
President Emeritus
The Ohio State University
April 1997

INTRODUCTION

Topophilia, or the love of place, is something all of us experience in various degrees of intensity for one or more important places in our lives. For most people, the place where they grow up retains a place of special affection in their hearts and minds. It is there that they were nourished and enriched by the landscape. But it is also possible for people who relocate to become very attached to the new environment and to draw renewed sustenance from this adopted landscape.

Such has been the experience of Bill and Margery Vandament, who, in the summer of 1991, relocated from sunny California to the human warmth of the Upper Peninsula. Their relocation was at first tentative and temporal—it was a relocation of the mind, not the heart. But that relocation soon became an extended stay and a love affair with the entire region. Bill and Margery not only accepted their new environment as they found it, they embraced it. In turn, they enriched it with their easy style and genuine graciousness. The water, the trees, and the terrain of the Upper Peninsula glisten in the seasonal skies and somehow both test and comfort those who accept the land as a companion in life. Such was the magical experience of the Vandaments in their adopted home of the Upper Peninsula. Margery, in fact, is said to have remarked to Bill on their return flight from Marquette following their initial visit that it was just like Camelot—they must have been dreaming.

And in many ways the Upper Peninsula is a state of mind, a dreaming while awake about the human experience with the land. This volume attempts to record some of the specialness of the Upper Peninsula, a region as distinctive as any in the United States and a fine laboratory for the serious student of regional culture. The settlement of the Upper Peninsula in the mid-nineteenth century built upon Native American foundations. The area provided ample opportunity for immigrants from all over Europe to bring with them a cultural diversity and history unmatched in the United States. Their diversity fostered a rich folklore, complete with regional story forms, folkways and foodways. Upper Peninsula residents learned to favor the tall tale which flourished in many an American frontier town and made it the essence of their humor.

The essays in this volume which explore this cultural specialness are presented as a tribute to Bill and Margery Vandament, who through their own openness to the Upper Peninsula encouraged such research and reflections. They are also a tribute to the people of the

Upper Peninsula who day after day allow all of us to enjoy their warmth, creativity, good humor, hard work, and cultural traditions as residents of a very special place. People of the Upper Peninsula are not isolated; they just honestly do not know why anyone would want to live anywhere else.

Russell M. Magnaghi
Michael T. Marsden
Marquette, Michigan
April 1997

A Sense of Place

Culture

The First Yoopers
The Archæological Evidence

Marla M. Buckmaster

Who were the first Yoopers? Were they French Canadians, Cornish, Italians, or Scandinavians? While all these ethnic groups were early historic residents of Michigan's Upper Peninsula, the honor of First Yooper is reserved for the Paleo-Indians, a term used by archæologists to identify the first human occupants in the New World. Most archæologists believe these early residents crossed over a land bridge which connected northeastern Asia and North America during the last ice age approximately twelve to fifteen thousand years ago.

Paleo-Indians built their homes, made tools, hunted, raised children, and died in a land quite different from the North America we know. Glacial ice still covered vast portions of Canada and the northern United States. As this ice receded, melt water fed a series of large glacial lakes covering vast portions of the upper Midwest. Mammoth, mastodon, and other large Pleistocene fauna roamed the Great Plains and adjacent lands. Because Paleo-Indians depended entirely on hunting and gathering for subsistence, they lived in small, widely scattered bands. Their possessions were few and their camps temporary. They left no written records and are known today by a meager archæological record.

Fortunately, their tools, particularly their projectile points, were distinctive. Their lance-shaped points were longitudinally channeled or fluted and executed with extraordinary workmanship on carefully selected raw materials. They were often ground along their lower lateral edges. These fluted points, as they are known, are found throughout much of North America. They are often exposed by erosion or by farmers tilling their fields. While usually recovered as isolated finds, they are occasionally found with other chipped stone tools. In the Great Plains and the American Southwest, they have been found with or occasionally embedded in the bones of large extinct Pleistocene mammals.

No one knows why Paleo-Indians fluted their early projectile points. It may have facilitated hafting (binding the point to the shaft), or it may have resulted in greater bloodletting on wounded animals. No matter the reason, it is a characteristic that disappeared approximately ten thousand years ago. After that time, projectile points, although retaining the same lance-shaped outline, excellence in workmanship, grinding, and careful selection of raw material, are stemmed rather than fluted. Although the point style changed, other early chipped stone tools as well as many aspects of this early hunting and gathering lifestyle persist in the archæological record. However,

1

archæologists recognize the stylistic difference in projectile points and refer to this period as Late Paleo-Indian.

While many individuals had speculated that Paleo-Indians lived and hunted in the Upper Peninsula, evidence to support these claims had eluded archæologists working in the dense second-growth forests of the Upper Peninsula. This evidence, however, was discovered in the early spring of 1987, when James Paquette and John Gorto, two former Northern Michigan University students and avocational archæologists, located a number of Late Paleo-Indian projectile points on the bottom of Deer Lake Reservoir. Aware of the significance of the find, they reported their discovery. Northern Michigan University's Archæological Laboratory responded. Using volunteers, the NMU archæological field crew battled a late spring snowstorm accompanied by strong winds, ice, and rain that left the site covered with more than two feet of snow to excavate two 2 x 2-meter test pits at the newly discovered Gorto site and documented the first evidence of Paleo-Indians in the Upper Peninsula. The excavation was ended when spring melt water began to refill the basin, which flooded the two excavation units.

A decade has passed since the unexpected find of these Late Paleo-Indian points. During this time, the university's Archæological Laboratory has focused attention on the central Upper Peninsula in an attempt to understand more fully the late Pleistocene/early Holocene occupation of this area by Paleo-Indians. This archæological attention has had mixed results.

The good news is that four distinct Late Paleo-Indian projectile point types are now extant from central Marquette County. By comparing these points with typologically similar points found in datable contexts in the Great Plains, one can develop a tentative chronological sequence. In addition, a small area of the Paquette site, located several miles southwest of Marquette, contains two separate and distinct early culture bearing strata. Finally, a large quartzite quarry has been located and a Carbon-14 sample recovered several feet beneath the surface in a 2 x 2-meter test unit.

The bad news is that no early sites have been found in locations suitable for excavation. The majority of the data comes from surface collections. Most sites are located in reservoir basins and found when water levels are unexpectedly low for brief periods of time. The assemblages recovered from the Gorto, Mesnard Quarry, and Paquette sites are exceptions. Unfortunately, none of these sites has provided anything close to an ideal opportunity for archæological excavation.

CULTURE: THE FIRST YOOPERS

Geology

The archæology of this early period is inextricably linked to the geology of the Upper Peninsula. The geology is particularly important in Marquette County, which embraces two distinct geological areas. The eastern portion of the county is low, relatively flat land, the result of successive water laid deposits, while the central and western regions of the county are dominated by the more rugged topography associated with the southern edge of the Laurentian or Canadian Shield.

Evidence of Paleo-Indians has been found only in the more rugged area of central Marquette County. This area begins several miles west of the city of Marquette and the Lake Superior shoreline. The land climbs steadily, and the rugged topography associated with the southern edge of the Laurentian or Canadian Shield is clearly visible as one travels west from the lake shore. Elevations in this portion of the county vary from fourteen hundred to approximately nineteen hundred feet above sea level. This entire upland region is dotted with numerous small lakes and is currently forested with dense second-growth forest. The Yellow Dog Plains are located immediately north of this area, while the Mulligan Plains form the east/northeast border of this area.

Ice from the Greatlakean substage, the last major ice advance of the Wisconsin Glacial Stage, covered vast portions of the Upper Peninsula, including central Marquette County. Farrand and Drexler (1985) indicate the uplands of central Marquette County were totally ice free by 8700 B.C. Carbon-14 dates obtained from lake sediments in the Michigamme Highlands, located immediately northwest of the study area, support this early date for the withdrawal of glacial ice from central Marquette County (Brubaker 1975). The rather recent discovery of a buried spruce and tamarack forest reported by Hughes and Merry (1978) in the Gribbon Basin, located in the study area, provides further chronological evidence of glacial activity. The forest, buried as a result of ice-marginal ponding caused by a glacial readvance, provides clear evidence of a later ice advance. The Marquette Stadial, the name proposed for this later ice advance, climaxed slightly less than ten thousand years ago. At that time, it is likely ice advanced southward as far as the southern edge of the current Yellow Dog Plains. Hughes, however, does not believe that it advanced into the rugged terrain of the study area. It is likely that melt water from a standstill of the Marquette Stadial located north of the Yellow Dog Plains deposited the outwash sands that formed this topographic feature, while the Mulligan Plains to the northeast of the study area were probably formed as a result of drainage from the Yellow Dog Plains (Hughes personal communication 1990). Although the Marquette

*Figure 1. Scottsbluff points recovered at the Gorto site
(photo courtesy of* The Wisconsin Archæologist*)*

*Figure 2. Scottsbluff-related points recovered at the Gorto site
(photo courtesy of* The Wisconsin Archæologist*)*

Culture: The First Yoopers

Stadial was responsible for creating some of the major topographical features surrounding the study area, it did not directly affect the rugged uplands of central Marquette County, which would have remained ice free. The retreat of the Greatlakean ice, variously estimated to have occurred between 9000 and 8200 B.C., therefore determines the maximum date for human occupation of central Marquette County.

Archæological Data

As previously stated, the first reported evidence of Late Paleo-Indians in the Upper Peninsula was found at the Gorto site. This site was discovered when Deer Lake Reservoir was drawn down as the result of a court-ordered environmental cleanup. Numerous Scottsbluff and Eden points and point fragments, often referred to as Cody Complex, were visible in the rocky matrix forming the Reservoir bottom in an area projected to be the shore of the original lake. Although a salvage program was begun immediately, weather, which included the two-foot spring snow storm, and academic commitments limited the time which could be spent at the site.

The initial surface collection of the site revealed several discrete concentrations or clusters of surface materials. Two 2 x 2-meter test pits were established and excavated in the area containing the largest and most dense concentration of surface materials. Work was nearly complete on these two units when spring melt water refilled the basin, flooding the site. A total of eighty-six points and point fragments exhibiting fine collateral to horizontal transverse flaking, lanceolate blade shape, and lower lateral edge grinding were recovered. It was possible to reconstruct and identify six Scottsbluff projectile points (see Figure 1 opposite) and eight Scottsbluff-related points that exhibited small basal projections or ears (Figure 2). Also recovered were two Eden (see Figure 3 next page) and four side-notched projectile points (Figure 4 next page). A majority of these points were believed to be manufactured from Hixton silicified sandstone, a raw material derived from Silver Mound in southwestern Wisconsin. The remainder of the points have been manufactured from quartz, chert, and an unidentified felsitic material. It should also be noted that only three of the points were complete when recovered. The remainder have been pieced together from fragments. Many of these fragments exhibit evidence they had been fractured by exposure to intense heat rather than by use. In addition, several of the fragments had been severely blackened and discolored by exposure to fire.

The partial outline of a circular feature was identified during the excavation of the two adjacent test pits. Soil differences only partly

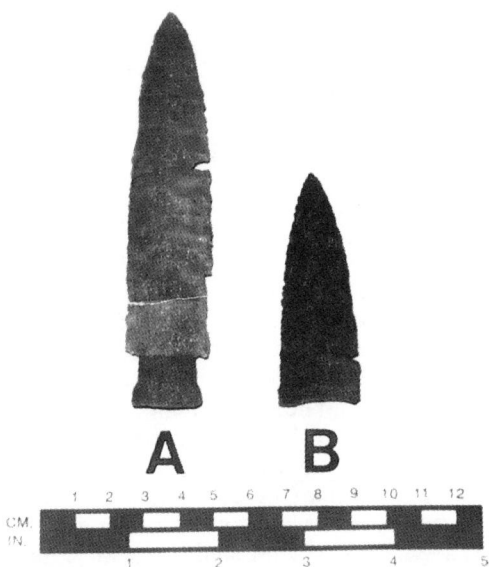

*Figure 3. Eden points recovered at the Gorto site
(photo courtesy of* The Wisconsin Archæologist*)*

*Figure 4. Side-notched points recovered at the Gorto site
(photo courtesy of* The Wisconsin Archæologist*)*

identified this feature in plan view. However, the feature was further identified by plotting the recovered points and point fragments. The resulting distribution identified a concentration of material associated with the slightly more sandy matrix of the feature and suggested the feature measured approximately 180 cm in diameter. In addition, two post molds were identified in the feature. Although no charcoal or burned bone was recovered during the excavation of these two test units, this feature has tentatively been interpreted as a cremation (Buckmaster and Paquette 1988).

While work proceeded on the Gorto site, several other sites were located within Deer Lake Basin. Caven Clark (1989) reported on the material collected from these sites. The presence of Hixton silicified sandstone and a number of early tool types, including a Scottsbluff projectile point, bifacial knives, and scrapers in the combined assemblages, led him to suggest many of these sites also have an early cultural affiliation.

Since finding these early sites at Deer Lake, efforts have been focused on locating additional sites within central Marquette County. These efforts have been hampered by several factors. A dense second-growth forest covers most of this region of the Upper Peninsula. There has been limited development, including farming, in this area that might expose sites, and access into and through the area is difficult.

However, during the summer of 1988, an unusual opportunity to explore Silver Lake Reservoir Basin presented itself. The drought that plagued most of North America also had a significant impact on the Upper Peninsula. Water levels dropped by as much as eighteen inches in the Lake Superior Basin. Throughout the central Upper Peninsula, reservoirs were drawn down to regulate stream flow for hydro-electrical plants. By late August, water levels reached unprecedented lows in Silver Lake Basin, exposing portions of the original lake shore. Unhampered by forest cover, volunteer field personnel located eleven sites. Two of these sites produced additional Cody Complex material. The base and shoulder portion of a Scottsbluff projectile point was collected from the Silver Lake Dam site. The stem of this point expands slightly at the base, forming the "ears" associated with Great Lakes Cody Complex. Silver Lake #4 also produced the base of a Scottsbluff projectile point.

Silver Lake #3 is the find spot of a single lanceolate projectile point. The point, manufactured from what is believed to be Hixton silicified sandstone, is a rather broad bladed lanceolate with contracting lower edges that are heavily ground. Careful inspection of these lower lateral edges reveals the presence of a stem and slight shoulder similar to the basal constrictions and shouldering displayed on Hell Gap points. Although this distinctive trait is not as pronounced on

A Sense of Place: Michigan's Upper Peninsula

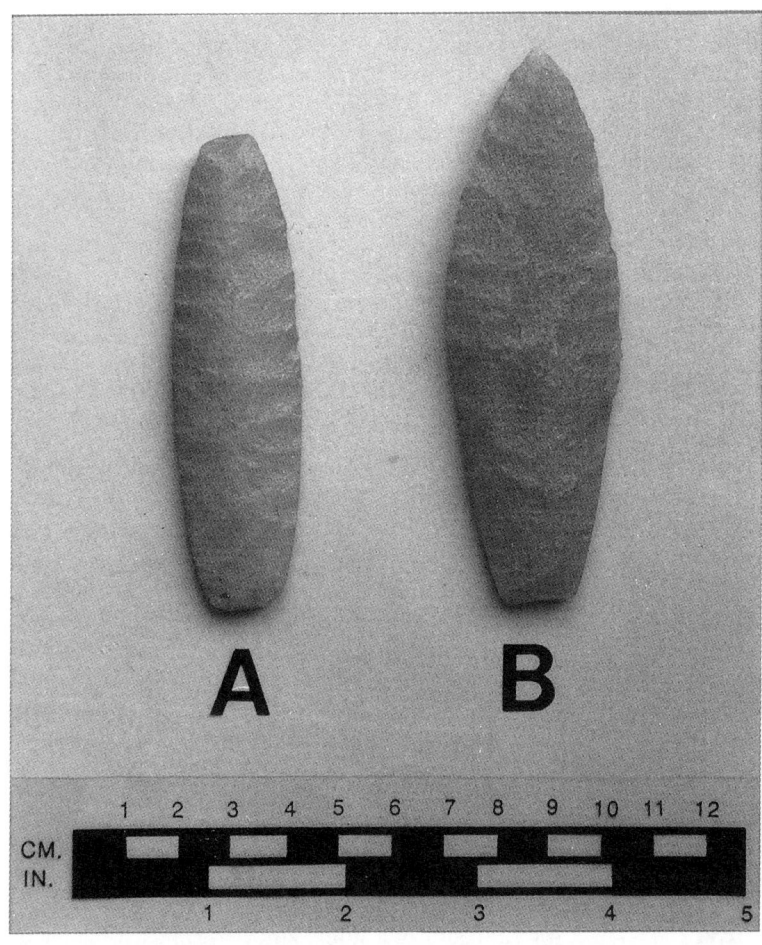

Figure 5. Agate Basin points recovered from Silver Lake #11 (A) Hell Gap points recovered from Silver Lake #3 (B) (photo courtesy of The Wisconsin Archæologist*)*

CULTURE: THE FIRST YOOPERS

the Silver Lake specimen as it is on some of the Hell Gap points described by Frison and Stanford (1984) and Morrow (1984), this particular point shares such close structural and technological affinities with the Hell Gap points from the Casper site (Frison 1974) and the Jones-Miller site (Stanford 1978) that there is little doubt the specimen is a product of this cultural complex (see Figure 5 opposite).

Silver Lake #11 is also the find spot of a single projectile point. This point, manufactured from Hixton silicified sandstone, is an Agate Basin point. The point exhibits well executed collateral to horizontal transverse flaking with fine marginal retouch. The point had been resharpened. In addition, examination of the blade revealed evidence that it had been further modified before it was abandoned. The distal end had been altered to form a narrow, chisel-like bit which is heavily abraded and polished from use (see Figure 5 opposite).

Several other sites at Silver Lake provide evidence of continued occupation of this area through the Early Archaic, the time period following Late Paleo-Indian. This evidence includes a variety of early notched projectile points with thinned and/or concave bases that in many cases had been ground. At least one of these points clearly resembles a Kirk Corner Notched point (De Regnaucourt 1992). Other evidence of the Early Archaic includes a trihedral adz and a variety of scrapers and drills manufactured from Hixton silicified sandstone.

Unfortunately, none of this material has been found in a datable context. However, the discovery of four distinct Late Paleo-Indian projectile points, which are widely recognized as prehistoric time markers, allows us to begin formulating a working chronological sequence of early human occupation in the central Upper Peninsula of Michigan. This sequence, however, relies entirely on typological counterparts and dates from the Great Plains.

The recovery of an Agate Basin point extends the known distribution of this point type into the Upper Peninsula. This point type, like the other early point types mentioned in this paper, has not been found in an easily datable context in the Upper Great Lakes Region. Salzer (1974) cautiously dated Agate Basin-like materials, known as the Flambeau Phase materials from the North Lakes region of Wisconsin, as approximately nine thousand years old. Since the publication of Salzer's report, archæological data recovered from numerous sites on the High Plains suggest this initial estimate of the age for the Flambeau Phase/Agate Basin-related materials could be as much as one thousand years late. Stratigraphic evidence and radiocarbon dates from various sites on the Plains (Irwin-Williams et al. 1973, Frison 1978, Frison and Stanford 1982, Shelley and Agogino 1983) suggest that Agate Basin is currently the earliest Paleo-Indian projectile point recognized in the Upper Peninsula and may indicate occupation of the central Upper Peninsula prior to or immediately after the advance of the Marquette Stadial at slightly less than ten thousand years ago.

The recovery of a Hell Gap point very similar to those found on the Plains offers supporting evidence for this early occupation of the study area. Investigations at the Casper site (Frison 1974), the Jones-Miller site (Stanford 1978), the Carter-Kerr McGee site (Frison 1977), and the Agate Basin site (Frison and Stanford 1982) have provided important data regarding the relationships between Hell Gap and Agate Basin projectile points. Information from these sites not only strengthens early arguments favoring a direct lineal relationship between these two early point traditions but appears also to indicate they were at least partly contemporaneous and again suggests the possibility the Upper Peninsula could have been inhabited during or immediately after the Marquette Stadial.

The identification of Scottsbluff and Eden projectile points or Cody Complex materials at sites on both Silver Lake and Deer Lake documents a strong presence of this Late Paleo-Indian manifestation in the central Upper Peninsula. Unfortunately, like earlier Late Paleo-Indian point types, Great Lakes Cody points have not been found in a clearly datable context. Numerous radiocarbon dates are available for Cody components on the High Plains. A compilation of this data suggests dates of circa 9,200 to 8,600 years ago for this complex and suggest that the makers of the Scottsbluff and Eden projectile points at Deer and Silver Lakes may have occupied the area shortly after the last remnants of the Marquette ice sheet had melted away.

Two other sites deserve mention in this discussion of the early prehistory of central Marquette County. The first, the Paquette site, is a large site which produced a lithic assemblage somewhat reminiscent of the materials reported from the Sheguiandah site, located near the north shore of Lake Huron. Like Sheguiandah, the Paquette site produced a variety of quartzite tools, including large bifaces, choppers, cores, and large unifacially retouched flakes. A number of anvils and very battered hammerstones were also recovered. Unfortunately, both historic and contemporary use of the area had disturbed most of the site. Undisturbed deposits were found only on a small terrace overlooking Goose Lake. Test pits located on this terrace produced a number of small, steeply retouched chert scrapers in association with debitage (chipping debris) dominated by local quartzites. These materials were concentrated in two distinct, culture-bearing strata separated by as much as 15 cm of sterile sand. The presence of an encrustation of iron-cemented sand on the lithic materials from the lower level but not on the materials from the upper level suggest a significant chronological separation of the two strata. A single point with shallow side notches and a lanceolate blade and a drill were recovered from the site by James Paquette. Although this assemblage most closely resembles the material collected from Sheguindah and other early sites from the north shore of Lake Huron, detailed comparison of the assemblages is complicated by the lack of a comprehensive report on these north shore sites. There is, however, a Carbon-14 date of 9,130 years ago from the basal portion of a peat formation overlying an artifact-bearing stratum, which suggests a date for these materials.

Finally, some mention of the Mesnard site, a large quartzite quarry located within the city limits of Marquette, is necessary. A controlled surface collection in 1991 recovered biface fragments, cores, hammerstones, and considerable debitage, some of which is difficult if not impossible to distinguish visually from Hixton silicified sandstone. The following summer, several 2 x 2-meter test units were excavated on a terrace overlooking Lake Superior. A single feature was identified in unit 2. This feature had an amorphous outline and an irregular bottom. The feature had a total depth of 30 cm and extended 30 to 60 cm below the surface. It contained numerous small flakes of Mesnard Quartzite and charcoal. The recovered charcoal was divided into two samples. The first was sent to Beta Analytic, Inc. in Florida and dated at 5,280 years ago. The second sample was sent to WRC Radiocarbon Laboratory in Nevada and dated at 5,270 years ago. It is important to note that cultural material continued well below the feature. The team was still recovering debitage in level 14 seventy-five centimeters below the surface when the season ended, making it necessary to backfill the unit.

Conclusions

At this point, archæological research in central Marquette County has been able to document the presence of four distinct Late Paleo-Indian points representing three recognized Late Paleo-Indian stages as well as an artifact assemblage that resembles artifacts found on the north shore of Lake Huron. However, none of this data has been recovered under anything close to ideal circumstances. As a result, except for the single Carbon-14 date from the Mesnard quarry site, one is limited to typological comparisons with Late Paleo-Indian materials from the Great Plains for possible dates. If these dates are similar in the two areas, then portions of the central Upper Peninsula could have been occupied during or immediately after the Marquette Stadial by Paleo-Indians, giving them claim to the title "First Yoopers."

Bibliography

Agogino, George A. "A New Point Type From Hell Gap Valley, Eastern Wyoming." In *American Antiquity 26* (1961), 558–560.

Brubaker, Linda B. "Post Glacial Forest Patterns Associated with Till and Outwash in Northcentral Upper Michigan." In *Quaternary Research 54* (1975), 499–527.

Buckmaster, Marla, and Paquette, James. "The Gorto Site: Preliminary Report on a Late Paleo-Indian Site in Marquette County, Michigan." In *The Wisconsin Archæologist 69(3)* (1988), 101–124.

Clark, Caven P. "Plano Tradition Lithics from the Upper Peninsula of Michigan." In *The Michigan Archæologist 35(2)* (1989), 88–112.

DeRegnaucourt, Tony. *A Field Guide to the Prehistoric Point Types of Indiana and Ohio, Occasional Monographs of the Upper Miami Valley.* Ansonia, Ohio: Archæological Research Museum, 1992.

Drexler, Christopher W., Farrand, William R., and Hughes, John D. "Correlation of Glacial Lakes in the Superior Basin with Eastward Discharge Events from Lake Agassiz." Ed. J. T. Teller and Lee Clayton. In *Glacial Lake Agassiz*. Geological Association of Canada Special Paper 26, 1983, 309–329.

Ellis, Chris J., and Deller, D. Brian. "Post-Glacial Lake Nipissing Waterworn Assemblages from the Southeastern Huron Basin Area." In *Ontario Archæology* 45 (1986), 39–60.

_____. "Paleo-Indians. The Archæology of Southern Ontario to A.D. 1650." In *Occasional Publications of the London Chapter*. Ed. Chris Ellis and Neal Ferris. Ontario Archæology Society 5, (1990), 37–63.

Farrand, William R. and Drexler, Christopher W. "Late Wisconsin and Holocene History of The Lake Superior Basin." In *Quaternary Evolution of the Great Lakes*. Ed. P. F. Karrow and P. E. Calkin. Geological Association of Canada Special Paper 30, 1985, 17–32.

Frison, George C. *The Casper Site: A Hell Gap Bison Kill on the High Plains.* New York, NY: Academic Press, 1974.

_____. *Prehistoric Hunters of the High Plains.* New York, NY: Academic Press, 1978.

Frison, G. C. and Stanford, D. *The Agate Basin Site: A Record of the Paleo Indian Occupation of the Northwestern High Plains.* Ed. G.C. Frison and D. Stanford. New York, NY: Academic Press, 1982.

CULTURE: THE FIRST YOOPERS

Hawke, Richard. *A Guide to Rocks and Minerals of Michigan.* Midland, MI: Dick Hawke Science Service, 1981.

Hughes, V. D. and Merry, W. J. "Marquette Buried Forest 9,850 Years Old" (Abstract): *American Association for the Advancement of Science*, National Meeting, 144th Annual Meeting, Washington, D.C. File, 12–17, 1978.

Irwin-Williams, Irwin, C. H., Agogino, G. and Haynes, C. V., Jr. "Hell Gap: Paleo-Indian Occupation on the High Plains." In *Plains Anthropologist 18* (59) (1973), 40–53.

Mason, Ronald J. "The Paleo-Indian Tradition." In *Introduction to Wisconsin Archæology.* Ed. William Green, James B. Stoltman, and Alice B. Kehoe. The Wisconsin Archæologist 1986 #67 (3–4):181–206.

Mason, Ronald J. and Irwin, Carol, "An Eden-Scottsbluff Burial in Northeastern Wisconsin." In *American Antiquity 26* (1960), 43–57.

Morrow, Toby A. *Iowa Projectile Points.* Iowa City, IA: The University of Iowa. Special Publication of the Office of the State Archæologist, 1984.

_____. "Great Lakes Cody: A Case Study of Interaction Among Early Holocene Hunter-Gatherers" (unpublished manuscript).

Salzer, Robert J. "The North Lakes Project: A Preliminary Report. Aspects of Upper Great Lakes Anthropology." In *Minnesota Prehistoric Archæology Series 11* Ed. E. Johnson. 1974, pp. 40–54.

Shelley, Phillip H. and Agogino, George. "Agate Basin Technology: An Insight." In *Plains Anthropologist 28* (1983), 115–118.

Stanford, Dennis. "The Jones-Miller Site: An Example of Hell Gap Bison Procurement Strategy." In *Bison Procurement and Utilization: A Symposium.* Ed. Leslie B. Davis and Michael Wilson. *Plains Anthropologist 23*, 1978, 90–97.

Voss, J. "The Barnes Site: Functional and Stylistic Variability in a Small Paleo-Indian Assemblage." In *Mid-Continental Journal of Archæology 2* (1977).

A Sense of Place: Michigan's Upper Peninsula

CULTURAL TRACKS
Finnish Americans in Michigan's Upper Peninsula
Michael M. Loukinen

Due to its remarkable geographical isolation, Michigan's Upper Peninsula, the "UP," has remained a well-kept secret. Surrounded on three sides by lakes Superior, Michigan, and Huron, the UP had long remained inaccessible. After 1900, railroads finally forged economic and passenger links through Wisconsin; yet only when the seven-mile Mackinac Bridge was completed in 1957 did a more sustained degree of cultural contact occur between UP residents and the rest of the nation. It is a wilderness area still approximately 85 percent forested. People work in mining, forestry, commercial fishing, farming, tourist services, universities, hospitals, and clinics. New growth industries are Indian gambling casinos and prisons.

The UP has always been a tough place to make a stand. It is known for its endless winters with gloomy gray skies, deep burrowing black flies, mosquitoes, ticks, bone-breaking ice under a thin snow powder cover, and white-outs in the passing lanes. Children's boots and mittens are put on and taken off in a cycle of perpetual motion that is rumored to give kindergarten teachers a regionally specific carpal-tunnel syndrome. Wages and population density have something in common: They are low. Some of the counties are so sparsely populated that they come close to Frederick Jackson Turner's definition of the American Frontier that was supposed to have ended by 1890—fewer than two persons per square mile. In virtually all UP counties, deer outnumber people. Nevertheless, those who stay—and many who had to leave to find careers—maintain a profound love for this place.

Strange things happen in the UP that make headlines elsewhere. An Ann Arbor newspaper reported during the week of June 16, 1996 that a tourist had to explain to an Avis clerk in Detroit why he should not be charged for the damage to his rental car when an eagle landed an eight-pound sucker on his roof, leaving an impressive dent. That same week, a retiree stepped out of his morning shower to find a doe crashing through his picture window. Grabbing a butcher knife, he wrestled the dazed animal through the hallway into the living room where the craziness ended in a pool of blood. This land is different, and its people are different.

A distinctive feature of this region is that one of the smallest of the Euro-American ethnic groups in America is one of the largest ethnic groups in the UP. Americans reporting Finnish Ancestry in the 1990 United States Census totaled 658,870, about three-tenths of one percent of the national population. In the UP, the corresponding figure was 51,214 persons, amounting to 16.3 percent of the UP's population of 313,915 people. Hence, the proportion of Finnish Americans in the UP stands over fifty times their proportion in the nation as a whole. Finnish Americans in the UP are concentrated primarily in the north-central and northwestern counties, starting from Marquette County westward along the southern shore of Lake Superior. As one moves west, the proportion of Finnish Americans increases; in Marquette County 22.1 percent are Finnish Americans; in Baraga County, 34.6 percent; and in Keweenaw county the proportion increases to 49.9 percent.

Table 1. Finnish American Ancestry by UP Counties, 1990

Up Counties	Total Population	Finnish Ancestry Population	Percent Finnish Ancestry
Alger	8,972	1,478	16.5%
Baraga	7,954	2,752	34.6%
Chippewa	34,604	1,485	4.3%
Delta	37,780	2,038	5.4%
Dickinson	26,831	1,719	6.4%
Gogebic	18,052	5,155	28.6%
Houghton	35,446	13,199	37.2%
Iron	13,175	2,091	15.9%
Keweenaw	1,701	848	49.9%
Luce	5,763	416	7.2%
Mackinac	10,674	294	2.8%
Marquette	70,887	15,663	22.1%
Menominee	24,920	539	2.2%
Ontonagon	8,854	3,282	37.1%
Schoolcraft	8,302	255	3.1%
Totals	313,915	51,214	16.3%

These 51,214 Finnish Americans in the UP are actually nested in a regional "Sauna Belt" stretching from the north central UP around the western shore of Lake Superior to include another 8,177 Finnish Americans in the five northernmost counties in Wisconsin and 41,533 in five counties of northwestern Minnesota. Historically, the UP has been and still is the nation's primary settlement area for Finnish Americans, and they have left their cultural tracks on the region.

Folklorist Richard Dorson came to the UP in 1946 to interview ethnic storytellers and noticed the strong cultural presence of the Finns. He wrote in his classic *Blood Stoppers and Bear Walkers*:

CULTURE: FINNISH AMERICANS

The coming of the Finn has rocked the north woods country. He is today what the red man was two centuries ago, the exotic stranger from another world. In many ways the popular myths surrounding the Indian and the Finn run parallel. Both derive from a shadowy Mongolian stock—'just look at their raised cheek-bones and slanting eyes.' Both possess supernatural stamina, strength, and tenacity. Both drink feverishly and fight barbarously. Both practice shamanistic magic and ritual, drawn from a deep well of folk belief. Both are secretive, clannish, inscrutable, and steadfast in their own peculiar social code. Even the Finnish and Indian epics are supposedly kin, for did not Longfellow model 'The Song of Hiawatha' on the form of the Kalevala?

But where the Indians lost, the Finns have won the Peninsula. Streaming into America after the Civil War, Finns today live in every northern state from Massachusetts to Oregon but cluster most thickly in Michigan and Minnesota. Michigan has more Finns than any other state—63,671, and four-fifths of them live in the Upper Peninsula. (Dorson 1952:122)

Between 1880 and 1920 in rural Finland, life was difficult for the many landless people. Rapid population growth among the rural poor, technological and crop changes that reduced the need for farm labor, the breakdown of the traditional labor exchange and bartering system, and the periodic threat of starvation left only a few bad choices for them. One could starve, work long hours for meager benefits in a sharecropping-like arrangement with a rich, often authoritarian farmer, join a movement to overthrow the exploiting system, migrate to a Finnish city where many were unemployed, or emigrate to America (Kolehmainen 1951:3-21). When they emigrated, they were often accused by religious and political authorities of being unpatriotic (Hoglund 1977). Hence, a considerable number of immigrants carried a deep, life-long resentment toward the rich, the church, and the state. Nevertheless, most emigrated with the intention of earning enough money to return to Finland to buy a farm. A farm signified more than a way to make a living; it expressed a strong psychic attachment to ancestral landscapes blended with meadows, lakes, rivers, and forests.

The first traces of Finnish immigration to the UP began in 1864 when a copper mining consortium recruited a dozen or more Finns who had been working as miners in northern Norway. Many of these miners had been inspired by the charismatic botanist-ethnographer-preacher, Lars Levi Laestadius, who preached hard-core remorse and personal repentance within the congregation and urged separation from the world of alcohol, card play, and fleshly mire. Descendants of this group are found throughout the UP, with their largest congregation being the Old Apostolic Lutheran Church in Hancock, Michigan.

These miners had an unusually high literacy rate, and their numerous letters to friends and relatives in their rural villages in Finland telling of "American gold" precipitated a chain migration initially dominated by single males and later including females and families. By 1880, an estimated 1500 Finns lived in Keweenaw and Houghton counties, the northwesternmost part of the UP. Two decades later this area would become America's foremost copper mining region (Alanen 1975; Kaups 1975). Erkki Vuorenmaa, who was featured in the film *Finnish American Lives* (Loukinen 1984), emigrated from Töyssä in 1910 and joked on his ninety-second birthday in Ironwood, Michigan that he had thought that he "could just come here and shake dat money tree, shovel dat money and haul it home in a wheelbarrow." Edward Loukinen, who left Kittalä in 1903, was so obsessed with the "Amerika fever" that villagers joked that he left behind a wake of broken spruce limbs when he emigrated.

Subsequent Finnish immigrants also settled in the copper mining communities, especially in and around the boom town of Calumet in Houghton County. Although originally named "Calumet" after the Native American peace pipe, to the Finnish immigrants the town became known as "Pesapäikka" (nesting place). It was a place where they had first planted American roots, where they had felt at home, and where they would later return while between jobs. Many Finnish immigrant institutions such as churches, temperance societies, Finnish language newspapers, mutual benefit organizations, athletic teams, and other cultural organizations began in the Calumet area.

Finnish immigrants in Calumet found themselves in a very complex, multi-ethnic environment that included thirty-two different language groups in 1880. According to the United States Census of 1880, in Michigan's Houghton and Keweenaw counties, which circumscribed most of the copper mining activity at the time, 48.9 percent of the population were immigrants, of whom 5.8 percent were Finns. By 1900 in Houghton County, the area of the most copper mining activity, 42.6 percent of the total population were immigrants, 25.7 percent of whom were Finns (Kaups 1974:58). Hence, in the last two decades of the nineteenth century, the Finnish immigrant population increased fivefold in these copper mining counties.

Reaction to the growing immigrant population was mixed. Mining companies welcomed them as inexpensive workers, while the English-speaking Americanized population were feeling some anxiety. Such anti-foreigner sentiments as "race suicide" appeared in the local English language newspapers, especially when immigrant workers joined labor unions and went on strike (Thurner 1984:21; Lankton 1991:212). Consider a comparison with contemporary American society: In 1900, almost half of the population in Michigan's Copper Country were immigrants. Today, we are currently witnessing a wave of public hostility toward immigrants and some immigrant-bashing legislative initiatives when United States Census estimates suggest that in 1995 only 8.7 percent of the United States population were foreign born, with higher levels in California (25 percent), Florida (15 percent), and New York (16 percent). One can understand the anxiety felt by the Anglicized natives in the UP's mining communities, and Finnish immigrants felt it. They knew that they were not universally welcomed in their new land.

During the latter half of the nineteenth century, Finnish immigrant settlement extended to three iron mining ranges in the UP, all within about seventy-five miles of Calumet. This included the Marquette Iron Range towns of Ishpeming, Negaunee, Palmer, Champion, Republic, Humboldt, and the port city of Marquette (north central UP). In the early 1870s, Finns migrated southwest to the Menominee Iron Range towns of Iron River, Crystal Falls, Amasa, Stambaugh, Quinnesec, Norway, and Iron Mountain. By 1885, Finns were moving into the Gogebic Range towns in the western UP along the Wisconsin boundary of Ironwood, Bessemer, and Wakefield.

Between 1864 and 1924, an estimated 350,000 Finns emigrated to America. The 1930 United States Census documents the first drop in the number of Finnish immigrants, reflecting the sharp declines in immigration after the 1924 immigration restriction laws were enacted. This decline is also caused by the increasing mortality rates of the aging immigrant population, the largest portion of whom emigrated as teenagers and young adults during the period between 1880 and 1924.

Other than the early immigration of a small number of Finnish miners recruited from Norway, mining had been totally unknown to Finnish immigrants. Virtually all historians acknowledge an ethnic hierarchy in the mines between 1870s and the 1950s (Puotinen 1977; Lankton 1991:211). Foremen, security guards, and the higher paid miners were usually English-speaking Americans or Cornishmen. Finns, Croatians, Italians, Hungarians, and more recently arrived immigrants were more likely to work as "trammers," the poorly paid human mules who manually loaded copper and iron ore into steel cars. The work was dangerous, dirty, and incredibly exhausting—and all too frequently interrupted by cave-ins, explosions, or strikes. Violence begot violence, and threats produced counter-threats. Labor law during this period was "the law of the jungle," determined by the security guards' clubs or the barrel of the gun. Mainstream labor unions such as the American Federation of Labor ignored miners' requests for support because they were too busy organizing skilled workers in urban factories; hence, the more radical Western Federation of Miners from Montana moved into the vacuum to organize the unskilled immigrant miners (Thurner 1984). As compared to other immigrants, an usually high percentage of Finnish immigrants supported radical leftist organizations.

Between 1900 and 1920, an extensive back-to-the-land migration occurred from UP mining towns into the cut-over lands of the forested interior. During this period, there also began a migration to the copper mining areas of Arizona and Montana. UP Finns moved to major cities in the Midwest, especially Detroit, when in 1905 Henry Ford announced that he would pay workingmen five dollars a day. In Detroit, a "Finn Town" with a rich array of immigrant institutions eventually developed in the inner city during 1920 to 1950 (Loukinen 1982).

The Michigan Copper Country in the strike of 1913–1914 fueled the migration to the countryside as thousands of the disenchanted Finnish miners, many of them blacklisted, swarmed into the cut-over forest lands with hopes of clearing the enormous white pine stumps and establishing farms (Loukinen 1979). Recall that Finns initially emigrated with the idea of earning money to buy a farm. Close to the forests, the world somehow seemed right; they felt at home near lakes and rivers surrounded by trees. Land fever spread quickly among the miners. Railroad companies that had been given enormous tracts of land to build railroads and lumber companies who had cut their timber wanted to dump their lands. Much of the topsoil was thin and rocky, yet slick, Finnish-speaking real estate agents promoted its agricultural potential to the frustrated Finnish miners. The leading Finnish-American historian, A. William Hoglund, concluded that many of the Finnish immigrants who bought farms in the cut-over regions of the UP on the periphery of the mining towns were essentially deceived by a clever promotional campaign (Hoglund 1978).

Throughout the UP, Finnish immigrants carved farms out of the forests and built rural "language island" communities. They established dairy farms and worked as lumberjacks during the winter months. Some observers in Finland writing in Finnish language newspapers in America encouraged this back-to-the-land migration, since it offered the only hope of saving the Finnish language and nationality (Kolehmainen and Hill 1951:42). They had recognized that homogeneous Finnish rural communities would serve as bastions of support for immigrant culture, much in the way such communities had supported Norwegian and German culture. The Finnish language was spoken regularly in the homes, churches, labor halls, and cooperative stores until the 1950s (Loukinen 1980).

Many of these rural hamlets have Finnish names, indicating the preponderance of saunas next to farmhouses: Aura, Nisula, Kiva, Yalmer, Tapiola, Little Finland, Suomi, Toivola, Paavola, Elo, and Askel. Others have mostly Finnish residents but their names give no such clue: Pelkie, Baraga, Klingville, Arnheim, Chassell, Winona, Twin Lakes, Green, Mass City, Ontonogan, Trenary, Eben, Sundell, Rumley, Rock, Chatham, Lake Linden, Traprock, Ahmeek, Traverse Bay, Mud Lake, Bootjack, Princess Point, Jacobsville, Rabbit Bay, Rudyard, Newberry, Sugar Island, and Neebish Island. These communities served as cultural oases sustaining Finnishness until the second, third, and fourth-generation migrations to urban areas gradually diminished the presence of immigrant culture (Loukinen 1992).

By 1920, 47 percent of the Finnish immigrants in the United States lived in rural communities (defined as those having fewer than 2,500 people), and in 1940, 61 percent of the Finnish immigrant farmers lived in Michigan, Wisconsin, and Minnesota (Hoglund 1978:4). Finnish settlement in the remote mining regions in the western Lake Superior Region and their subsequent migration into adjacent farming communities made Finns the "most rural" of all of the Euro-American immigrant groups, with the exception of the Anabaptist Amish and Mennonite ethno-religious enclaves (Fishman 1966).

What were some main sociological characteristics of the Finnish immigrant population in the western Lake Superior Region? Most of the men went through a similar occupational pattern:

(1) Their childhood was spent on an economically impoverished, rural, labor-intensive farm in Finland.

(2) Grueling underground copper or iron mining work was their first job in America, for which they were unprepared from previous occupational experience.

(3) Accustomed to living in culturally homogeneous rural villages in Finland, they found themselves suddenly thrust into an extremely multicultural environment in UP mining towns.

(4) They participated in a secondary migration to a rural community on the outskirts of a mining town and worked dreadfully long hours clearing fields in cut-over forested areas to establish small-scale dairy farms. Men left home to work as lumberjacks or part-time miners during the winter months.

(5) The immigrant community was split by a political-religious schism: "Church Finns" were pro-company and anti-union, while "Red Finns" were anti-clerical and pro-union.

On the women's side,

(1) single and some married women in towns worked as domestic workers for wealthier families, they were slower than the men to learn the English language, and they raised large families.

(2) On the farms, women worked in the barns and fields and cared for even larger families. During the winter months, while their husbands were working in lumber camps, they milked and butchered cows, chopped wood, cooked, washed, cleaned, read to their children, and did nearly everything that was to be done on a small dairy farm covered with three feet of snow.

Depending upon the exact time period of measuring immigrants' literacy, the Finns were the first or second most literate of all of the immigrants from Europe, surpassing or sometimes losing by a mere percentage point to eastern European Jews (Fishman 1966). Literacy (in Finnish) among these immigrants was 96 to 99 percent. One scholar estimates that by 1930, 350 different Finnish language newspapers and periodicals were published in America (Hoglund 1979). Aside from this exceptionally high literacy rate, a large Finnish language print industry was due to the tendency for Finns to get into bitter religious and political internecine quarrels. Following a dispute, a faction would leave to start a new group and establish their own newspaper (Ollila 1975). Curiously, these most literate Finnish and Jewish immigrants also placed first and second, respectively, in the proportion of their group that supported the American Workers' Communist Party (Kostianen 1978; Kivisto 1984).

Americanized neighbors thought the Finns were clannish and secretive. They were distinct from other immigrant groups in the mining town environments in the UP, insofar as they had found it far more difficult and less necessary (since there were so many of them) to learn to speak English.

After having lived in America for ten years, nearly all of the other immigrant miners had learned to speak English, but there were still 25.9 percent of the Finnish miners [in Calumet, Michigan] who were speaking only their ancestral language" (Loukinen 1982:170).

This linguistic distance from other European immigrants and assimilated Americans made them socially distant as well. Americanized English speakers disliked their clannishness, and this became a central feature of the stereotype of the Finns, who, in turn, referred to all other immigrants with the words *toisenkielliset* (other tongues). Their language served to define themselves as different and separate from others.

This social distance from non-Finnish immigrants and English-speaking, American-born persons contributed to the exceptionally high endogamy rate within the Finnish immigrant community. Although their are no studies of intermarriage of Finns in UP mining towns, other studies can inform us. An 1895 count of 176 married Finns in Duluth, Minnesota revealed that only forty-six (26.1 percent) were married to non-Finns (Kaups 1982:78). A study in New York City in 1921 reported a 92 percent endogamy rate among immigrants. A study in rural Minnesota in 1942 found an 87 percent endogamy rate (Nelson 1943). Using a sample of 1980 Census, "single Finnish ancestry" reports of respondents and their year of birth (before 1920) to infer that these persons were likely to have had both parents be Finnish immigrants, Stoller and Karni estimate that there was an 84 percent immigrant endogamy rate in America (Stoller and Karni 1992). Community studies combined with estimates based upon census ancestry reports suggest an extremely high degree of endogamy among Finnish immigrants, higher than that of nearly any other European immigrant groups. When a second ancestry was reported, it was usually of another Scandinavian group. Ten percent said they were Swedish and Finnish (Stoller and Karni 1992).

The Second Generation (American-born children of immigrants)

These clannish immigrants were busy breeding once they moved into rural settings. Based on one study of Pelkie, a rural community in Baraga County, the average number of children born to Finnish immigrant parents (the "second generation") surviving beyond the first year was 6.5, the same as in Old Order Amish farming communities in rural Pennsylvania (Loukinen 1979). Nearly all of the rural second generation had spoken Finnish at home and had learned English in a one-room school where they were punished if they were caught speaking Finnish. They were given the impression that speaking Finnish was un-American. Approximately one in ten also spoke Swedish, about the same proportion as back in Finland (Loukinen 1982). Those born between 1900 and 1930 in the rural areas completed eight grades of education in one-room schoolhouses, until roads and school buses in the mid-1930s permitted them to travel to nearby towns where they completed high school, and some went on to college. Based on a national sample of United States Census ancestry report data, among second-generation Finns born before 1916, 29.6 percent of men and 40.6 percent of women were high school graduates; 13.4 percent of the men and 14.4 percent of women had some college; and 4.5 percent of men and 3.6 percent of women were college graduates. Those living in mining towns and in cities were more likely to complete high school and college (Stoller and Karni 1992).

Leftist political radicalism was discredited and almost completely disappeared in the second generation. It was replaced with a more moderate, pro-union, liberal ideology supporting the Democratic Party. In some communities, Church Finn and Red Finn distinctions still served as slight barriers between residents, but it disappeared in most places.

Based on a study of 359 second-generation Finnish Americans from Pelkie, three out of four of the second-generation Finnish Americans had migrated in search of urban employment. Of these migrants, 42 percent had returned within ten years to live in Pelkie (Loukinen 1982). This remarkable attachment to their rural community of origin is exceptionally high among second-generation Finnish Americans from the UP. So many of them had migrated to Detroit between 1920 and 1950 that they were able to visit with relatives, neighbors, and friends from back home. Migration to the city did not mean breaking the bonds with their home community; it actually served to strengthen such attachments. Friends from home helped new migrants find jobs and lodging. Many persons married others whom they had known back home after dating them in Detroit. When asked where he had liked to hang out after work in the 1940s in Detroit, one man said, "Where I could find a ride home." Another said that he had seen more Pelkie people on Woodrow Wilson—a street running through the heart of Detroit's Finn Town—than he had ever seen in the village area in Pelkie (Loukinen 1982).

My own family's experience reflects this deep attachment to the UP. Both of my parents are second-generation Finnish Americans who grew up on small farms in Houghton County and migrated to Detroit in 1939. Whenever work schedules permitted, they returned home. My father often worked an afternoon shift, and when we were to go to the UP, he came home shortly after midnight to wake us up with the call, "Daylight in the swamp!" It was an echo from his youth that he had heard while working in the lumber camps on the Keweenaw Peninsula. The car had already been packed, and after a shower, we would hit the road. I can remember the sense of excitement as we approached the Straits of Mackinac and waited for the ferry boats. Seagulls filled the windy sky, sometimes hanging motionlessly on air currents. Indians roamed from car to car selling smoked fish wrapped in newspaper to passengers waiting for the next boat. Dad usually slept in the car during the ferry boat ride to

Culture: Finnish Americans

St. Ignace, while my mother, sister, and I roamed the decks searching through the fog for a glimpse of the UP.

I can still remember the clanking sounds of the steel ramps of the ferry boat falling onto the dock in St. Ignace and the sounds of eager passengers starting their engines. It was always a thrill to reach the UP. Dad rolled down the window as he swung west on US 2 toward Lehto's Pasty Shop, and fresh, surprisingly cool air filled the car. We breathed in deeply, and as we took in the lake air mixed with cedar, pine, and ferns, we exaggerated its virtues. We had passed into another world. We were home where we really belonged. We had been freed from our exile in the Detroit metropolitan area where my parents worked and my sister and I attended school. The UP had always been our psychic homeland.

My family made its annual pilgrimage to the UP every summer vacation over a period of thirty years, on most deer hunting seasons, during layoffs, and labor strikes. Immediately upon my father's retirement in 1972, he and my mother moved to the UP and built a retirement home on the shore of Portage Canal near their childhood homes. Virtually all my aunts and uncles and all my parents' childhood friends and acquaintances have followed an identical pattern. Like spawning salmon, the retired second generation had returned to their birth place. The vast majority of second-generation Finnish Americans who had left the UP in search of employment never really left the UP in terms of their social and inner lives. When people ask me, a third-generation American of Finnish ancestry, where I am from, it is a complicated question. I grew up primarily in the Detroit metro area and partially in the UP, but I have always felt that I am from the UP. Many third- and fourth-generation Finnish Americans whose parents were from the UP but migrated elsewhere have had the same experience.

Of the rural-born, second-generation UP Finnish Americans from Pelkie, 73 percent married other Finnish Americans (Loukinen 1982). Another study of the second generation in urban Conneaut, Ohio focused on those born between 1926 and 1935. It reported a 43 percent endogamy rate (Kolehmainen 1936). Most sociologists would claim this sharp difference in second-generation endogamy estimates between the rural UP and urban Conneaut was the result of differences in the relative proportions of Finnish Americans available in the marriage market, but the author of the 1936 study insists that it was due to a form of youthful rebellion against immigrant parents and to the tendency for women to seek mates belonging to more prestigious Americanized groups. No such sex differences in rates of in-group marriage were evident in the Pelkie study. The national estimate of second-generation endogamy based upon single-ancestry reports by persons assumed to be the third generation, that is, those born between 1945 and 1960, is 37 percent (Stoller and Karni 1992).

According to one analysis of a national sample of 1980 United States Census ancestry data, the second generation were more geographically dispersed than their immigrant parents, and their occupations reflect this trend (Stoller and Forster 1992). More than 40 percent of the employed, adult, second-generation Finnish American men born before 1930 worked in white-collar positions, as did 70 percent of the women in this cohort. Forty-one percent of the men, and 21 percent of the women worked in blue-collar jobs. Only 19 percent of the men and 7 percent of the women worked in mining, farming, fishing, and forestry, the occupations typical of their immigrant parents. Among those born after 1930, more were likely to work in white-collar occupations and fewer likely to work in blue-collar jobs. This is especially true for the males. Relative to other Euro-American ethnics, an exceptionally large number of women became teachers (Stoller and Forster 1992).

Today, the second generation is passing into history. Many are either deceased, living in assisted-living apartments, or in nursing homes. Some, whose health permits, are trying to teach their children about family history and cultural traditions. Most of their children, the third generation, are largely unaware of their heritage and are too busy spending and earning to learn.

The Third Generation

Some of the Americanized grandchildren of the immigrants retain a few images of the immigrant generation through memories of grandparents. Grandmother fired wood stoves, knitted wool mittens and socks; served them a buttermilk-like soup, a salt-cured fish, prune tarts, and a sweet bread called *nisua*; took them blueberry picking; canned berries, meats, and vegetables; and pounded rag carpets on a squeaky wooden loom. She drew black crosses over the heads of deceased people in old photographs and slathered Mrs. Juntunen's stinky salve on cut fingers. Grandfather bought them Orange Crush soda at the store, fired the sauna, and filled the white enamel water tubs. On his belt, he carried an enormous knife in a leather sheath and disappeared into the woods to make sauna *vihta* (switches). He scorched the kids with the water he poured onto the sauna rocks so that they squealed and climbed down close to the floor. For some reason, he talked Finnish while feeding and brushing his horses. In later years, he let his grandchildren drive the tractor during hay making. Even on those breezeless Saharan days in July, he wore woolen long underwear. He dug worms behind the barn by the manure pile, slipped them into a Prince Albert tobacco can, and took his grandchildren brook trout fishing, often carrying them home on his shoulders. Sometimes he slipped out into the night with a flashlight and a rifle. They heard their grandparents speaking Finnish at the kitchen coffee table where grandfather inserted a sugar lump on his tongue and drank coffee from a saucer. It seemed as if they were always talking at the coffee table. It was so frustrating to wait for them. Just as their talking seemed to end, they started all over again. These children also heard Finnish when their parents were telling secrets. It was almost whispered, as though the kids might understand. Later in their adult lives, some of the third generation would come to recognize these peculiar foods and customs as being a part of their vanishing cultural heritage.

Two studies of the third-generation Finnish Americans, the grandchildren of immigrants, show considerable educational achievement. One study of 194 third-generation Finnish Americans born in Pelkie is shown in the following table:

Table 2. Education: Third Generation Finnish Americans From Pelkie, Michigan

	male (n=96)	female (n=98)	total (n=194)
less than 12 years high school	10%	1%	6%
high school graduate	35	26	30
less than 4 years college	21	29	25
college graduate	25	22	24
graduate study	8	22	15
	100%	100%	100%

National estimates based on the assumption (a good one) that those born between 1946 and 1955 reporting Finnish ancestry are members of the third generation show that 95 percent had graduated from high school, 67 percent had some college, and 33 percent were college graduates (Stoller and Forster 1992). Hence, the UP pattern of Finnish American educational achievement is similar to the national picture.

An estimated seven out of ten of this UP third generation have left their home community following career dreams. While their parents migrated primarily to Detroit, where they could visit fellow ethnics, this third generation is now widely dispersed throughout all of metropolitan America. Many live far away, and they are not returning to live in the UP as many of their parents did. They come home for Christmas, weddings, funerals, and some summer vacations, but these visits begin to subside when their parents die. When they do return, everything seems changed: New people live in a former neighbor's house, and "No Trespassing" signs are posted on trees.

While most second-generation Finnish Americans returned to the UP upon retirement, very few of the third generation intend to do so. Whereas four out of ten of their parents had returned within ten years after migrating, only one of fourteen of the third generation had returned within a similar time period (Loukinen 1994). The tendency to pursue an education and move away forever is the story of rural America; it is not unique to the UP.

Third-generation Finnish Americans' occupations are spread throughout the American economic system. Based upon 1980 United States Census reports of Finnish ancestry, assuming that those born between 1946 and 1955 are members of the third generation, 20.9 percent are in administrative or management positions; 20.4 percent are in the professions; 18.3 percent are elementary and secondary school teachers; 7.3 percent are in the semi-professions; 4.2 percent are writers or artists; 8.4 percent are in sales, 8.9 percent are in administrative support positions; and 11.5 percent are in pink/blue-collar occupations (Stoller and Forster 1992).

They are just a little clannish. The in-group marriage rate for this third generation is four out of ten; for their parents it was seven out of ten; and for their grandparents, close to nine out of ten. If a member of this rural-born but now geographically dispersed third generation married another Finnish American, about half said they had tried to pass some sense of Finnish culture on to their children; for those marrying outside their ethnic community, this proportion declined by about 10 percent. Sociologists have long known that interethnic marriage has a way of erasing an ethnic identity and encouraging assimilation into the commercial mass culture of American society. Ethnic foods are replaced with McDonald's hamburgers.

Generational status—the kinship distance from the immigrant generation—is not the sole determining factor in Finnish American assimilation. Cultural experience of different cohorts (individuals born within a designated time period) is even more critical. Those members of the third generation (grandchildren of immigrants) who were born earlier were more likely to have had sustained contact with Finnish immigrant culture, because more immigrants were still living during their youth. This is reflected in their propensity to transmit the culture of their ancestors. Among those third-generation Finnish Americans born in Pelkie between 1935 and 1953, 53 percent said they had tried to pass Finnish culture onto their children; for those born between 1954 and 1972, this had fallen to 35 percent (Loukinen 1996).

Culture: Finnish Americans

The third and fourth generation lives without strong community or institutional support for their cultural traditions. The rate of contemporary Finnish immigration is insufficient to sustain a vital immigrant culture. Virtually all recent Finnish immigrants speak English fluently, so they do not contribute to the maintenance of an ethnic language. The Finnish language is heard in monthly church services attended by fewer and fewer elders, and the Finnish Evangelical church in America has merged with other Lutheran bodies such that there is no longer Finnish symbolism in the weekly services or doctrine. The rural Finnish co-ops have almost all closed or have been sold to private operators. Three generations of out-migration of Finnish Americans and recent in-migration of non-Finns has to a great extent depleted the presence of Finnish culture in the rural communities of the western UP. In addition, the third generation is now so scattered throughout America that few can interact with other Finnish Americans enough to sustain a sense of ethnic community.

Some media support for a Finnish American identity exists. Two Finnish language newspapers are being published, and the *Finnish American Reporter*, an English-language monthly, is published in Superior, Wisconsin. Many books and videos about Finland and Finnish American history and culture are marketed to Finnish Americans. *Saloampi,* a language and culture educational summer camp for youth, operates every summer in northwestern Minnesota. A weekly television program, *Suomi Kutsuu*, has been aired on WLUC-TV in Negaunee, Michigan since 1962.

In 1982, Finnish Americans created an annual, geographically rotating, national ethnic festival, FinnFest USA, whose purpose is to develop a sense of understanding and appreciation for the cultural heritage of Finnish Americans. Three FinnFests have been held in the UP—two in Hancock, Michigan at Suomi College in 1985 and 1990, and one at Northern Michigan University in Marquette, Michigan in 1996. In 1985, 1,493 registered, and in 1996 there were 6,221 fully registered and another ten thousand partially registered. Compared with previous FinnFests, a larger proportion attending the 1996 FinnFest were third- and fourth-generation Finnish Americans, because a special effort was made to attract them by encouraging scheduling of family reunions coincidental with FinnFest and offering free "Educare" services for youth (day care combined with Finnish American cultural education). About 488 children age seventeen and under attended FinnFest USA '96. Over 130 lectures, family history and genealogy workshops, films, ethnic crafts, dance and cooking workshops, and over thirty concerts were packed into a five-day period of enjoyable cultural education. The long-range cultural impact of such ethnic revitalization festivals remains to be seen.

Today, Finnish Americans are scattered throughout America. Based upon 1980 United States Census ancestry estimates, 33.4 percent live in rural areas (fewer than 2,500 inhabitants); 14.4 percent live in small towns; 32 percent live on the urban fringe; and 19.9 percent live in central cities. About 17.1 percent live in Michigan; 19.1 percent live in Minnesota, North and South Dakota; 9.4 percent live in California; 7.2 percent live in Washington; 6.1 percent live in Wisconsin; 5.7 percent live in Massachusetts; and 4 percent live in Oregon. (Stoller and Karni 1992). Many Finnish Americans still live in the upper Midwestern states. Michigan's Upper Peninsula, the first place where Finnish immigrants had planted roots in American soil, still has the highest concentration of them. What will persist of their cultural tracks across the UP landscape remains to be seen. The winds of cultural change are making them harder to find.

CULTURE: FINNISH AMERICANS

Bibliography

Alanen, Arnold. "The Development and Distribution of Finnish Consumer's Cooperatives in Michigan, Minnesota and Wisconsin, 1903–1973." In *The Finnish Experience in the Western Great Lakes Region*. Ed. by Michael Karni, et al. Turku, Finland: Institute for Migration, 1975, pp. 103–129.

Dorson, Richard. *Blood Stoppers and Bear Walkers*. Cambridge, Mass.: Harvard University Press, 1952.

Fishman, J. *Language Loyalty in the United States*. London: Morton, 1966.

Halkola, David. "Finnish-language Newspapers in the United States." In *The Finns in North America*. East Lansing, Mich.: Michigan State University Press, 1969, pp. 73–90.

_____. "Kielikysymys: The Language Problem in the Suomi-Synod." In *The Faith of the Finns*, Ed. Ralph J. Jalkanen. East Lansing, Mich.: Michigan State University Press, 1972, pp. 275–290.

Hoglund, William, *In the Trek of the Immigrants*. Ed. O. Fritiof Ander. Rock Island, Ill.: Augustana College Library, 1964.

_____. "Breaking With Religious Tradition: Finnish Immigrant Workers and the Church." In *For the Common Good*. Superior, Wis.: The Työmies Society, 1977.

_____. "Flight from Industry: Finns and Farming in America." *Finnish Americana*. (1978), Ed. Michael Karni. New York Mills, Minn.: Parta Printers, Inc.

_____. *Finnish Immigrants in America 1880–1920*. New York, NY: Arno Press, 1979.

_____. "Finns." In *Harvard Encyclopedia of American Ethnic Groups*. Ed. Stephan Thernstrom, Ann Orlov, and Oscar Handlin. 1980.

Hummasti, George. "The Workingman's Daily Bread: Finnish-American Working Class Newspapers, 1900–1921." In *For the Common Good*. Superior, Wisconsin: Työmies Society, 1977, pp. 167–194.

Jalkanen, Ralph J. Ed. *The Faith of the Finns: Historical Perspectives on the Finnish Lutheran Church in America*. East Lansing, Mich.: Michigan State University Press, 1972.

Jutikkala, Eino. *A History of Finland*. New York: Frederick A. Praeger, Inc., 1962.

Karni, Michael. "The Founding of the Finnish Socialist Federation and the Minnesota Strike of 1907." In *For the Common Good.* Superior, Wis.: The Työmies Society, 1977.

Karni, Michael G. and Ollila, Douglas J. Ed. *For the Common Good.* Superior, Wis.: The Työmies Society, 1977.

Kaups, Matti. "The Finns in the Copper and Iron Ore Mines of the Western Great Lakes Region, 1864–1905: Some Preliminary Observations." In *The Finnish Experience in the Western Great Lakes Region: New Perspectives.* Ed. Michael Karni, et al. Turku: Institute for Migration, 1975, pp. 55–88.

____. "Finns in Urban America: A View from Duluth." In *Finnish Diaspora II: United States.* Ed. Michael G. Karni, 1982, pp. 63–86.

Kero, Reino. *Migration From Finland to North America in the Years Between the United States Civil War and the First World War.* Turku, Finland: Institute of General History, 1974.

Kivisto, Peter. *Immigrant Socialists in the United States.* Cranbury, NY: Associated University Presses, 1984.

Kolehmainen, John. "A Study of Marriage in a Finnish Community." In *American Journal of Sociology* 42 (November 1936), 371–382.

____. "The Finnicisation of English in America." In *American Sociological Review* 2 (1937), 62–66.

____. "The Retreat of Finnish." In *American Sociological Review* 2 (1937), 887–889.

____. "Finnish Newspapers and Periodicals in Michigan." In *Michigan History Magazine* 24 (1940), 119–127.

____. *The Finns in America.* Hancock, Mich.: Lutheran Book Concern, 1947.

Kolehmainen, John and Hill, George. *Haven in the Woods: The Story of the Finns in Wisconsin.* Madison, Wis.: The State Historical Society of Wisconsin, 1951.

Kostiainen, Auvo. *The Forging of Finnish-American Communism, 1917–1924.* Turku, Finland: University of Turku.

Lankton, Larry. *Cradle to Grave: Life, Work, and Death at the Lake Superior Copper Mines.* New York, NY: Oxford University Press, 1991.

Loukinen, Michael M. "The Maintenance of Ethnic Culture in Finnish-American Rural Communities." In *Finnish Americana* 2 (1979), 8–27.

_____. "Sociolinguistic Structure of Finnish America." In *Theory in Bilingual Education*, 2. Ed. Raymond Padilla, Ypsilanti, Mich: Eastern Michigan University Press, 1980. pp. 159–176.

_____. "Second Generation Finnish American Migration from the North Woods to Detroit, 1920–1950." In *Finnish Diaspora*, Toronto, Canada: 1982.

_____. *Finnish American Lives*, 60 min. documentary film. Marquette, MI: Up North Films, Northern Michigan University, 1984.

Lowrey, Nelson. "Intermarriage Among Nationality Groups in a Rural Area of Minnesota." In *American Journal of Sociology* 48 (5) (1945), 585–592.

Niitemaa, Vilho. "The Finns in The Great Migratory Movement From Europe to America 1865–1914." In *Old Friends—Strong Ties*. Ed. Vilho Niitemaa. et al. Turku, Finland: Institute for Migration, 1976.

Ollila, Douglas Jr. "From Socialism to Industrial Unionism (IWW): Social Factors in the Emergence of Left-Labor Radicalism Among Finnish Workers on the Mesabi, 1911–1919." In *The Finnish Experience in the Western Great Lakes Region: New Perspectives*. Ed. Michael Karni, et al. Turku, Finland: Institute for Migration, 1975, pp. 55–88.

Puotinen, Arthur. "Early Labor Organizations in the Copper Country." In *For the Common Good*. Superior, WI: The Työmies Society, 1977.

Stoller and Karni. "Where Do Finns Live? Geographical Distribution of Finnish Americans." "Education." "Census Article on Occupations." In *Finnish American Reporter*. 1992.

Thurner, Arthur W. *Rebels on the Range: The Michigan Copper Miners' Strike of 1913–1914*. Privately published by Arthur W. Thurner, 1984.

Thurner, Arthur W. *Calumet Copper and People: History of a Michigan Mining Community 1864–1970*. Privately published by Arthur Thurner, 1974.

Works Cited

Loukinen, Michael M. "Continuity and Change Among Third Generation Finnish Americans From a Small Rural Community." The Making of Finnish America (International Conference), University of Minnesota, November 6, 1992.

Loukinen, Michael M. "From Language Island to Metropolitan America: Finnish American on the Move." Eighty-second Annual Meeting of the Society for Advancement of Scandinavian Study, University of Minnesota, St. Paul, MN, May 1, 1992.

Loukinen, Michael M. "Family History May Be the Key: Surveying the Values and Behaviors of Third Generation Finns in Pelkie, Michigan." FINNFORUM V. Towards the New Millennium, Prospects and Challenges, Laurentian University, Sudbury, Ontario, May 25, 1996.

Stoller and Forster, Lorna. "Ethnicity and Social Stratification: Finnish Americans in the 1980 Census." *The Making of Finnish America* (International Conference), University of Minnesota, November 6, 1991, (1992).

Iron Mining and Immigrants
Negaunee and Ishpeming, 1870–1910

Judith Boyce DeMark

The iron industry marks one of the most significant aspects of the economic history of the United States. Iron provided the natural resource needed for the rapid industrialization of post-Civil War America through its use in the railroad industry and as a component in the steel-making process. While iron ore was mined in other parts of the United States, it was in the Upper Peninsula of Michigan that the first large deposits of iron ore were discovered in the 1840s. From 1850 to 1920, the mines of the Michigan iron ranges were the most productive in the United States.

Iron ore was first discovered in the Upper Peninsula by William Burt and a group of surveyors working near the Teal Lake area. The discovery led to the eventual opening of three Michigan iron ranges, the Marquette, the Menominee, and the Gogebic. The Marquette Range lies a few miles west of the present-day city of Marquette. The first iron mining company on the Marquette Range was the Jackson Mining Company, organized in 1845.

Word spread rapidly, and within one year there were 104 companies formed for the purpose of prospecting minerals in the Lake Superior region. With the mining companies came miners to work the large open pits and to push beneath the surface to find underground deposits.

In 1855, there were only twelve men living year-round at what would become Negaunee. The first communities were actually "locations," or housing areas built within walking distance of individual mines. The largest communities on the Marquette Range were Negaunee and Ishpeming. This study focuses on the people who settled there, particularly those residents who immigrated to the Upper Peninsula from other countries.

By 1870, there were over three thousand people living in Negaunee Township. The community of Ishpeming began with several miners and their families living at the Cleveland mine location in the late 1840s; by 1870, there were almost four thousand residents of Ishpeming. Thus, within fifteen years, the two communities had grown by over six thousand people.

The population grew steadily from 1855 to 1870, due to transportation improvements and the growth of the mining industry. The Jackson Mining Company built a dock with ore pockets in 1857 at Marquette. In that same year, the Soo Canal was opened. The greater ease in shipping ore led to a decrease in shipping costs and so helped spur the mining industry. These two factors in turn helped population growth.

One of the most interesting aspects of Upper Peninsula history is the heavy concentration of immigrants; this was certainly true in Negaunee and Ishpeming. The United States Immigration Commission, in describing the characteristics of iron mining on the Marquette Range in 1911, stated that the history of immigration was a history of the development of the iron-mining industry. Histories of mining communities throughout the Midwest and the West generally include a discussion of the large number of foreign-born who helped work the mining areas. Immigrants were in such places as Butte, Montana; Cherry Creek, Colorado; and Silver City, Nevada. In those places, the foreign-born comprised from one-third to one-half of the total population. What makes the Marquette Iron Range unique is that immigrants made up an even larger percentage. For example, according to the Census of 1870, communities such as Negaunee were over 70 percent immigrant.

The largest immigrant groups in Ishpeming and Negaunee in 1870 were Irish, English, German, and Canadian. There was also a relatively large community of Swedish immigrants in Ishpeming in that year, although no Swedes were living in Negaunee at that time. Most of the English immigrants were from Cornwall, a famous mining area in the southwestern part of Great Britain. The Cornish miners were well known for their mining expertise. Cornwall had both tin and copper mines, and the miners from that region were valued for their experience and tended to form the largest percentage of mining captains, a position of great importance in the mines.

The labor force that worked in the mines was comprised of immigrants from England and from many other countries. From the beginning of the iron ore industry in the Upper Peninsula until well into the twentieth century, a majority of miners were born outside the United States. Immigrants came from more than forty different countries. They brought many aspects of their native culture with them, and this diversity created a unique blend of religions, languages, and customs. Many of the newcomers, such as the Cornish, brought a wealth of experience in mining and mining technology that would vastly improve mining methods in the Upper Peninsula.

In Ishpeming in 1870, the largest number of workers were Irish-born immigrants and their children. Out of 551 employed Irish-Americans, some 216 worked as miners. According to some earlier studies of Upper Peninsula mining, the Irish had little experience in mining and tended to be unskilled laborers. The statistics in the Census of 1870 appear to conflict with earlier assumptions. To be

CULTURE: IRON MINING AND IMMIGRANTS

sure, there were Irishmen who worked as laborers; however, the Irish held a variety of positions. They were saloonkeepers, mine overseers, mine foremen, blacksmiths, shoemakers, carpenters, and law enforcement officers. This would indicate that many of the Irish who arrived on the Marquette range had some training in skilled jobs prior to their arrival. And if they did not have skilled experience before they got to the area, many learned new skills once on the iron range. In a list compiled in 1903 of employees who had been with the Lake Superior Iron Company, there were several men who had been working on the Marquette Iron Range as early as 1870. Four of the men were Irish. One was John McEnroe, who in 1870 was a thirty-eight year old mine foreman. He began his career in Negaunee in 1858. There was also Thomas Enright, who in 1870 was sixteen years old and working as a laborer.

Although the Irish in Michigan iron mining history have not been focused on in most previous histories, the one group that has received a great deal of attention is the English. The United States Immigrant Commission reported that most of the English who immigrated to the Upper Peninsula were experienced miners from Cornwall, England. The Cornish and their children were employed in the mines in larger percentages than any other group. For example, in 1870 in Ishpeming, an overwhelming 74 percent of the English immigrants and their sons were miners.

Large numbers of all immigrant groups were miners, because mining companies employed the largest number of workers, and the immigrants also helped in the town-building process. A sense of community began to flourish on the Marquette Range by 1870, and both communities showed their ethnic diversity. Religion had come to both towns, with varying denominations according to the religion of the newcomers. There were Catholic and Methodist churches in Ishpeming and Catholic, Methodist, Episcopal and Baptist churches in Negaunee. Early explorers were instrumental in bringing Catholicism to the Upper Peninsula in the seventeenth century, and French Canadian immigrants helped build the first Catholic churches in Negaunee and Ishpeming in the nineteenth century. The Cornish immigrants were responsible for introducing Methodism to the Marquette Range, and Swedish immigrants were instrumental in the arrival of the Baptist church. School districts were formed, and the first school buildings were completed. Several businesses were started in the two towns, including a brewery, a flour mill, and mercantile establishments. However, none of these early enterprises enjoyed long-term success.

Successful businesses take time to grow, and life was far from easy for the residents of the iron range in 1870. The winters in northern

Michigan are noted for their severity, and it was no different in the nineteenth century. Supplies were scarce in the winter months, as there was no shipping out of Marquette harbor—the nearest port—from October until May, due to freezing in Lake Superior. Many homes were overcrowded, and families in those days had no modern conveniences. Water had to be hauled in, and there was no indoor plumbing. Because of dangerous mining conditions, there was always the threat of severe injury or death for those who worked in the mines.

While the majority of men worked in the mines or in mine-related jobs, a few of the immigrant women of Ishpeming and Negaunee held a variety of other occupations. Women generally worked at such service-related positions as waitresses, milliners, cooks, or domestic servants. One young woman, the daughter of a miner, worked as an ore weigher at one of the mines. Few women actually worked in the mines; superstitious miners considered them bad luck underground. Some women were, however, entrepreneurs or had property in their own names. For example, Mary Carr, the twenty-one-year-old daughter of Irish-born Bernard Carr and his English wife Elizabeth, lived at home with her parents. Mary was a milliner, and the Census of 1870 indicated that she had twelve hundred dollars worth of personal property, a handsome sum in those days. Mary A. Crocker, wife of Negaunee attorney J. M. Crocker, did not work outside her home but had almost three thousand dollars of personal property. Wilhelmina Koster, a German immigrant, owned her own boardinghouse and had five thousand dollars in real estate and personal property. Some women worked as school teachers. Most women, however, listed their occupation as "keeping house," a term used to describe married women or single women who still lived at home.

When looking at the number of boarding houses and families with boarders in Ishpeming and Negaunee in the nineteenth century, it is obvious that the immigrant women were indeed working, contributing members of the household. In the community of Ishpeming in 1870, there were over two hundred immigrant families who took in boarders, and for every one of those families it can be assumed that it was the wife who cooked, washed clothes and linens, made beds, and probably did numerous other chores such as record keeping and sewing.

Families were generally large in the mid-nineteenth century, and this was certainly true in the Upper Peninsula in 1870. Of the 890 families in Ishpeming and Negaunee, 792 contained at least one child, with a total of 2,347 children. The average number of children per family was three. German and Irish families tended to be larger than other immigrant families. Both groups averaged 3.3 children per family. Swedish families were the smallest with an average of 2.2 children. Swedish immigrants in the Upper Peninsula were younger than most other newcomers, and this accounted for the smaller family size. Some families had many more children than the average. In Negaunee in 1870, for example, there were 23 families that had at least seven children. This figure does not take into account the families with adult children who had married or who had moved out on their own.

Schools were built for the children of Ishpeming and Negaunee by 1869. While there were schools at both communities early in town development, there was a real disparity in school attendance according to the Census records. In Ishpeming, only about half of the school-age children were attending school, and there were differences among ethnic groups in the percentage of children in school. For example, 60 percent of English and Irish children were in school in 1870, whereas a much lower percentage of Swedish and Canadians between eight and sixteen attended. One possible reason for this difference is the number of Swedish and French Canadian children who did not speak English; many of those children had been in the United States only for a short while. Perhaps their families kept them at home until they were older or had learned English.

There was not a compulsory school attendance law in Michigan until 1871; thus, parents did not feel compelled to send their children to school. In addition, many children of immigrants were needed to help supplement the family income. It was not until 1885 that the state of Michigan would forbid the employment of children under fourteen who had attended school fewer than four months in the previous year. In 1870, there were several young boys working at various occupations, particularly in the mines. Seven sons of Swedish immigrants worked in the mines, and two of those boys were only twelve years of age. Three thirteen-year-old sons of English immigrants also worked in the mines. Some sons helped their fathers or mothers in retail businesses and were not in schools. There were also several girls under the age of sixteen who worked as domestics in either Negaunee or Ishpeming.

With many children working rather than attending school, one can assume that in most cases the extra money was needed for daily living expenses. Since few women worked outside the home, the money earned by a young boy or girl might be the only income the family had, especially if the father had died and the children were being raised by their mothers. When a miner was killed in a mining accident, the wife and children were allowed to live rent free in company housing for several months. But there would still need to be money for food, and one young person's wages would certainly help feed the family.

In addition to working children and the ever-present threat of mining accidents, other factors show the difficult life faced by immigrants on the Marquette Iron Range in the early years. While there were many women in the community by 1870, there were few social institutions such as ethnic societies and little time for outside entertainment until much later. Women as well as men were occupied with the day-to-day struggle of living in the first few years of town development.

By 1910, life was much easier for the immigrant families of the iron range. Schools, services, ethnic clubs, and community businesses flourished. An early twentieth-century business directory indicated how much the area had changed in forty years. There were banks, a hospital, several small manufacturing plants and mercantile stores, and numerous churches. The Cornish immigrants had introduced Methodism to the Upper Peninsula, and the Swedes and Finns brought the Lutheran church to the area. There was daily mail delivery in the early twentieth century. By 1910, there were three newspapers in Ishpeming. All of the Ishpeming papers were Republican owned, including the *Superior Posten*, a Swedish language paper that had been established in 1888.

The number of ethnic clubs had grown dramatically, indicating the variety of immigrant groups. Meetings were held by such groups as the Finnish National Brothers' Temperance Union, the Scandinavian Aid and Fellowship Society, a chapter of the Ancient Order of Hibernians, the Swedish Home Society, and *L'Union Canadienne Française*. Women had formed several clubs, including the Daughters of Rebecca and a ladies' auxiliary to the Order of Hibernians. There were nine religious societies according to a business directory of 1910. In Ishpeming there were sixteen churches, with the largest percentage being Lutheran. The Sisters of St. Joseph lived and worked at St. John's Convent. There were several musical groups, including a Scandinavian band.

It would appear from the variety of recreation in both communities that families in 1910 had more leisure time. There were three theaters in Ishpeming. Skiing was also an important form of recreation, just as it is today. Immigrants on the iron range were, in fact, responsible for bringing organized skiing to the United States. The Norden Ski Club was founded in Ishpeming in 1887 and was one of the first ski clubs in the United States. In 1904, Carl Tellefsen, a Norwegian immigrant, was the instigating force behind the organization of the National Ski Association. Tellefsen became its first president.

CULTURE: IRON MINING AND IMMIGRANTS

The Ishpeming Snow Shoe Club was organized in November of 1886. Another popular Upper Peninsula sport began to grow in the late nineteenth century with the creation of the Wawonowin Golf Club, which was organized in 1888 with twenty members. Women formed several bridge or whist clubs, and many women found time to volunteer in church or other local benevolent societies.

Educational institutions had grown dramatically by 1910. In 1903, Negaunee High School graduated its twentieth class. There were eight graduates. The class president, secretary, and treasurer were all girls. A girl was valedictorian, and another young woman was salutatorian. According to the school yearbook, there were several student organizations, including a literary society and a debating club. There was a girls' indoor basketball association that fielded four teams in 1903. The faculty included three women and two men. In Ishpeming in 1910, there was one public high school, eight other public schools, a school for the hearing impaired, a manual training academy, and one Catholic school.

The ethnic composition of the Marquette Iron Range began to change dramatically toward the end of the nineteenth century. So many Finnish immigrants arrived after 1890 that over three thousand Finns lived in Ishpeming and Negaunee by 1910, and they comprised the largest foreign-born group in the two communities. In fact, more than five thousand Finnish immigrants lived throughout Marquette County, accounting for almost one-third of all foreign born in the county. There were other new ethnic groups as well. Following a trend throughout the United States in that era, the Italians had become a major ethnic group on the Iron Range. There were over one thousand Italian-born residents of Ishpeming and Negaunee, and there were even larger numbers of Italians on the Menominee Iron Range around the community of Iron Mountain. The English and Swedish continued to immigrate by the hundreds, but the number of Irish, Canadian, and German immigrants had dropped considerably.

Thus, one can see that a variety of ethnic groups were instrumental in the settling of the Marquette Iron Range. Without the immigrants from northern and southern Europe, the Upper Peninsula would be a much different place today.

Bibliography

Beard's Directory and History of Marquette County. Detroit, MI: Hadger and Bryce, 1873.

Holbrook, Stewart H. *Iron Brew: A Century of American Ore and Steel.* New York, NY: Macmillan, 1939.

Holmio, Armas K. E. *Michiganin Suomalaisten Historia.* Hancock, Mich.: The Book Concern, 1967 (English typescript at Finnish-American Historical Archives, Suomi College, Hancock, MI.).

Mulligan, William H., Jr. *Historic Resources of the Iron Range in Marquette County, Michigan, 1844–1941.* Marquette, MI: The Economic Development Corporation of the County of Marquette, 1991.

Rubenstein, Bruce A. and Lawrence E. Ziewacz. *Michigan: A History of the Great Lakes State.* St. Louis, MO: Forum Press, 1981.

Rydholm, C. Fred. *Superior Heartland: A Backwoods History.* Marquette, MI: C. Fred Rydholm, 1989.

United States Census Office. *Population Schedules of the Eighth Census of the United States, 1860* (Microfilm Reel 554, Michigan, Vol. 13, Marquette County, Pt. 1–74).

United States Census Office. *Population Schedules of the Twelfth Census of the United States, 1910* (Microfilm Reel 662, Michigan, Vol. 58, Marquette County, Pt. 1–257).

United States Immigration Commission. *Reports of the Immigration Commission. Vol. 3. Statistical Review of Immigration, 1819–1910, Distribution of Immigrants.* Washington, DC: Government Printing Office, 1911. Reprint ed., New York, NY: Arno and the New York Times, 1970.

Young, Otis E., Jr. *Black Powder and Hard Steel: Miners and Machines on the Old Western Frontier.* Norman: University of Oklahoma Press, 1976.

A Sense of Place

History

A Sense of Place: Michigan's Upper Peninsula

PRE-STATEHOOD PERCEPTIONS
Michigan's Upper Peninsula

Russell M. Magnaghi

Popular perceptions of many geographical regions of the United States have remained clouded and poorly described and thus incorrectly perceived for years before their reality became known. The Great Plains, today considered a source of agricultural abundance, were labeled "The Great American Desert" in the early nineteenth century. Utah's Great Salt Lake Basin was viewed as unfit for human habitation and the lake as a terrible salt sea. Then settlers arrived, developed irrigation, introduced agriculture, and prospered; later they found industrial uses for the minerals of the Great Salt Lake. And so it is with Michigan's Upper Peninsula, a scenic wilderness inhabited by Indians and bound on the north by the cold, clear waters of Lake Superior. It was and remains a land isolated and little understood, even by Michiganians of the Lower Peninsula.

By the time Michigan became a state in 1837, a considerable body of scholarly and popular literature had been published about the Upper Peninsula and its resources. However, some people—like John T. Blois—did not take time to check the record. When he introduced the region in the *Gazetteer of the State of Michigan* in 1838, he wrote:

> *Of this portion of Michigan, very little satisfactory information is to be had, and that which is known, is of a character devoid of much interest.*[1]

In 1887, fifty years after statehood, a number of individuals reflected on the value of the Upper Peninsula with such statements as, "It wasn't worth eighteen pence," or it was "not worth a dollar." Even Governor Alpheus Felch, addressing a semi-centennial celebration of statehood, said that in 1836 "of the upper peninsula, nothing was known and nothing expected from it."[2] John Harris Forster, writing in 1886, said in reflection, "The acquisition [of the Upper Peninsula in 1836] was regarded as worthless, yet it was thought by some that the white fish of Lake Superior might be a fair offset for the lost bull-frog pastures of the Maumee [River]."[3] Alex Campbell writing at the same time noted:

> *At that time [1836-1837] it was considered a comparatively worthless territory, its geographical position being unfavorable to agriculture, its climate frigid and unfriendly to all the pursuits we had come to regard as necessary in the settlement of a State.*[4]

Was the Upper Peninsula so remote and infrequently visited that there was little or no information available to the public regarding the land, its people, and its resources in 1837? It is the object of this study to review the pertinent literature available at that time on the Upper Peninsula in order to illustrate the fact that, although the information was readily available, it was ignored.

The scholarly and popular knowledge concerning the region revolved around five topics:

(1) mining
(2) fishing
(3) scenic beauty and resulting tourism
(4) lumber
(5) agriculture

In the past, these resources built the Upper Peninsula, and today portions of them remain important resources for renewed economic growth and development.

The Indians of the St. Lawrence River Valley at Montreal provided the first information concerning the copper of the Upper Peninsula to the French explorer Jacques Cartier in 1535. They told him that in the country of "Sagueway," which was bordered on the west by Lake Huron, red copper was to be found. When Cartier left Canada for France, the Indians presented him with a great knife of red copper from Sagueway.[5] This copper was not native to the shores of Lake Huron but had been carried by traders from the primitive mines operated by the Indians in the Keweenaw Peninsula, as this was the only source of pure copper in North America. Later, when Samuel de Champlain made his first voyage to Canada in 1603, he was told by the Indians, "There is toward the north a mine of pure copper," and they showed him some copper bracelets which had been obtained from the Hurons.[6]

The French Jesuit missionaries who began to enter the Lake Superior country in the mid-seventeenth century left a valuable chronicle of the land, its people, and resources. The Jesuits had curious and scientific minds and kept accurate records of what they saw. They wrote in detail about the Indians and their way of life and described the water quality of Lake Superior, its fisheries, the blueberries, and wild rice. Furthermore, they created an extremely accurate map of Lake Superior that was not improved until the nineteenth century.[7] Unfortunately, much of their knowledge and information concerning the Upper Peninsula was relegated to French archives and libraries, and what was published was not generally available to the English-speaking public. Other French archival depositories held official government correspondence and reports that also shed light on the Upper Peninsula, but these were never published and thus were unavailable to all but diligent scholars.8

After the French and Indian War in 1763, the British took possession of Canada, which still included the future state of Michigan, and a new era of chronicling and popularizing the Upper Peninsula began. Alexander Henry was one of the first British traders to leave Albany, New York and settle at the Straits of Mackinac in 1761. Over the years, he survived Pontiac's Rebellion, traveled extensively throughout the region, and left accurate descriptions of the Peninsula. In 1809 he published the record of his observations entitled *Travels and Adventures in Canada and the Indian Territories between the Years 1760 and 1776.* This account was read extensively by Henry Rowe Schoolcraft and has been described as containing detailed information about the Indians in the Great Lakes region. Henry presented a clear and detailed picture of the Upper Peninsula. At Mackinac Island he wrote of the famed white fish and trout fisheries and then described the lands bordering the St. Mary's River and the village of Sault Sainte Marie. Making a constant problem then and now were the abundant and pesky mosquitoes and black flies that were "so numerous as to be a heavy counterpoise to the pleasures of hunting." Henry went on to describe a near-paradise. "Pigeons were in great plenty, the streams supplied our drink; and sickness was unknown." On April 25, 1763, he wrote of Sir Robert Dover whom he described as an English gentleman "on a voyage of curiosity." Thus we have an early indication of an individual coming to the Upper Peninsula as a tourist.9

The copper resources in the vicinity of the Ontonagon River were not overlooked. Henry noted "the abundance of virgin copper" that "presented itself to the eye, in masses of various weight. The Indians showed me one of twenty pounds." He went on to note that the Indians used to process the red metal "into spoons and bracelets for themselves." In 1766, Henry canoed up the Ontonagon River and saw the Ontonagon Boulder, the object of curiosity to many visitors to Lake Superior. He said that it weighed "no less than five tons. Such was its pure and malleable state, that with an ax I was able to cut off a portion weighing a hundred pounds." Although there was copper available to the manufacturer, it would be difficult to extract because of the isolated nature of the land:

> The copper-ores of Lake Superior can never be profitably sought for but local consumption. The country must be cultivated and peopled, before they can deserve notice.10

This statement by Henry provides some insight as to why, in 1837, Michiganians overlooked the valuable copper deposits. The copper was there, but the isolated sites in relationship to the markets made it nearly valueless, and thus it was ignored.

Henry also described the shipyard at Point aux Pins, some six miles up the St. Mary's River from Sault Sainte Marie on the Canadian side of the river. The shipyard and assaying furnace established there made the pine-covered point the first industrial site in the Lake Superior country. Henry briefly discussed the industrial capacity of the region as well.[11]

A second English traveler and writer in the Upper Peninsula was Jonathan Carver, who was active in the late 1760s. His journals were "widely read in Great Britain, in America, and in Europe, achieving for its author recognition as an important traveler to the hinterland of America." Although Carver did not travel extensively in the Upper Peninsula, he did write of aspects of the region. He found the sturgeon of Green Bay as being "counted here the best fish." The ducks and wild fowl of the region along with the wild rice were also described. He also wrote of the abundance and great weight of the various fish—white fish, trout, cisco—in the Straits of Mackinac.

Mackinac Island, the center of the fur trade in the Great Lakes country, was discussed at length by Carver. He wrote about the garrison and the commercial activities on the island. The nature of the land in the vicinity was also the object of his reporting:

> *The land about Michilimackinac for some miles has a sandy dry, barren soil, so that the troops and traders can scarcely find sufficient for gardens to raise greens on; yet there is [sic] spots of tolerable good pasturage for sheep and cattle.*

Then he continued:

> *The land about Lake Huron is very poor and barren and unfit for cultivation excepting some spots at the entrance of rivers, and between Lake Huron and Lake Michigan for near an hundred miles in length is a very high plain lying north and south from which rise several rivers heading near each other that discharge themselves into both of these lakes. The timber that grows here is spruce, pine, hemlock, and fur [fir], some beach [beech], pople [aspen], and birch which last is very useful for the Indians in making their canoes.*

The land north of Lake Michigan was described by Carver as being much the same as that of Lake Huron. Further, he noted small sand cherries growing on the banks of Lake Michigan and other lakes that were the size of sweet fern bushes.[12]

HISTORY: PRE-STATEHOOD PERCEPTIONS

The popularity of Carver's work provided Americans and Michiganians with insights into the region and the quality of its land. Schoolcraft found the book useful and indicated that from his personal experiences, Carver had visited the places that he wrote about.[13]

The American geographer Jedidiah Morse published *The American Geography; or A View of the Present Situation of the United States of America* in 1789. This classic work was read and studied by many Americans. In it he discussed the copper, the fishery of Lake Superior, and the beauty of Sault Sainte Marie. Although he inaccurately located the copper deposits in the Chequemegnon area and on islands in the eastern end of Lake Superior, he did provide a route for its passage to New York. He concluded by stating, "The cheapness and ease with which any quantity of the ore may be procured, will make up for the distance and expense of transportation." Of the Lake Superior fishery he continued, "This lake abounds with fish, particularly trout and sturgeon; the former weigh from twelve to fifty pounds, and are caught almost any season of the year in great plenty." The terrible savage storms of the lake were described as making navigation dangerous. Morse concluded with a note for the tourist: "The entrance into this lake from the straits of St. Marie, affords one of the most pleasing prospects in the world."[14]

At approximately the same time, J. Long visited the Lake Superior country and in a work published in 1791 described many aspects of the Upper Peninsula. He noted that Indian corn and hard grease were "the food all traders carry to the upper country." However, he was also impressed by the abundance of the fish—pickerel, trout, and "white fish of an uncommon size"—in Lake Superior. He also wrote of the great size of Lake Superior and noted that its water was so clear that sturgeon could be clearly seen to a great depth.[15]

The land which became the state of Michigan remained in British control until the ratification of Jay's Treaty. According to the terms of the treaty, the British agreed to evacuate their military posts in the Great Lakes region by June of 1796, which they did. American control over the region was slowly imposed. Mackinac Island continued as the military, governmental, and commercial center for the Upper Peninsula.

Even at this early date, many Americans, including government officials, became acquainted with the resources of the region. A map of the United States produced by Samuel Lewis in 1795 showed "copper mines" to exist on the south shore of Lake Superior.[16] Four years later, New York Congressman William Cooper had specimens of this metal in his possession and brought them to the attention of the Congress. The assayer of the United States tested some of the samples and reported that this copper was "pure malleable copper, fit for the manufactors." At this time the economy of the nation needed a local source of copper, because an Anglo-French war had restricted importation of British copper. Congress authorized President John Adams to send an expedition to Lake Superior to confirm the presence of copper and if true to arrange a treaty with the Indians in order to obtain the copper-rich land for the United States. Due to a series of unfortunate delays, the designated leader of the expedition, Richard Cooper, never set forth. Later in 1801, due to political considerations and biases, newly inaugurated President Jefferson canceled the expedition. Although there was knowledge of Lake Superior copper in Philadelphia and Washington, DC, it remained untapped.

Dr. Francis Le Baron, a surgeon at Fort Mackinac, was the next individual to question whether the copper of the Upper Peninsula could be exploited. He began his correspondence on the subject in 1809, and by September 1810 he addressed a letter to the Secretary of War "on a Subject which has long since occupied my mind, relative to the probable existence of rich and valuable Copper mines, in & about Lake Superior & its navigable waters." From a long residence in the region, Dr. Le Baron had not only heard of copper deposits in the region but had seen specimens from different locations. He concluded that with government assistance these copper deposits could become "an inexhaustible source of wealth to those who engage in the working of them, and unparalleled prosperity to this part of Our western possessions." Dr. Le Baron also sent specimens of copper found in the western Upper Peninsula to John Davis of Boston and Colonel P. B. Porter, a member of Congress.[17]

Nothing seems to have developed from Dr. Le Baron's inquiry. However, in 1810 Secretary of Treasury Albert Gallatin wrote in a report, "State of Domestic Manufactures," that information about the copper had appeared in library journals and other publications, and there were widespread expectations for its development by Americans. Settlement in the Great Lakes country, especially in the south, however, was slowed because of the Indian hostility led by Tecumseh and the Shawnee Prophet. The coming of the War of 1812 brought settlement of the region to a complete halt; however, specimens of Upper Peninsula copper continued to be assayed and reports written on its purity and potential industrial use. William Eustis was minister plenipotentiary to the Netherlands from 1814 until illness forced his retirement in 1818. During his stay in the Netherlands, he sent specimens of Lake Superior copper to an assayer at Utrecht. A portion of the assayer's glowing report stated:

HISTORY: PRE-STATEHOOD PERCEPTIONS

> *From every appearance, the piece of copper seems to have qualified for rolling and forging; and that its excellence is indicated by its resemblance to the copper usually employed by the English for plating.*

The report continued that the copper "...has proved that it does not contain the smallest article of silver, gold, or any other metal." Late in 1820, Schoolcraft further noted that some Lake Superior copper had also been sent to the University of Leyden for analysis and was found to be of "uncommon purity."[18]

In the years following the War of 1812, with the Indian threat gone, the American people began their westward migration in earnest and naturally showed a burning interest in the land and its resources. This attitude can be seen in a petition written by Lewis Bringer seeking to have Congress pass a law which would allow individuals to develop gold, silver, lead, and copper mines in the United States.[19] Although Bringer was primarily interested in developing lead mines west of the Mississippi River, this spirit prevailed throughout the nation.

Dr. Le Baron was now in a position to petition Congress to allow him a concession to exploit the copper of the Upper Peninsula. He felt that the development of these deposits would "contribute to the prosperity and independence of these United States." His request attracted Congressional interest, and on December 24, 1816 he answered a series of questions probably requested by a Senate committee concerning the region, transportation, the Indians, and naturally the copper. Dr. Le Baron further felt that the development of these copper deposits would bring about a strong American presence and eventual domination of a region whose Indian inhabitants were then dominated by British fur traders and thus pro-British in their allegiance. Dr. Le Baron continued by saying:

> *In a few years a Colony would be formed of a hardy, industrious, and brave people, attracted to the Government of the United States and forming a Barrier on that Frontier which would give confidence to New Adventurers, and would produce a speedy settlement of the intermediate territory between the shores of Lake Superior & Detroit.*[20]

In order to extract the mineral wealth, Dr. Le Baron proposed a unique interaction of workers in this region with an extremely sparse population. Fur traders would continue to gather furs in the winter and work in the mines during the summer "until there are excavations made in the earth that will contain men so within its bowels as to produce a temperate climate." Unfortunately, nothing came of

Dr. Le Baron's enthusiasm, but more information on the region reached the public.

Mineral resources of the region were not the only items discussed in scientific publications. In the summer of 1810, the youthful botanist Thomas Nuttall visited and collected specimens in the vicinity of Mackinac Island. He eventually published his findings in 1818 under the title, *The Genera of North American Plants, and a Catalogue of the Species, to the Year 1817*. Here he described three species new to science from the Upper Peninsula: a dwarf species of iris (*Iris lacustris*) found on the shores of northern Lakes Michigan and Huron; a large-headed tansy (*Tanacetum huronense*) named for Lake Huron; and a thimbleberry (*Rubus parviflorus*) occurring in the northern Great Lakes and found in the West.[21]

By this time, information about the Upper Peninsula began to appear in a variety of popular publications. Andrew Miller's emigrant guide, *New States and Territories . . . in 1818*, labeled the region of the Upper Peninsula as the "Northwestern Territory" and stated that it "lies west of Michigan Territory and Lake. It is bounded by Lake Michigan on the east, Superior and the grand portage north, Mississippi river west and Illinois territory south." As if to paraphrase earlier chroniclers, Miller wrote: "... the territory derives its chief importance at present from its mines, wild game, fish, fowl, and wild rice. Virgin copper," he continued, "has also been found in several places, and iron ore."[22] In 1819, Daniel Blowe published an emigrant guide again calling the Upper Peninsula the Northwestern Territory. Writing about Pointe aux Pins, he noted that shipbuilding continued to be carried out there and that there were places along the St. Mary's River that had the potential of becoming mill sites. Neither Mackinac Island nor the copper deposits were forgotten. He noted that his British audience should not be surprised to learn that Americans were finally entering the region to work the copper deposits and that the British should take heed of the possibilities. Finally, he wrote that in November 1816 a company was formed in the United States to develop these deposits which "ensures the future commercial consequence of this territory."[23] The third and last descriptive study of the Upper Peninsula to be reviewed was the result of a trip taken by Estwick Evans during the winter and spring of 1818. In his work, Evans described Mackinac Island and praised its fish: "The Michilimackinac trout are bred in Lake Michigan and are celebrated for their size and excellence; they sometimes weigh 60 to 70 pounds." His account continued:

> The tract of country lying between Lake Michigan and Lake Superior is rather sterile. The falls of St. Mary situated in the strait between Lakes Huron and Superior, are mere cascades. In this

HISTORY: PRE-STATEHOOD PERCEPTIONS

strait there are several islands. Below the falls is situated [the site of] Fort St. Mary. In this strait are caught fine fish of many kinds.

Evans went on to write of the Indians and ended by saying that "...the vicinity of this place [Sault Sainte Marie] is a perfect wilderness."[24]

The year 1820 was pivotal in the historical perception of the Upper Peninsula. Up to that time, a surprisingly large amount of accurate data about the environment and resources had been gathered and made available to the public through published works, government reports, and specimens. All of this knowledge about the region had been gathered by individuals, but an official government expedition with professional scientists and artists had never visited the area to develop detailed reports and drawings.

The nationalistic territorial governor of Michigan, Lewis Cass, was well aware of the Upper Peninsula, its resources, and Indian difficulties. On November 18, 1819 he wrote to Secretary of War John C. Calhoun proposing that he head an expedition through the little-known area to the south of Lake Superior, to the headwaters of the Mississippi River, and back through Chicago. Cass was primarily concerned with acquiring accurate geographical knowledge of the region and obtaining the cession of Indian lands in the area.[25] In response to this request, Calhoun wrote on January 14, 1820 that the expedition had his sanction, but financing would have to come from Cass's Indian superintendency budget and a supplemental one thousand dollars from the War Department. Calhoun concluded: "Feeling as I do great interest in obtaining correct Topographical, geographical and military survey of our Country, every encouragement consistent with my means will be given by this department."[26] A few weeks later, he wrote to Cass attaching Henry R. Schoolcraft to the expedition so that the minerals of the country could be properly studied.[27]

The fact that the Cass expedition was in the process of being organized was promptly reported by the newspapers. The *Detroit Gazette* of March 3 published an article praising Calhoun's foresight in having authorized such a beneficial expedition that would help to reduce the nation's ignorance of its own geography. This article reached a much larger audience when it was reprinted by the *Nile's Weekly Register* in April.

Individual territorial officials were also interested in the expedition and its results. William Woodbridge, the Michigan territorial secretary, wrote to Calhoun in February, concerned about the purpose of the expedition and the importance of the government's obtaining the Indian cession to the copper-rich lands.

In June 1820, the Cass expedition moved into the north country. Stops were made at Mackinac Island and then at Sault Sainte Marie. At the latter stop, a treaty was made with the Indians ceding land for a future military post, but no mention was made of the copper deposits to the west. The flotilla of canoes passed along the south shore of Lake Superior making accurate observations. Much of what they saw and wrote about merely pointed to the accuracy of the earlier reports.

It is one thing to make reports and another to get the information published and out to the public so that perceptions of the land are created. At first, the data uncovered were written up in the form of official reports. In a letter written to Calhoun on October 1, Schoolcraft discussed the copper deposits and related matters. First he noted that the lands belonged to the Ojibwe Indians and their title would have to be extinguished. However, Schoolcraft pointed out that these copper lands were the least valuable to the Indians for hunting purposes because they were rocky and rough. As a scientist, he stated that the "copper is abundantly found on the southern shore of Lake Superior...." As he continued, he noted the remote location of the copper and the lack of a labor force but pointed out that the richness of the copper would attract the capital and energy needed for this process; in turn this would greatly aid the American economy. Schoolcraft sought to allay fears of developing these deposits because of the distance and went into a detailed study of the distance and obstacles between the Ontonagon River and New York City and ended his comments with the fact that imported copper was shipped from great distances into the United States.[28]

In November, Schoolcraft again wrote to Calhoun identifying the locations of potential copper deposits: Isle Royale, the northeast branch of the Ontonagon River, the Keweenaw Peninsula, and the Porcupine Mountains. However, his notices of other locations such as east of Point Abbaye at the entrance to Huron Bay, in the vicinity of the city of Marquette at Pictured Rocks, and at Lake Court Oreilles in northern Wisconsin proved to be fanciful. He had prefaced his listing with the fact that he had either seen or had been told of deposits of float copper.[29]

Once the Cass expedition returned from its western expedition, there was scholarly interest in the publication of its records and observations. Benjamin Silliman of Yale University sought to publish Calhoun and Schoolcraft's views "respecting more especially the mineralogy and geology of the regions explored by Gov Cass &

Party...."[30] These notes were to be published in the *American Journal of Science and Arts*, which Silliman was quick to point out had an extensive scholarly audience in both Europe and America, and recently Secretary of State John Quincy Adams had requested a set of the journal for the library of the State Department. Calhoun agreed that the journal was the best way to get this "valuable paper" to the public.[31] In a letter to Schoolcraft, Calhoun wrote, "The report will be a valuable addition to the scientific [literature] of our Country."[32] Schoolcraft was in total agreement with having his "Report on the Northwestern Copper Mines" released for a publication which would soon be in the hands of scholars.[33] Earlier in January, continuing a tradition, Schoolcraft sent Calhoun a specimen of copper so that it could be viewed in Washington by a curious public.

Of the numerous scientists who accompanied the Cass expedition, only Schoolcraft rushed to have his *Narrative Journal of Travels from Detroit Northwest through the Great Chain of American Lakes to the Sources of the Mississippi River in the Year 1820* published. This action quickly angered his colleagues. If the reader missed the book, there was always an extensive book review in *The North American Review* which went into descriptive detail about Mackinac Island, Sault Sainte Marie, Lake Superior, Pictured Rocks, and, naturally, the all-important copper deposits.[34]

The immediate result of the Cass expedition was a new and strong American presence at Sault Sainte Marie, where the Ojibwe Indians were openly pro-British. In 1822, Fort Brady was established on land ceded by the Indians two years earlier. The fort not only brought together officers, soldiers, and their families, but they were followed by contractors and merchants, allowing better communications with Detroit. At the same time, the War Department decided to establish an Indian agency at Sault Sainte Marie, and Henry Rowe Schoolcraft was made superintendent. He interacted well with the Indians and spent his time studying their life and culture and visiting the far-flung parts of the Upper Peninsula. After this time, Schoolcraft was the chief source of information on the region reaching the public in Lower Michigan. Over the decades, everyone from journalists to congressmen sought his opinions and insights on the Upper Peninsula, and he readily complied with their requests.

Information concerning the Upper Peninsula was not restricted to Schoolcraft and government reports. On July 13 and 26, 1822, the *Detroit Gazette* carried a series of interesting letters from an unidentified gentleman who had traveled to Sault Sainte Marie. Noting the agricultural potential there, he pointed out, "Potatoes, oats, pease, and garden stuffs generally, succeed with certainty every year." Locally, George Johnston proved to be a fine farmer planting 1,200 bushels of potatoes along with oats, peas, and hardgrass. Johnston also had a vegetable garden with radishes, lettuce, and carrots, along with a flower garden filled with roses and pink and violet hyacinths surrounded by fields of strawberries. In the L'Anse area he wrote that John Holiday was raising corn, peas, and garden vegetables, "all of which are said to flourish well" and that there was other land available with rich soil and well adapted for the development of an agricultural settlement.

Next, our mysterious author wrote of the fishery in the St. Mary's River. The garrison at Fort Brady and the civilian neighbors daily ate "the most delicious fish, the *poisson blanc*, or white fish, and also the salmon, trout, pike, carp, and sturgeon. The small spotted trout and several kinds of small pan fish are also found in the waters of that vicinity." The woods were filled with passenger pigeons, which provided a constant daily food supply for the garrison. During the harvest season, the wild rice attracted the "most delicious wild fowl," which also entered the local diet.

Building materials and pasture grasses were also described. There was an abundance of timber available for the construction of Fort Brady. The closest limestone was located down river at Neebish Rapids, and it was hoped that the flat sandstone at the rapids could be utilized for building purposes. On Sugar Island, there were natural meadows where an adequate supply of hay could be cut for the horses and oxen, and there was also pasturage in the woods, while that on the common was considered of fine quality.

After the return of the Cass expedition, Congress became interested in the copper deposits of the Upper Peninsula. One of the leading figures in this movement was Senator Thomas Hart Benton of Missouri, who was considered a leading advocate of frontier expansion. Benton entered the Senate in December 1821 and was named to committees on Public Lands and Indian Affairs. Between 1823 and 1833, Benton was the chair of the Committee on Indian Affairs.[35]

Knowledge of and interest in copper on the southern shore of Lake Superior was of concern to many Congressmen because of its economic potential for the United States. On May 8, 1822, the Senate passed a resolution seeking data on the "copper mines on the south shore of Lake Superior. . . ." In response to this request, in October Schoolcraft completed a report and sent it to the Senate "embracing the principal facts known respecting them [the copper deposits] ensisting [sic] on their value and importance, and warmly recommending their further exploration and working."[36]

HISTORY: PRE-STATEHOOD PERCEPTIONS

This was followed by correspondence between the apostle of expansion, Senator Benton, and Michigan territorial governor Lewis Cass. In a letter dated January 19, 1823, Cass wrote that copper could be found "between Lake Superior, and the streams which descend to Green Bay and the Mississippi [River]...." He continued:

> *The present state of our knowledge of that country* [Lake Superior] *is not such as to enable us to determine where this metal can be found in sufficient abundance to defray the expense of collecting and transporting it to market.*[37]

Through the year of 1824, the two continued a correspondence on Lake Superior copper. Then Cass indicated that Benton should correspond directly with Schoolcraft, the budding authority on the region and its resources. Schoolcraft received mineralogical specimens from George Johnston, the aforementioned Sault Sainte Marie resident, and other travelers who visited the region. As a result, he was able to create a mineral cabinet or exhibition case in the Indian agency which was seen by many passing visitors over the years.[38] As Schoolcraft's fame spread, federal officials and Congressmen sought his expertise. In April 1824, Schoolcraft received a letter from M. M. Dox, collector of customs at the port of Buffalo, concerning the potential development of the copper deposits and the essential markets which would expand the American economy. Schoolcraft optimistically answered:

> *All accounts concur in representing the metal in that quarter of a superior quality, and furnish strong indications that it may be obtained, in quantities, with more than ordinary facility.*[39]

He proceeded in discussing in some detail the possibilities of developing these deposits.

Thus it transpired that on March 14, 1826 Benton wrote Schoolcraft that ten thousand dollars had been appropriated by the Senate to further implement a clause in the Prairie du Chien Treaty of 1825. He proposed that a government delegation should meet with the Indians "so that the copper mine business is arranged."[40]

So it was that in the summer of 1826, Cass was heading an expedition accompanied by the Commissioner of Indian Affairs, Thomas McKenney, to Fond du Lac (modern Duluth) to treat with the Indians. In July and August the treaty was arranged, and Article 3 accomplished what Senator Benton sought:

A Sense of Place: Michigan's Upper Peninsula

> The Chippewa tribe grant to the government of the United States the right to search for, and carry away any metals or minerals from any part of their country.

However, the Indian title and jurisdiction to their lands was maintained.

While the treaty negotiations were underway, to the east along the Ontonagon River a group was unsuccessfully attempting to dislodge the famed Ontonagon Boulder. When the equipment that they brought proved insufficient for the task, they tried to melt some pure copper from the boulder. Finally, they were able to crack off some specimens. Schoolcraft expressed his horror at the mutilation of "the noblest specimen of native copper on the globe."[41]

Commissioner McKenney left a detailed account of various locales along the shoreline of the Upper Peninsula. Concerning Mackinac Island, he wrote a description worthy of an advertising agency:

> Mackinac is really worth seeing. I think it by no means improbable, especially should the steamboats extend their route to it, that it will become a place of fashionable resort for the summer. There is no finer summer climate in the world. The purest, sweetest air—lake scenery in all its aged and grand magnificence, and the purest water; white fish in perfection, the very best fish, I believe in the world, and trout, weighing from five to fifty pounds. No flies, and no mosquitoes, nothing to annoy, but every variety for the eye, the taste, and the imagination, with all that earth, and water, and sky can furnish, (except good fresh meat, and where such fish are plenty, this can be dispensed with) to make it agreeable and delightful. There are no bilious fevers here; and temperate people may, with something like certainty, if not organically diseased, spin out life's thread to its utmost tenuity. But in winter I would prefer not to be here; and that would form an exception, as to temperature, of at least seven months out of the twelve.[42]

McKenney went on to discuss a variety of aspects of the Upper Peninsula. Passing Drummond Island in the St. Mary's River, he was impressed with its "picture of barrenness" and sterility. At Sault Sainte Marie, he felt that the "rheumatic" problems affecting some members of the military garrison of Fort Brady were caused by the vapors rising from the rapids. "The staples of the place, are the white fish and maple sugar, and some few, but not many furs." Although he had read about the sterility of the land at Sault Sainte Marie, he was impressed by the fine quality of potatoes, oats, peas, strawberries, and other unmentioned vegetables which were cultivated in George Johnston's garden and that of the garrison. He concluded that what he experienced, despite the short growing season and northerly location,"demonstrate that man can accomplish much, even over the most forbidding state of things, and in the very face of nature, who frowns, as she certainly does here, upon all such efforts." As the boats passed along the shore, McKenney continued to make comments about the nature of the land. The formation now known as Pictured Rocks National Lakeshore was duly recognized and noted as were the barren "peaks" in the vicinity of modern Marquette. At a later point in his writing he concluded, "I consider this whole region doomed to perpetual barrenness."[43]

In the summer of 1831, Schoolcraft was authorized to lead an expedition into the Lake Superior country and Northern Wisconsin. The expedition consisted of Schoolcraft, George Johnston, Douglass Houghton, M. Woolsey, an escort of ten soldiers from Fort Brady at Sault Sainte Marie, and a few Ojibwe who conveyed the provisions. They left Sault Sainte Marie on June 25 and returned on September 4, thus traveling 2,308 miles in seventy-two days. Their destination was the confluence of the St. Croix and Yellow Rivers in Northern Wisconsin, where they met the Ojibwe and Sioux in council to discuss recent hostilities.

Schoolcraft was unimpressed with the dissemination of geographical information about the Upper Peninsula up to that time. He noted the lack of information in the numerous errors found on contemporary maps. The records kept and published by members of the expedition upon their return would hopefully fill the void.[44]

In his *Personal Memoirs* Schoolcraft noted that on the Keweenaw Peninsula members of the expedition blasted to check the minerals lying underground while others explored the interior seeking specimens with which they returned. He concluded that the Peninsula was "highly metalliferous."[45] Dr. Douglass Houghton, a geologist, submitted a special report to Lewis Cass concerning the copper of the Upper Peninsula. He began the report:

> *It is without doubt true that this subject has long been viewed with an interest far beyond its actual merit. Each mass of native copper which this country has produced, however insulated, or however it may have been separated from its original positions, appears to have been considered a sure indication of the existence of that metal in beds; and hence we occasionally see, upon maps of that section of our country, particular portions marked as containing "copper mines," where no copper now exists.*

He continued that in general, although the public had been misled by inaccurate information, this did not diminish the fact "that a greater quantity of insulated native copper has been discovered upon the borders of Lake Superior, than in any other equal portion of North America." Concerning the Ontonagon Boulder, he wrote that the "ore of that metal has long been known to the lake traders as the green rock ...." In conclusion, he noted that he was unable to make a thorough investigation of the copper resources of the region and one would have to be made in the future. However, he did bring some scientific credence to the status of Upper Peninsula copper.[46]

The role of tourism is a bit more difficult to identify. However, there are indications in the 1820s that there were tourist vacationers and health seekers in the Upper Peninsula. Thomas McKenney, Commissioners of Indian Affairs, fell into the latter category. He wrote that when he started his trip to Duluth, he was in poor health but found that the environment improved him. He also noted that in the summer of 1826 there was a visitor to L'Anse who was there seeking to improve his health.[47] A few years later, Schoolcraft noted that M. Woolsey of the 1831 expedition was in the Upper Peninsula as "an admirer of nature, seeking health."[48]

In the 1820s and 1830s, Mackinac Island was evolving from a fur trading center to a tourist destination. Martin Heydenburk observed the change which had taken place by 1833:

> *Mackinaw was the seat and center of the American fur trade. It was then in the height of its prosperity, but soon after the [American Fur] company disbanded, and those connected with it left. This changed the place from a commercial to a pleasure-seeking community, and an entire change of inhabitants resettled.*[49]

In his position as Indian agent at Sault Sainte Marie and authority on the region and its people, Henry R. Schoolcraft was visited by many early tourists. In September 1834, Captain Tchehachoff of the Russian Imperial Guards was in the eastern Upper Peninsula. Two years later, Lewis Cass—now Secretary of War—and his daughter visited, while Baron de Behr, minister of Belgium, traveled to Sault Sainte Marie to see the entrance of Lake Superior. Other visitors in the 1830s included Baron Mareschal and Count de Colobiano, the Austrian and Sardinian ambassadors to Washington respectively, and Catholic Bishop Frederick Rese of Detroit, to name but a few prominent individuals who visited Schoolcraft at Sault Sainte Marie or Mackinac Island.[50]

Although most of these individuals remained in the eastern part of the Upper Peninsula, some individuals ventured into the more remote areas and described places like the area that would become

HISTORY: PRE-STATEHOOD PERCEPTIONS

Pictured Rocks National Lakeshore. In 1826, McKenney was impressed with Grand Sable, an "extraordinary mountain of sand ... which varies in height from 100 to 300 feet; and stretches along the shore of the lake, at the base of which is a beach." He went on to describe Doric Rock and Pictured Rocks in general.[51] Nine years later, Chandler R. Gilman visited Pictured Rocks and left his recollections in the first book written on the area.[52] Others hoped for the day when travel would be readily available to ordinary citizens who would not have to brave the difficulties of travel faced by the missionaries, fur traders, and explorers.

On the eve of statehood, Schoolcraft summed up the growing importance of the Great Lakes region as a tourist destination:

> The great lakes can no longer be regarded as solitary seas, where the Indian war-whoop has alone for so many uncounted centuries startled its echoes. The Eastern World seems to be alive, and roused up to the value of the West. Every vessel, every steamboat, brings up persons of all classes, whose countenances the desire of acquisition, or some other motive, has rendered sharp, or imparted a fresh glow of hope to their eyes. More persons, of some note or distinction, natives or foreigners, have visited me and brought me letters of introduction this season [1836] than during years before. Sitting on my piazza, in front of which the great stream of ships and commerce passes, it is a spectacle at once novel, and calculated to inspire high anticipations of the future glory of the Mississippi Valley.[53]

Although more accurate and glowing accounts of the Upper Peninsula were reaching the public in various forms of print, the negative but realistic views continued. As we have seen, Thomas McKenney noted the barrenness of the land of the central Upper Peninsula and wrote that at Sault Sainte Marie, during the 1825 to 1826 season, snow fell from October to April to the depth of approximately seventeen feet. McKenney also noted the poor travel accommodations en route.[54] A short time later, the Territorial Legislative Council of Michigan was seeking to create the Territory of Huron out of a portion of the Upper Peninsula. In its report to Congress, the Council noted the weather: "At the most favorable season of the year, the intercourse between the eastern & western sections is extremely difficult & in the winter season in a measure impracticable; the inconvenience of which has long been sensibly felt by both sections." However, in a positive light, the Council proposed that two separate governments could exist because "...so far as our knowledge extends, there is no section in the northern latitudes of the United States superior to it in point of climate, soil, timber, and water privileges." Because of these attributes, the Council added that the federal government could make money selling the public lands.55

We have seen how information was gathered, but it is important to understand how these data entered the popular consciousness, especially of the people of Michigan. By the early 1830s, data on the Upper Peninsula was reaching an audience in Detroit. In 1834, the book *Historical and Scientific Sketches of Michigan* was published with a series of lectures presented by Cass (September 18, 1829) and Schoolcraft (June 4, 1830) that discussed the Indians in depth. Schoolcraft, talking about "Natural History," mentioned the gypsum deposits of St. Martin's Islands north of Mackinac but did not mention copper. Concerning the fish resources, Schoolcraft told his audience "…the most important of our lake fishes considered in reference to its value in commerce, is the white fish." Further, he pointed out that in 1830 eight thousand barrels of white fish valued at forty thousand dollars were taken from Lake Superior. As if to complement Schoolcraft's observations on white fish, during the summer of 1834 L. Godard of Detroit offered white fish from Sault Sainte Marie for sale.56

Not only were descriptions and observations of the Upper Peninsula appearing in print, but a variety of specimens were beginning to be placed on display in Detroit where the public could observe them. The recently established (1828) Michigan State Historical Society became the depository of a number of collections related to the Upper Peninsula. On March 6, 1831, Schoolcraft donated "a collection of minerals, specimens and organic remains with a catalogue; he also donated a number of specimens of Indian work." Society records show that "General Cass presented a collection of specimens illustrating the geology and mineralogy of the country visited by him during his expedition of 1820." The Society's display area was located in the Territorial Council House in Detroit and thus readily available to the curious public.57

Henry R. Schoolcraft, now a noted authority on the Upper Peninsula, in 1831 wrote four lengthy letters describing portions of the region which appeared in news print. These "Albion Letters" appeared in the *Detroit Journal and Michigan Advertiser* weekly between March 23 and April 27, 1831. In the first installment, when describing the "northwestern territory," Schoolcraft said that it "will form an upper peninsula" in the future. This could possibly be the first time that the term "upper peninsula" appeared in print. Referring to a trip taken in 1824 to Tahquamenon Falls, he depicted the upper falls as presenting "some of the most picturesque scenery of the north." He also noted the isolation of the region when describing Mackinac Island:

> The American flag displayed from the fort [Mackinac]...reminds the visitor that he is far away from the ordinary haunts of civilization where it is still necessary to exhibit the arm of power to maintain order among the different tribes who periodically meet here.

In other issues, he wrote of the rocks and minerals found on Mackinac Island, the beauty of Lakes Huron and Michigan and the march of progress and civilization coming from the south. His last letter concentrated on Sault Sainte Marie but cautioned summer visitors:

> Those who are pleased with looking upon skies and woods and waters, may be happy during a summer residence here. But it is the Siberia of the American Army. It has no post route. Papers and reviews are received when it pleases the postmaster at Detroit to send them, or when he has an opportunity of doing so.[58]

Due to his knowledge of the land and people of the North, Schoolcraft was called into service to lead an expedition during the summer of 1832 whose purpose was to discover the source of the Mississippi River. One of his secondary goals was to gather and disseminate information about portions of the Upper Peninsula. Lieutenant James Allen noted in his diary:

> I have been particular in describing this part of our route [Keweenaw Peninsula] because it is the least known of any part of the lake [Superior]. Its rocks and minerals are no where accurately described and its topography is falsely represented on all the maps of it that I have seen.[59]

This expedition attracted considerable interest in the newspapers of the time, and Dr. Douglass Houghton contributed a series of reports for the *Detroit Journal and Michigan Advertiser* from various points along the route. The reports were published as they were received and reprinted in other newspapers as well. On October 8, 1832, a summary article appeared which analyzed the importance of the expedition in terms of the copper resources and the possibilities of tourism:

> The investigations made at Keweenaw Point by Mr. Schoolcraft and Doctor Houghton on their late expedition to the sources of the Mississippi, though only superficial, warrant inferences that copper ore will be found there in such abundance as to invite and reward future exertions. The mineral associations are there all of a promising character, and the specimens brought back are rich in variety

and beauty. The determination of such an important fact is highly to be estimated. It may have a mark'd influence on the coming prosperity of Lake Superior.

And then the article continued:

...and we may anticipate that Lake Superior will in the course of a few more years be nearly or quite as well known as its sister Lakes below; and that its mineral wealth, its picturesque and often sublime scenery, will have the witnesses and admirers than the rare few who have the enterprise of Mr. Schoolcraft and his associates.[60]

The record shows that by 1835 the value of the Upper Peninsula should have been known to officials, politicians, scholars, and the general public in Michigan; however, in the heat of the political debate to include the western Upper Peninsula within the proposed state, tempers rose to a fever pitch, and the land was condemned as frozen, worthless, and not worth a dollar. In the midst of the struggle, however, farsighted individuals prevailed.

The heart of the problem lay in the fact that the original boundary separating Michigan and Ohio, known as the Toledo Strip and encompassing 468 square miles, had been incorrectly surveyed. During the presidential election year of 1836, the politically powerful state of Ohio pushed aside the surveying errors and Michigan's legal claim.

Did Michigan have any claim to the Upper Peninsula? During the debates to draft a state constitution conducted in the spring of 1835, the western boundary was noted. It ran up through the center of Lake Michigan, across the Upper Peninsula, and bisected the international boundary in Lake Superior. The eastern half of the Upper Peninsula was to be included in the new state.[61]

In Washington, the debates over Ohio's claim to the Toledo Strip seemed to be a lost cause for Michigan. On January 22, 1836, Colonel D. Goodwin of Detroit wrote Lucius Lyon, the delegate to Congress,[62] suggesting that Lyon look into securing more land to the west in compensation for the loss of the Toledo Strip. Lyon replied that he had no doubt that the Senate Judiciary Committee would "be willing to give us all the country west of Lake Michigan and north and east of the Menominee river of Green Bay and the Montreal river of Lake Superior, thus giving us the greater part of the coast of that lake, which may at some future time be valuable."[63] In a subsequent letter, he seemed to have mixed feelings about the land and its prospects:

HISTORY: PRE-STATEHOOD PERCEPTIONS

> ...the [Senate Judiciary] committee will probably give us a strip of country along the southern shore of Lake Superior, where we can raise our own Indians in all time to come and supply ourselves now and then with a little bear meat for delicacy.[64]

In some ways, Lyon had to be careful because Michigan Whigs, through their organ the *Detroit Journal*, supported the Ohio claim to the Toledo Strip.[65] On February 21, 1836, Lyon had his opportunity to put forth the claim to attach the western Upper Peninsula to the future state before the Senate Judiciary Committee. His request:

> ...all the country we can get on Lake Superior and Michigan without producing serious inconvenience to the inhabitants that may now or hereafter reside there; and I have no doubt the committee will recommend that our western boundary be so altered as to run down Lake Michigan to the Fox Islands, thence along the main ship canals into Green Bay and up the Bay to the mouth of the Menominee River, thence up said river to the head of the branch nearest *Lac Vieu Dessert* [Lac Vieux Désert], thence through said lake down the Montreal river of Lake Superior.

Although his fellow delegates John Norvell and Isaac E. Crary were opposed to the addition, Lyon felt "...if we are to lose so much on the south we ought at least to have something on the west and north." He then rather prophetically continued:

> My opinion is that within 20 years the addition proposed will be valued by Michigan at more than forty millions of dollars, and that even after ten years the State would not think of selling it for that sum.[66]

In a letter to Senator Charles C. Hascall, Lyon stated:

> This will give Michigan about 20,000 square miles of land, together with three fourths of the American shore of Lake Superior, which may at some future time be esteemed very valuable. A considerable tract of country between Lake Michigan and Lake Superior is known to be fertile and this with the fisheries on Lake Superior and the copper mines supposed to exist there may hereafter be worth to us many millions of dollars. At any rate it can do us no harm and I am in favor of getting it while we can, for at best, if we are cut down on the south as we certainly shall be, our State will be quite poor and small enough.[67]

Finally, in a March 31 letter to the *Detroit Free Press*, Lyon further highlighted the value of the Upper Peninsula:

65

> *The upper peninsula is known to contain vast forests of the very best pine, which is even now much wanted in Ohio, Indiana, Illinois, and the southern part of Michigan and Wisconsin, and must very shortly furnish the material of a highly valuable trade.*[68]

In the course of these debates in the Senate Judiciary Committee, Henry R. Schoolcraft, who was in Washington working on a treaty with the Indians of northern Michigan, was invited by Silas Wright to offer expert testimony on the geography and natural resources of the Lake Superior region to members of the Committee.[69]

As the discussion on the incorporation of what became known as the Upper Peninsula continued, it had to draw to a close so a decision could be made. A map was produced similar to one drawn by L. Judson and published in 1838 by order of the Wisconsin territorial legislature. Senator William Preston of South Carolina drew his finger from the Montreal to the Menominee River, which was thought to be a natural highway between Green Bay and Lake Superior. Preston thought that this was a fair division of land so that a future state of Wisconsin would not be too large, and Michigan would be adequately compensated yet sized in keeping with the other states of the time.[70] Thus, on March 1, the Judiciary Committee decided on the boundary question in Michigan's favor and sent it to the Senate for final approval.

The *Detroit Free Press* took a vehement anti-Upper Peninsula stand:

> *If the committee in Congress who reported the Dismemberment Bill imagine that the people of Michigan can be reconciled to its provisions by extending their jurisdiction over the region of perpetual snows—the ultimate Thule of our national domain on the North—they are much mistaken....*

As it continued in a similar vein, it was obvious that the *Detroit Free Press* was mirroring the feelings of its readers:

> *We have made it our object to ascertain the feelings of our citizens on this subject; and we find them unanimous in the opinion, that the mere extension of our jurisdiction over that territory, if not an injury, would not be a benefit to Michigan, in the present generation. If Congress annex it to us, they must not suppose that it will be regarded, in any measure as an equivalent for the rights of which they propose to despoil us. If they should determine to take away from us our bread, and give us, in return a stone, let them not offend us by calling it a compromise....*[71]

Events began to move rapidly. On March 22, there was a meeting of the citizens of Detroit concerning the inclusion of the western half of the Upper Peninsula into the state of Michigan. In their memorial to Congress, they protested the incorporation "of the sterile region on the shores of Lake Superior destined by soil and climate to remain forever a wilderness."[72]

During the debate in the Senate, Thomas Hart Benton noted that some people objected to the size of the new Michigan, but he felt that, since it was a frontier state facing Canada and the Indians, it needed the extra territory so that it would be strong. In terms of sustaining its population, he felt that the inclusion of this territory of "16,000 or 18,000 square miles" would be of little importance for agricultural purposes, but the land was chiefly desirable for its mineral resources, of which copper was the most important.[73] Benton was one of the few people whose views on the incorporation mentioned the copper resources in the region.

As these debates were underway in Washington, the *Detroit Free Press*, a voice of popular sentiment, suddenly found one of its reviewers reversing his position. On June 1, the *Press* published a book review of Gilman's *Life on the Lakes*. The reviewer briefly discussed the work and then added:

> *Besides some agreeable tales founded upon Indian tradition, which the author picked up in his tour, the volumes before us contain some very interesting facts in relation to the country on Lake Superior which Congress proposes to annex to Michigan. If the sketches of the author are faithfully drawn, the country lying on the Southern shore of the great lake is far more valuable than we anticipated for mines and timber, Copper ore, almost without alloy, majestic oaks and...gloomy forests of lofty and moaning pine, are often spoken of by our author.*

John Norvell sought the support of Schoolcraft, to whom he wrote on August 2. The result was the publication of two lengthy but detailed letters on August 17 and 24 in the *Detroit Free Press*. In them, Schoolcraft listed the natural resources of the region and its value to Michigan and the nation. By this time, even the editors of the *Detroit Free Press* were impressed and noted that the ideas presented were being ignored by the rival and anti-annexation *Journal of Michigan*.

A writer, simply signing "Common Sense" in the August 17 issue of the *Detroit Free Press*, wrote this response:

> *No man can read this letter...without coming to the conclusion, that the lake coast and territory added to Michigan on lake Superior, with the resources which they furnish for agriculture, minerals, shipbuilding, navigation, fisheries and commerce, constitute a splendid*

> acquisition. With regard to the climate, it is sufficient to remark that it is equal to that of the state of Maine, one of the most thriving and prosperous states of the Union.

Schoolcraft left Mackinac Island on October 27 and arrived in Detroit three days later. He noted that:

> Political feeling still ran high respecting the terms of admission proposed by Congress to Michigan, and the convention, which recently met at Ann Arbor, refused their assent to these terms, under a mistaken view of the case, as I think of rash and heady advisors; for there is no doubt in my mind that the large area of territory in the upper country, offered as an equivalent for and importance to the State than the "seven mile strip" surrendered—an opinion, the grounds of which are discussed in my "Albion" letters.[74]

By this time, the people of Michigan could do little to change the course of history. Congress had decided to attach the Upper Peninsula to the new state, and on June 15, 1836 a bill was passed which admitted Arkansas and Michigan to the Union. However, Michigan's admission was conditional on its acceptance of the Upper Peninsula annexation. People protested, as we have seen, but finally political expediency won out and on December 14 and 15, a group of Democrats at their "Frost-Bit Convention" accepted the compromise. After that, it was a matter of routine, and on January 26, 1837 President Andrew Jackson signed the bill making Michigan the twenty-sixth state in the Union.

It seems strange that the perceptions of the Upper Peninsula were so limited during the debates and public discussion on incorporating the region into the new state. From scholarly to popular articles and books, from government reports and mineral specimens and artifacts in displays in the city of Detroit, there was abundant knowledge of the region.

The heart of the problem lay in the fact that Michiganians felt they were being forced to take action which other states had never been required to do, namely, to attach the Upper Peninsula to the new state. As a result, the people and leaders ignored the positive facts available concerning the Upper Peninsula and instead stressed the negative aspects of the region: long, cold winters; the sterility of the soil; the idea of a perpetual wilderness; and the watery break between the peninsulas at the Straits of Mackinac. They overlooked the fact that the region had abundant mineral wealth in the form of copper, indications of iron, gypsum, fish, timber, scenic beauty for a possible tourist trade, and even some good land for agriculture.

HISTORY: PRE-STATEHOOD PERCEPTIONS

Although these resources have been exploited and certain activities continue to aid the local economy, some people continue to view the Upper Peninsula as a hidden corner of the United States and isolated from the rest of Michigan. In 1983, Mary Ann Harrell wrote an article for the National Geographic Society which begins, "All through Michigan's Upper Peninsula runs a sense of ultimate outpost, the most distant community, the limit of human things." As Bruce Johanson of Ontonagon told Harrell, "This is not the edge of the world, but you can see it from here."[75] Despite this legacy, the Upper Peninsula has become a unique cultural and social region within the nation and has certainly lived up to the expectations of its historic friends and promoters.

A Sense of Place: Michigan's Upper Peninsula

NOTES

1 John T. Blois. *Gazetteer of the State of Michigan.* Detroit: Sydney L. Rood & Co., 1838, pp. 16–17.

2 Edward W. Peck. "Disputed Questions in the Early History of Michigan," *Michigan Pioneer and Historical Collections.* [hereafter cited: MPHC] 11 (1887), 158.

3 John Harris Forster. "Early Settlement of the Copper Regions of Lake Superior," MPHC. vol. 7 (1886), 183.

4 Alex Campbell. "The Upper Peninsula," MPHC. 3 (1881), 247.

5 Jacques Cartier. *A Shorte and Briefe Narration of Two Nauigations and Discoueries to the Northweast Partes Called Newe Fraunce.* London: H. Bynneman, 1580, pp. 32, 55, 63, 76.

6 W.P. Ferguson. "Michigan's Most Ancient Industry: Prehistoric Mines and Miners of Isle Royale," *Michigan History.* vol. 8 (1924), 155-70; H.P. Biggar, ed. *The Works of Samuel de Champlain.* 2 vols. Toronto: The Champlain Society, 1922, I:164.

7 Two studies which deal with this work of the Jesuits: Russell M. Magnaghi. "The Jesuits in the Lake Superior Country," *Inland Seas.* 41:3 (Fall 1985), 190-203; Robert Karrow, Jr. "Lake Superior's Mythic Isles," *Michigan History.* 69:1 (January-February 1985), 23–31.

8 Reuben G. Thwaites, ed. *The Jesuit Relations and Allied Documents.* 70 vols. New York: Pageant Book Company, 1959, I, viii.

9 Alexander Henry. *Travels and Adventures in Canada and the Indian Territories between the Years 1760 and 1776.* New York: I Riley, 1809, pp. 54–55, 57–59, 61–63, 68–70.

10 *Ibid.,* p. 232.

11 *Ibid.,* p. 230.

12 Jonathan Carver. *The Journals of Jonathan Carver and Related Documents, 1766–1770.* Edited by John Parker. St. Paul: Minnesota Historical Society Press, 1976, pp. 1, 74, 75, 71, 72.

13 Henry R. Schoolcraft. *Personal Memoirs of a Residence of Thirty Years on the American Frontier.* Philadelphia: Lippincott, Grambo, 1851, p. 168.

14 Jedidiah Morse. *The American Geography; or A View of the Present Situation of the United States of America.* Elizabethtown: Shepard Kollock, 1789, pp. 37–38.

15 J. Long. *Voyages and Travel* . . . [1768–1782]. (Originally published in London in 1791). Edited by Reuben G. Thwaites. *Early Western Travels.* 32 vols. Cleveland: The Arthur H. Clark Company, 1904–1907, VI:79-81.

16 The following material can be found in: Magnaghi. "The Aborted Cooper Expedition to the Lake Superior Country, 1800," *Inland Seas.* 36:2 (Summer 1980), 80–86.

17 Clarence E. Carter, compiler and editor. *The Territorial Papers of the United States.* vol. X. *The Territory of Michigan, 1805–1820.* Washington, D.C.: Government Printing Office, 1942, pp. 271, 328; Magnaghi. "Le Baron's Attempt at Exploiting Upper Peninsula Copper," *Harlow's Wooden Man.* 16:3 (Fall 1980), 5–7.

18 Schoolcraft to John C. Calhoun, Vernon, New York, November 6, 1820, "A Report to the Secretary of War on the Number, Value, and Position, of the Copper Mines on the Southern Shores of Lake Superior," in *Message from the President* [Monroe] *of the United States.* Washington D.C.: Gales and Seaton, 1822, pp. 20, 8, 17.

19 "Lands Containing Precious Metals Communicated to the House of Representatives, February 13, 1816," in *The New American State Papers, Public Lands.* 8 vols. Wilmington, Delaware: Scholarly Research, 1973, V:588.

20 Magnaghi. *Harlow's Wooden Man* (Fall 1980), 6.

21 Edward G. Voss. *Botanical Beachcombers and Explorers: Pioneers of the 19th Century in the Upper Great Lakes.* Contributions from the University of Michigan Herbarium volume 13, Ann Arbor, 1978, pp. 4–5.

22 Andrew Miller. *New States and Territories . . . in 1818.* [n.p.], 1819, pp. 76, 78.

23 Daniel Blowe. *A Geographical, Commercial and Agricultural View of the United States of America Forming a Complete Emigrant's Directory.* Liverpool: Henry Fisher, 1819, pp. 703–05.

24. Estwick Evans. *A Pedestrious Tour of Four Thousand Miles through the Western States and Territories during the Winter and Spring of 1818.* [Originally published: Concord, NH: Joseph C. Spear, 1819]. Edited by Reuben G, Thwaites. *Early Western Travels.* VIII: 231–32.

25. Lewis Cass to John C. Calhoun, Detroit, November 18, 1819, in W. Edwin Hemphill, ed. *The Papers of John C. Calhoun.* 13 vols. Columbia: South Caroliniana Society, 1969, IV:415.

26. Calhoun to Cass, Washington, D.C., January 14, 1820, in *Ibid.*, IV:573.

27. Calhoun to Cass, Washington, February 25, 1820, In *Ibid.*, IV:684.

28. Schoolcraft to Cass, Sault Ste. Marie, October 1, 1822, in *Message from the President of the United States*, (1822), 8, 12–13.

29. Schoolcraft to Calhoun, Vernon, New York, November 6, 1820, in *Ibid.*, 27.

30. Benjamin Silliman to Calhoun, New Haven, Connecticut, January 5, 1821, in Hemphill. *The Papers of John C. Calhoun*, V:534.

31. Calhoun to Silliman, Washington, DC, January 13, 1821, *Ibid.*, V:556.

32. Calhoun to Schoolcraft, Washington, DC, February 28, 1821, in *Ibid.*, V:652.

33. Schoolcraft to Calhoun, Albany, New York, January 30, 1821, in *Ibid.*, V:581.

34. Schoolcraft. *Narrative Journal of Travels from Detroit Northwest through the Great Chain of American Lakes to the Sources of the Mississippi River in the Year 1820.* Albany: E & E Hasford, 1821; *The North American Review.* 15 (July 1822), 224–50.

35. William M. Meigs. *The Life of Thomas Hart Benton.* Philadelphia: J.B. Lippincott Company, 1924, 121, 146–47; William Nisbet Chambers. *Old Bullion Benton, Senator from the West: Thomas Hart Benton, 1782-1858.* Boston: Little, Brown & Company, 1956, 107, 111.

36. Schoolcraft. *Personal Memoirs.* p. 122.

37. Cass to Thomas Hart Benton, Detroit, January 19, 1823, in Carter. *The Territorial Papers.* XI:331–32.

HISTORY: PRE-STATEHOOD PERCEPTIONS

38 Schoolcraft. *Personal Memoirs.*, pp. 137, 182.

39 *Ibid.* p. 192.

40 *Ibid. Personal Memoirs.* pp. 203, 241.

41 *Ibid. Personal Memoirs.* p. 245.

42 Thomas McKenney. *Sketches of a Tour to the Lakes.* Edited by Herman J. Viola. Barre, MA: Imprint Society, 1972, p. 326.

43 *Ibid.*, pp. 139, 147, 158–61, 192-93, 311.

44 Schoolcraft to Governor George B. Porter, Sault Ste. Marie, October 1, 1831; Schoolcraft to Secretary of War Elbert Herring, Sault Ste. Marie, September 21, 1831, in "Henry R. Schoolcraft—Expedition into the Indian Country," 22d Congress, 1st Session. House of Representatives, Doc. no. 152, pp. 2–3.

45 Schoolcraft. *Personal Memoirs.* p. 360.

46 Douglass Houghton to Lewis Cass, Fredonia, New York, November 14, 1831, in "Henry R. Schoolcraft—Expedition into the Indian Country," 22d Congress, 1st Session. House of Representatives, Doc. no. 152, pp. 17–19.

47 McKenney. *Sketches of a Tour.* p. 287.

48 Schoolcraft. *Personal Memoirs.* p. 588.

49 Martin Heydenburk. "Mackinaw Re-visited—How It Looked 40 Years Ago—Petoskey and the Camp Meeting." MPHC. 7 (1887), 197.

50 Schoolcraft. *Personal Memoirs*, pp. 493, 516, 544, 550, 559, 566–67.

51 McKenney. *Sketches of a Tour.* pp. 183, 185–86.

52 Chandler Robbins Gilman. *Life on the Lakes: Being Tales and Sketches Collected during a Trip to the Pictured Rocks of Lake Superior.* 2 vols. New York: George Dearborn, 1836, II:55.

53 Schoolcraft. *Personal Memoirs.* p. 522.

54 McKenney. *Sketches of a Tour.* pp. 161–62, 192, 203.

55 "Memorial to Congress by the Legislative Council," April 1827, in Carter, ed. *Territorial Papers.* XI: 1074–76.

56 *Historical and Scientific Sketches of Michigan.* Detroit: Stephen Wells & George L. Whitney, 1834, pp. 169, 181, 191; J.C. Holmes. "The Michigan State Historical Society." MPHC. 12 (1888), 316–17, 319; *Detroit Free Press,* July 30, 1834.

57 Holmes. MPHC. 12 (1888), 316–50.

58 Henry R. Schoolcraft. "Sketches of the Upper Peninsula or 'Albion Letters' March 23, 30, April 6, 13, 27, 1831" from transcripts from the *Detroit Journal and Michigan Advertizer* filed with the Marquette County Historical Society, Marquette, Michigan.

59 Philip P. Mason, ed. *Schoolcraft's Expedition to Lake Itasca The Source of the Mississippi River.* East Lansing: Michigan State University Press, 1958, p. 178.

60 *Ibid.,* p. 366.

61 "Report of the Committee to Draft a Constitution," Detroit, May 15, 1835 in Harold M. Dorr, ed. *The Michigan Constitutional Conventions of 1835–1836.* Ann Arbor: The University of Michigan Press, 1940, p. 463.

62 The future Upper Peninsula had a friend and able ally in Lucius Lyon. He was familiar with the eastern portion of the land, as in 1827 he had surveyed Bois Blanc Island in the Straits of Mackinac for the government; he was familiar with Cass and Schoolcraft; and knew the land and the people. Lucius Lyon to Mrs. Mary Thompson, April 2, 1841, in L.G. Stuart, ed. "Letters of Lucius Lyon." *MPHC 27* (1897), 541.

63 Lyon to Colonel D. Goodwin, Washington, DC, February 4, 1836, in *Ibid.,* p. 475.

64 Lyon to Dr. A. Philes (of Galena, Ill.), Washington, DC, February 18, 1836, in *Ibid.,* pp. 477–78.

65 *Democratic Free Press,* March 16, 1836.

66 Lyon to Colonel Andrew Mack (of Detroit), Washington, DC, February 21, 1836, *Ibid.,* p. 479.

67 Lyon to Charles C. Hascall, Washington, DC, February 21, 1836, *Ibid.,* pp. 479–80.

68 Lyon to Morese and Bragg of the *Detroit Free Press,* Washington, DC, March 31, 1836 in *Ibid.,* p. 494.

69 Schoolcraft. *Personal Memoirs.* p. 547.

70 Detailed studies on the boundary question include: Reuben Gold Thwaites. "The Boundaries of Wisconsin." *Magazine of Western History*. 6:5 (September 1887), 489–504; Claude S. Larzelere. "The Boundaries of Michigan." *MPHC 30* (1905), 1–27.

71 *Detroit Free Press*, March 23, 1836.

72 24th Congress, lst Session, House of Representatives, Doc. 207, p. 2; Carter, ed. *Territorial Papers*. 12, p. 15 [March 18, 1836]

73 *Detroit Free Press*, May 18, 1836.

74 Schoolcraft. *Personal Memoirs*. p. 547.

75 Mary Ann Harrell. *America's Hidden Corners: Places off the Beaten Path*. Washington, D.C.: National Geographic Society, 1983, p. 92.

A Sense of Place: Michigan's Upper Peninsula

The fifteen counties in the Upper Peninsula of Michigan and those generally lying north of the 45th parallel in Wisconsin were proposed to make up the State of Superior during the movement of the 1970s.

UP Statehood
Efforts Span Many Decades

James L. Carter

Independence has run deep in the fiber of the people of Michigan's Upper Peninsula for generations. This remote, rugged land has forged in its inhabitants a spirit of self-reliance born of a certain necessity imposed by geography and climate. This resilience of spirit has been strengthened through the rigors of hard work required in mining, lumbering, and commercial fishing, the Peninsula's time-honored occupations.

From the beginning, then, it was not unreasonable that this independent spirit should manifest itself in a decades-long quest for self-government as a state separate from the Lower Peninsula of Michigan, in a strong desire for their own star in Old Glory as the State of Superior!

Statehood for the Upper Peninsula and adjacent counties in northeastern Wisconsin is not a subject for much serious consideration as the twentieth century draws to a close. For much of the 1800s, however, it was a major issue attracting the attention of the entire nation and the support of many leaders in this region.

The Upper Peninsula was included in the Northwest Territory when it was organized in 1781. Soon, new political units began to be established within the territory, and by 1809 the Upper Peninsula had been divided into three sections. In the east, parts of present-day Chippewa and Mackinac counties were in the Michigan Territory which had been set up in 1805. The central area was included in the Indiana Territory, and the western section was a part of the Illinois territory. Then, in 1818, the Michigan Territory was expanded to include the entire Upper Peninsula.

The movement to include the Peninsula in a territory apart from Michigan began in the 1820s. A widely circulated petition prompted James Duane Doty, a Michigan territorial judge, to draft a bill to establish what was to be called the Huron Territory. By 1823, Doty's judicial district included Michilimackinac, Brown, and Crawford counties, which then covered much of Michigan and all of Wisconsin. The Huron Territory (or Huronia) would include the Upper Peninsula, what was to become Wisconsin, and parts of Minnesota and northern Illinois. Influential Senator Thomas Hart Benton of Missouri, a leading supporter of Michigan statehood, introduced the bill, but the effort faltered before any Congressional action was taken.

The cause came alive again in 1827 when Austin E. Wing of Monroe, who had been elected a Michigan Territorial Delegate to Congress in 1823, introduced a bill similar to Doty's. It also had the backing of

Senator Benton and Michigan Territorial Governor Lewis Cass. The bill passed the House in 1829, but Wing's third term expired later that year and the Senate took no action.

In 1830, another bill was introduced, including only part of the Upper Peninsula in the proposed territory, but it failed to gain the support of many Lower Michigan residents. Michigan was preparing for statehood, and there were already indications it would be awarded the Upper Peninsula if it was not successful in its claim to the Toledo Strip. Many Michiganians were coming to regard the territory east of the Menominee-Montreal Rivers as a potential part of their future state. Therefore, Congress did not want to stir up the already murky waters of the Michigan-Ohio controversy, and once again it failed to take action.

With the border problem with Ohio finally resolved, Michigan gained statehood in 1837, and all of the Upper Peninsula was included. Of the new state's 175,000 inhabitants, only about three thousand lived north of the Straits of Mackinac. There were perhaps one thousand white residents, with the remainder mainly Ojibwas or persons of mixed blood. During the decades of the 1830s and 1840s, there were no calls for statehood from the Upper Peninsula, which Henry Clay once said was "as remote as the moon." The fur trade was in rapid decline, and prospects for development of other resources to many seemed dim.

The one glimmer of hope came from the Lake Superior copper deposits, which were known to exist since the early years of European exploration of the region. Native people had mined and traded copper throughout North America for several thousand years. Attempts by the French and British to mine copper were made as early as the 1700s. However, it was not until State Geologist Douglas Houghton's report, following his 1840 expedition along Lake Superior's south shore, that interest in copper mining began to grow. In fact, by the mid-1840s, the nation's first mineral rush sent hundreds of would-be miners to the Keweenaw Peninsula in search of copper. Exploration and development of iron mines on the Marquette Range would soon follow. The industrial age had reached the Upper Peninsula.

By 1850, there were 5,659 inhabitants in the Upper Peninsula's seven counties. (Chippewa, 828; Houghton, 126; Keweenaw, 582; Mackinac, 3,598; Marquette, 136; and Ontonagon, 389. Schoolcraft County was attached to Marquette County for administration and was not reported separately.) While the population was small in comparison to Michigan's total of just under 400,000, its representatives in the state legislature were already lobbying for support of roads and port improvements, schools, and other state services.

HISTORY: UPPER PENINSULA STATEHOOD

Although the idea was still widespread that the Upper Peninsula was a remote wilderness of little value, Governor Robert McClelland thought differently. He told a joint session of the Michigan House and Senate in 1853, "There is no part of the State which deserves more your fostering care than the mineral region of Lake Superior."

One of the big complaints of Upper Peninsula residents was the method of taxing mining companies, which were required to pay taxes directly into the state treasury. They charged that Lansing was reluctant to return a fair share of the mining revenues to the areas that generated them. Tax laws also tended to discourage investment of new capital needed to expand the mining industry.

Senate Mines and Minerals Committee Chairman L. W. Clark, following his committee's report in 1853, acknowledged the state's difficulty in governing the remote Upper Peninsula. He reminded legislators that the only communication with the Upper Peninsula in winter was "...carried on by means of the dog-train, and snowshoes, and the mail and travel are forced to pass through portions of three states to get to or from the Capitol."

Clark also took note of a statehood movement in the northern region but did not think residents really wanted separation from the rest of Michigan "...unless unequal laws and an oppressive policy shall drive them to it."

The several newspapers in the Upper Peninsula at Ontonagon, Houghton, and Sault Sainte Marie had joined the call for statehood. The first paper to take up the cause was the *Lake Superior Journal* at the Sault, which headed an article in an 1851 issue, "North Michigan—A New State." Senator Abner Sherman's *Upper Peninsula Advocate*, published in Ontonagon, was particularly vocal in support of the statehood movement. Sherman had become chairman of the important Senate Committee on Mines and Minerals.

By the mid-1850s, the region's population had grown to approximately ten thousand. In 1857, Senator Sherman presented to the Legislature a petition signed by seventy-seven prominent residents that the Upper Peninsula be set off into a new "Territory of Superior."

This renewed activity for statehood prompted legislators and other leaders to respond more seriously to Upper Peninsula needs. They were particularly interested in tying the two peninsulas together by better transportation and communication. The Saint Marys Falls Ship Canal was completed in 1855 at Sault Sainte Marie, providing greatly improved commercial shipping; it was a boon for the mining industry. Building of a rail line linking the Lower and Upper Peninsulas stirred much activity; several companies were incorporated, but it would be more than twenty-five years before rails would actually be laid.

Surprisingly, the Upper Peninsula statehood movement gained national attention, largely through the staunch backing of Horace Greeley, the noted journalist/abolitionist and owner of the *New York Daily Tribune*. Greeley had visited the Copper Country in the summer of 1847. Part of his support for Upper Peninsula statehood came from the fact that it would enter the Union as a free state at a time when the free state-slave state balance was one of the country's most controversial political issues. Much of the press looked favorably on the effort. The *Philadelphia American* commented in 1857 that "...the project for erection of a new commonwealth to be called Superior ... seems to be assuming definite shape and importance." Not surprisingly, major newspapers in the Lower Peninsula, such as the *Grand Rapids Herald* and the *Detroit Daily Free Press*, were much against the State of Superior proposal.

Importance of the Lake Superior district's mines increased greatly during the Civil War, when the nation's and the region's attention was focused on the war effort. The Upper Peninsula's first steam railroad had been built between the Marquette Range mines and the port of Marquette in 1857, and the urgent need for iron ore during the war spurred completion of the Peninsula Railroad by Chicago and North Western interests from the Lake Michigan port of Escanaba to the Marquette Range mines in 1864. Some military roads were also built.

After the war, attention turned once again to the statehood issue. The movement had built up such a head of steam that a territorial convention was held in Houghton in 1868. The delegates included many of the region's most prominent leaders. For example, heading the Marquette County delegation were such noted personages as Peter White, Hiram A. Burt, M. H. Maynard, James E. Dalliba, and T. T. Hurley. Delegates drew up a lengthy memorial to the Michigan House and Senate, setting forth the reasons for formation of a new territory, but it met little enthusiasm in the Legislature. In 1869, a minority resolution approving the secession of the Upper Peninsula was submitted to the House of Representatives by its Committee on Federal Relations, but it was tabled, and no action was taken.

As the Legislature balked at the idea of statehood, residents of the Upper Peninsula continued to feel they were coming out on the "short end." Taxes, roads, schools, mail service, revenues, lack of legislative concern: All remained vital issues to proponents for statehood.

HISTORY: UPPER PENINSULA STATEHOOD

By 1875, another territorial convention was being planned. This time it was held in Austin's Hall in Ishpeming on March 11. Representatives arrived from all Upper Peninsula counties except Mackinac. Alfred P. Swineford, publisher of the Marquette *Mining Journal*, called the convention to order. Again, delegates were made up of the region's leading citizens. Although the convention proposed the formation of a separate state, the Legislature once again took no action. There was little encouragement in the state's press outside of the Upper Peninsula. Swineford, who was to become a widely recognized expert on iron ore and later governor of the Alaska Territory, continued to be a strong proponent of the State of Superior well into the 1880s.

The economy of the Upper Peninsula expanded significantly after the Civil War, although the decade of the 1870s was rather sluggish. Transportation improved, and by 1872 the Peninsula Railroad was connected to the Chicago and North Western system by a line from Escanaba through Menominee to Green Bay, joining the Upper Peninsula to the national rail system. Then, in 1881, the Detroit, Mackinac and Marquette Railroad was completed from the Straits of Mackinac westward to Marquette, connecting the two Michigan peninsulas. In 1888, the Minneapolis, St. Paul and Sault Ste. Marie Railroad (Soo Line) was completed across the southern part of the Peninsula. Lake transportation also flourished, and the region's logging industry reached its zenith. With its growing economic base came increased political influence in Lansing. Little by little through the decades of the 1880s and 1890s, the issues that had fueled Upper Peninsula statehood efforts were resolved.

One of the last serious efforts to gain statehood for the Upper Peninsula during that time had its base in Sault Sainte Marie. In July of 1892, the *Sault Ste. Marie News* carried an article entitled "The State of Superior," written by William M. Snell, a Sault resident studying law in Washington, DC. He pointed out that the Upper Peninsula, with more than 180,000 residents, ranked ahead of five states in population and four of the five in valuation. "Enough has been said," he wrote, "to show that the Upper Peninsula of Michigan has a treasure in territory, wealth, population, and institutions, eminently fitting her to a place among the free, sovereign and independent states of the Union."

Snell's article sparked a flurry of supporting articles in the Peninsula's press, but one, at least, was a bit skeptical. The *Ontonagon Herald* commented that, "[the statehood proposal is] rather a good scheme if it could be carried out, and it seems we have heard of it before."

But with its growing influence and population, the Upper Peninsula began looking to develop a larger role within Michigan rather than as a state apart. Some of the Peninsula's most able citizens were elected or named to state offices, climaxing in 1910 when *Sault Sainte Marie News* publisher Chase S. Osborn won the post of governor.

The last serious effort of the early 1900s to promote Upper Michigan statehood came from the opposite end of the Peninsula—Menominee, and Roger Andrews, publisher of that city's daily newspaper, the *Herald-Leader*. Andrews was one of the leaders in the effort to transform the Upper Peninsula from a largely cut-over timber-producing region to one of bountiful agriculture. With leading citizens from every county, he helped found the Upper Peninsula Development Bureau in 1911 to promote the region as "Cloverland." It later played a key role in helping develop the region's tourist industry.

Andrews gave a rousing speech at the annual banquet of the Calumet Business Men's Association in January of 1916 declaring, "The Upper Peninsula of Michigan, our Cloverland, should be a separate state of the United States of America." The speech was reported on all the major wire services and was picked up by newspapers across the country. Andrews's ringing conclusion to his speech struck a chord throughout the region. "There is room in Old Glory for another star. And that star, 'The State of Superior.'"

Citing statistics similar to those Snell had published at the Sault in the early 1890s, Andrews's speech caused a lively debate in the Lower Michigan press. The *Saginaw Herald* was impressed. "But all this does not constitute an argument for a separate state. The plan for the future must be closer relations between the two peninsulas, rather than a severance." Although Upper Peninsula editors generally praised Andrews's speech for the national attention it gained for the region, few thought it was any longer a practical idea. How times had changed! The Ishpeming *Iron Ore* mused, "...away down in our hearts we do not wish to divorce ourselves from our neighbors south of the straits."

As the years went on, the idea of Upper Peninsula statehood became more and more a novelty. In the 1950s, Pat Hays, proprietor of Escanaba's House of Ludington, flew a State of Superior flag over his hotel. Ironwood attorney, Theodore G. Albert, filed a humorous "Bill of Complaint in Action for Divorce" in a Dickinson County court in 1959 with the Upper Peninsula being the plaintiff and Lower Michigan the defendant. The document was widely noted and commented on in the media. But what started in jest soon became a serious cause for attorney Albert, who drew on considerable support in adjacent Wisconsin counties that also favored joining a State of Superior. At this time the Upper Peninsula Independence Association promoted gambling as a means of supporting a new state. Although it

HISTORY: UPPER PENINSULA STATEHOOD

gained wide national attention, the proposal was supported by only one of the region's papers—the *Daily Mining Gazette* in Houghton. Taking a look in 1962 at the revived statehood efforts, the *Mining Journal* in Marquette snorted editorially: "The proposal to carve a new state out of the Upper Peninsula is a threadbare plan.... The way to solve our differences is not in separate statehood, but in closer cooperation."

The 1970s saw the most recent widespread interest in Upper Peninsula statehood. Attorney Ted Albert revived his efforts by incorporating "The 51st State of Superior," headquartered in Ironwood. At the same time he incorporated a similar organization in northern Wisconsin. State Senator Joe Mack of Ironwood requested the Michigan Senate make a study comparing the revenue produced in the Upper Peninsula with state expenditures in the region. Longtime state representative Dominic Jacobetti of Negaunee actually suggested that statehood be seriously considered. All this prompted a flurry of public response, some serious, but much was in the vein of good-natured humor. Posters, bumper stickers and tee-shirts proliferated.

Once again, the movement gained national attention. The *Philadelphia Inquirer* observed, "[the idea] is becoming a serious movement toward separatism...talk of a 51st state has moved into the action stage." The *Rhinelander* (Wisconsin) *Daily News* complained that "Madison and Lansing don't give a damn about us because we don't have the votes or the kind of tax base that makes legislatures sit up and take notice.... We get lip service and not very much of that."

The statehood proposal was actually put on the ballots in Marquette and Iron Mountain in 1975, where it was soundly defeated. That year a *Detroit Free Press* poll showed 62.9 percent were against the proposal, while 37.1 percent favored it. The district's congressman, Phil Ruppe of Houghton, said he had "very serious reservations about making the Upper Peninsula a separate state. I fear that statehood...would place a tremendous tax burden on Northern Michigan citizens.... There is very little likelihood that the Michigan Legislature and the United States Congress will ever approve of statehood for the Upper Peninsula."

Michigan Attorney General Frank Kelley issued a key document on statehood in his twenty-page Opinion No. 4911, addressing the legalities and containing much historical background. His opinion had been requested by Upper Peninsula lawmakers. Kelley concluded that the region could become a state, but it had to follow some definite procedural steps in the process.

A Sense of Place: Michigan's Upper Peninsula

SUPPORT YOUR 51ST STATE

JOIN THE CAUSE

Decked out in red, white and blue, this poster made a bid for Upper Peninsulans' support during the 1970s.

HISTORY: UPPER PENINSULA STATEHOOD

Representative Jacobetti succeeded in getting the Legislature to approve a five thousand dollar study on the feasibility of establishing a new state, and the debate continued. The *Flint Journal* had this to say: "If [the Upper Peninsula] did suddenly find itself a state...it would rank 42nd in size and 49th in population—and, opponents of the idea say, 51st in wealth."

Statehood efforts of the 1970s climaxed on March 8, 1978, when Representative Jacobetti introduced House Bill No. 6115 "to separate the Upper Peninsula from the state of Michigan; to adjust certain boundary lines between the Upper and Lower Peninsulas; and to provide for a referendum." The bill was referred to the House Appropriations Committee which Jacobetti headed but was never brought to a full vote of the House.

Newspapers across the country took note of the issue. "As days grow longer and the snow begins to melt, a secessionist movement has come out of hibernation once again in Michigan's Upper Peninsula," quipped the *Albuquerque* (New Mexico) *Journal*. But Upper Peninsula papers were not so kind. A Marquette *Mining Journal* editorial was headed "51st State: Where Will the Money Come From?" The Iron Mountain *Daily News* titled its editorial on the statehood issue more bluntly: "Ignore It."

Most of those who took a serious look at Upper Peninsula statehood concluded that it was not economically feasible. The late Jim Trethewey, veteran Upper Peninsula journalist and former editor of the *Mining Journal*, called statehood "a pie-in-the-sky dream." In the mid-1970s, he did a survey and found that the costs of education, capital expenditures, highways, and social programs far outweighed the amount of revenue the region generated. The various studies done at the request of Upper Michigan legislators were quietly dropped when they produced similar results. After taking an extensive tour of the Peninsula in 1976, Leo Hertzel wrote in the *North American Review*, "Looking out of the window at the unbroken stretches of wilderness I was driving through, I felt that it was evident this area would need something special if it was going to become financially self-sufficient...."

The late Jean Worth, well-known historian, commentator, and editor of the Escanaba *Daily Press*, probably summed it up best in an editorial when he said the State of Superior is "...a state of mind. Being and remaining a part of Michigan is a state of reality."

Superior, the elusive state,
Wayward kin of Michigan;
The Badger State's rebellious North,
Nemesis of Madison.

Will it someday find a place
Proud among the states, united?

Is Superior a mirage,
The fiction of a Northwoods dream?
Or is it the vision
Of a future state?

Who knows! Dreams often guide our destiny,
And visions forecast our fate.

A Sense of Place

Economy

A Sense of Place: Michigan's Upper Peninsula

CRUCIAL CROSSROADS
The Economy At Century's End

Harry Guenther

Introduction

The year-end turning of the calendar has no special significance in the real-world course of events. Nevertheless, it often is seized upon by pundits, critics, and philosophers of various stripes to remark on the recent past and what it bodes for the future as though it represented a meaningful turning point. This tendency is even stronger at century's end and nearly irresistible at the end of a millennium.

In discussing the economy of Michigan's Upper Peninsula as we approach the end of the millennium, however, there may be more than calendar relevance to the notion of a turning point. The region's economy is in the midst of major forces of change, change that represents either threats or opportunities, depending on how the region's institutions and communities respond to these forces and on how the region's constituent groups envision the region's future. As the year 2000 approaches, the Upper Peninsula may be facing an economic turning point as significant as the discovery of iron ore or the beginning of timber harvesting in the nineteenth century.

The Upper Peninsula's history compels us to think in terms of natural resource extraction when we consider the nature of the region's economy—furs, fish, game, timber, ores. Of course they are still important, especially the latter two. In addition, timber harvesting and iron ore mining create some of the most visually prominent sources of economic activity. Trucks loaded with massive stacks of logs, seemingly precariously secured, lumber past us on highways, side roads, and in town; massive ore docks dominate the Marquette coastline; and ore boats are frequently seen at the docks or offshore.

Yet, despite their visual presence and continued importance, the structure of the Upper Peninsula economy has been radically transformed since the days when resource extraction dominated the economy. The shifting characteristics are especially notable over the last three decades for which we have detailed statistical data for the region. Since the mid 1960's, the private sector has experienced slow employment growth of only a little over 2 percent per year compounded. The economy has benefited additionally, however, from quite strong public sector (federal, state and local) employment growth, said employment totalling some 38,500 jobs in mid-1996— over a quarter of total employment. During the period since the 1960s, almost all private sector employment growth, some 80 percent, has been concentrated in just two categories: retail trade and services. These two sectors together currently account for nearly 40 percent of private sector employment. While manufacturing employment has risen over this period, today it constitutes only about one percent of Upper Peninsula empoyment. If we lump together private sector services and the finance, insurance, and real estate sector with public sector employment, including military, and call this "all services," then the region's economy is primarily a service economy, with retailing playing a major supporting role. While on the one hand this is a source of strength, because services and retail trade are less subject to wide cyclical swings or interruptions due to labor-management conflicts, it also may involve certain weaknesses. Many (though by no means all) service jobs imply relatively low skills and low pay and do not offer career opportunities to keep the best and the brightest in the region. Also, the portion of our broader category of services that consists of public sector employees does have unstable ingredients, namely military downsizing and state and local budget constraints.

These factors have much to do with the tendency in some quarters to view the outlook for the Upper Peninsula economy as being less than rosy. Military bases have been closed, federal funds flowing to state and local entities are falling to the budget axe, and state government is seeking to reduce its outlays for a variety of social programs. At the same time, mining production, due to rising costs, lower ore grades, and cheaper sources of supply in third world countries, has an uncertain future at best. Additionally, some of the same factors influencing mining raise questions regarding the wood and wood products sector of manufacturing—if not its viability, at least its ability to expand significantly.

Charting the Path Ahead

In contemplating the possible nature of further regional economic development, it is natural to think in terms of what can be appended to what is already in place—in other words, what businesses might fit or find synergies with businesses currently operating in the region. Another version of this strategy, especially in a region with significant dependence on resource extraction, is to endeavor to capture more of the value added in the stream from raw materials to finished product. While both versions of this strategy can be viable approaches to regional economic development, they tend to be backward-looking (that is, they focus on the nature of the economic structure to date) and, thus, often ignore opportunities which may be quite different from current business endeavors. This tendency is strengthened by the fact that people in the region comfortable with, or at least accustomed to, the economy's present structure and the region's communities' power structures usually have a significant vested interest in the status quo. The result can be an unwillingness to think about a region in new ways or an antipathy to new ideas about the direction of economic development.

Because of these kinds of impediments to growth through change, when opportunities do appear on the horizon, advantage of them is not taken unless the community's vision of the future is changed. This generally is a slow process at best, unless forceful entrepreneurs compel a new vision by virtue of the success of their own ventures that seize these opportunities—or unless outside forces compel new visions. As we near the end of this century, the Upper Peninsula is blessed with the second of these; if those forces succeed in changing the economic culture of the region, the needed forceful entrepreneurs may emerge as well.

The principal outside forces to which I refer are three in number:

(1) the Canada-U.S. Free Trade Agreement (CUSFTA) and, to a lesser extent, its extension to Mexico via the North American Free Trade Agreement (NAFTA);
(2) aggressive outsourcing as companies seek to become more efficient and competitive; and
(3) the closure of K. I. Sawyer Air Force Base (KIS).

CUSFTA

The significance of CUSFTA to the Upper Peninsula does not lie in tariff reductions which will benefit or harm important firms in the region. Rather, it lies in the forces the treaty has set in motion that create opportunities for the region which have no special relationship to the tariff barriers faced by specific goods manufacturers. These forces perhaps are best exemplified by the growing volume of trade between the two countries as shown in Table 1 below. Canadian exports to the United States have grown in value by 84 percent since CUSFTA came into force and United States exports to Canada by 80 percent. The significance of this growth in trade to the Upper Peninsula can be inferred from data on commercial traffic across the International Bridge at Sault Sainte Marie. These data, presented in Table 2, show that commercial vehicle bridge traffic has increased by 79 percent since enactment of CUSFTA through the end of 1995.

It readily is apparent that this increased traffic is not primarily a function of delivery origins or destinations in the Upper Peninsula. Rather, it stems from the fact that the Upper Peninsula constitutes an important link in a trade corridor running east-west and connecting eastern Canada and the northeastern United States with western Canada and the northwestern United States. This can be better appreciated by a look at the highway mileage figures in Table 3. It is frequently shorter to travel via the Upper Peninsula between eastern Canada and the northwestern United States than it is to travel south of the Great Lakes; it even is shorter by this route from some northeastern U. S. cities to the Northwest or to western Canada. It also is shorter to travel via the Upper Peninsula from eastern Canada to western Canada than it is to travel north of Lake Superior.

While the trade corridor through the Upper Peninsula exists, is used, and is growing in traffic volume, no objective, regional strategy has been developed to take advantage of the opportunities associated with it. Other regions in the United States have developed strategies and organized efforts to take advantage of the opportunities associated with the existence of trade corridors (The Red River Trade Corridor in Manitoba, the Dakotas, and Minnesota and the Route 35 corridor through Texas into Mexico are two examples.). However, to date, the Upper Peninsula has been only a passive beneficiary of the traffic through the region.[1]

The types of opportunities associated with a trade corridor strategy have been spelled out in greater detail elsewhere (Guenther 1995). It is sufficient to note here that they revolve around trans-shipment, inter-modal transportation, logistical planning and control, warehousing, inventory control, component production, and sub-assembly.

Table 1
Canada's Merchandise Foreign Trade, Total and with the United States, 1990-1995 (in billions of Canadian Dollars)

	(a) Total Exports	(b) Exports to the US	(c) a/b	(d) Total Imports	(e) Imports from the US	(f) e/f
1990	145.6	109.2	.750	136.9	94.0	.687
1991	140.2	105.8	.755	136.6	94.4	.691
1992	155.4	120.4	.773	149.2	105.8	.710
1993	181.3	144.9	.799	171.9	125.8	.732
1994	217.9	177.4	.814	203.0	151.7	.747
1995	253.8	202.0	.800	225.4	169.0	.750

Table 2
Sault Ste. Marie International Bridge Commercial Vehicle Traffic Count

	1990	1991	1992	1993	1994	1995	1996
1st half	33501	31394	35736	42024	50763	58021	60848
2nd half	29438	34982	38137	44461	53922	54794	

Source: International Bridge Authority

Table 3
Road Miles Between Selected North American Cities via Alternate Routes

From ↓ ← To →

		Toronto	Ottawa	Montreal	Quebec	Portland[1]	Boston	Buffalo	Albany	New York
Fargo	N	1111	1165	1297	1456	1588	1630	1216	1523	1579
	S	1193	1462	1594	1753	1756	1676	1208	1510	1490
Duluth	N	856	910	1042	1201	1333	1375	961	1268	1324
	S	1009	1278	1410	1569	1572	1492	1024	1326	1306
Minneapolis	N	979	1033	1165	1324	1456	1498	1084	1391	1547
	S	953	1222	1354	1513	1516	1436	968	1270	1250
Pierre	N	1457	1511	1643	1802	1934	1976	1562	1869	2025
	S	1321	1590	1661	1820	1884	1804	1336	1638	1618
Madison	N	858	912	1044	1203	1335	1377	963	1270	1426
	S	680	949	1081	1240	1243	1163	695	997	977
Green Bay	N	721	775	907	1066	1198	1240	826	1133	1289
	S	617	886	1018	1177	1180	1100	758	934	914
Milwaukee	N	838	892	1024	1183	1315	1357	943	1250	1406
	S	626	895	1027	1186	1189	1109	641	943	923
Portland[2]	N	2599	2653	2785	2944	3076	3118	2704	3011	3067
	S	2653	2922	2993	3152	3216	3136	2668	2970	2950
Seattle	N	2526	2580	2712	2871	3003	3045	2631	2938	2994
	S	2588	2857	2928	3087	3151	3071	2603	2905	2885

[1] Portland, ME
[2] Portland, OR

N=northern route via Sault Ste. Marie
S=southern route via Chicago

Source: Rand McNally Road Atlas, *1994; adapted from a table in Guenther, H.,* Opportunities to the Upper Peninsula Resulting from North American Economic Integration *(1995), unpublished.*

Outsourcing

As individual national markets become integrated into binational, multi-national, or global markets, competition intensifies. In response, companies seek efficiencies through a variety of strategies. One of the most important of these in the United States for several years and more recently in Canada has been aggressive outsourcing. This no longer includes only the traditional professional services such as accounting, legal, or marketing but also any aspect of the planning, design, production, distribution, and servicing chain when an outside firm can provide the service cheaper. Coupled with technology, many activities that formerly had to be performed on site now can be conducted or controlled from remote locations. Geography loses significance in these situations.

With Canadian-United States trade expanding and Canada desiring to take advantage of free trade with Mexico, it becomes crucial for Canadian firms to become fully competitive with their United States counterparts. As they seek to do this, outsourcing by Canadian firms will intensify, creating opportunities for efficient suppliers. Given the proximity of the Upper Peninsula to Canada, especially to Ontario, which constitutes some 40 percent of Canadian GNP, and assuming a strategy to seize the opportunities associated with a trade corridor concept, there are opportunities for existing or new firms in the Upper Peninsula to benefit from that outsourcing.

Closure of K. I. Sawyer

Many in the region continue to focus on the harm to the economy caused by the base closure or the risks associated with aspects of developing a strategy for its reuse. A prime example has been the lengthy handwringing and procrastination in deciding to move the Marquette County Airport to the former base. The closure of the base actually provides the region with a wonderful gift in the form of a set of opportunities and valuable investment in buildings and infrastructure that the community could never have afforded to put in place. This is a once-in-many-lifetimes opportunity and one which neatly dovetails with the two factors mentioned above, the trade corridor and outsourcing. KIS represents an ideal hub for the implementation of a trade corridor strategy and a base from which to become a player in the effort by Canadian firms to become more competitive.

ECONOMY: AT CENTURY'S END

Creating a Growth Vision

The opportunities for accelerated economic growth of the Upper Peninsula exist, but they necessitate new strategies to take full advantage of them. The development of a strategy, in turn, depends on the vision which the communities of the region and their leaders have for the future of the Upper Peninsula—a vision which should recognize the strengths of the region relevant to an advanced-technology, service-driven, global economy and which embraces perceptions about the region often at odds with traditional perceptions.

The region's strengths perhaps best can be explored with a matrix based on three basic characteristics—geography, physical resources, and human resources—and two contrasting visions—one, the traditional resource extraction-based economy; the other, that of a service-driven economy. This is shown in Figure A below:

Figure A

Upper Peninsula Characteristics as Strengths and Weaknesses
Based on Contrasting Economic Visions

Regional Characteristics	Economic Visions	
	Extractive	Service Driven
Geographic Location		
1. Absolute	W	S
2. Relative	W	S
Natural Resources		
1. Physical	S	S
2. Aesthetic	W	S
Human Resources		
1. Physical	S	NR
2. Intellectual	NR	S

W = weakness, S = strength, NR = not relevant

Source: Adapted from Guenther, H., *Opportunities for the Upper Peninsula Resulting from North American Economic Integration (1995, unpublished).*

Looked at in this way, it is easy to understand why the Upper Peninsula is often viewed as plagued with disadvantages in connection with economic development. Historically, when the vision of the region's economy was one of resource extraction, most of these characteristics *were* disadvantages. The absolute geographic location meant a cold, harsh winter with heavy snowfall and frozen transportation routes and very wet, muddy, insect-ridden springs and early summers; the relative geography meant that the natural resources were a long way from the sites where they were ultimately used. The natural resource characteristics were mixed; the physical resources, as the basis for the extractive activity, were a major strength; on the other hand, the aesthetic resources (remoteness, numerous lakes, rivers, waterfalls, and bogs, dense forests—in short, all the things that lend beauty to the region) acted as impediments to moving the extracted resources to market. The physical subcategory of human resources was a strength—the early settlers of the region often were attracted by the work associated with resource extraction and the climate and so were suited to it. The intellectual resources, while perhaps in limited supply, were irrelevant to the economic activity in any event.

Looking at these same resources in a service-driven economy, we find that all are advantages except for one: the physical subcategory of human resources, which is not directly relevant. The absolute location is an advantage for exploiting a diverse variety of cold-weather and energy-efficiency technology as well as wind power generation. The relative location can be an advantage in terms of rapidly growing Canada-United States trade and the mileage advantages of an Upper Peninsula route in east-west traffic movements. The physical resources are advantageous in applying new technology to resource extraction, to environmental protection and remediation, and to various aspects of wildlife and habitat management. The aesthetic resources are a major advantage not only to tourism—already a major component of the present service economy—but also to attracting people to the area who have the technical skills a high-tech service economy of the future will need and who are fed up with the problems of urban and suburban living. With regard to human resources, while the physical side is probably irrelevant to a service-driven economy, the intellectual resources are the lifeblood of a viable service economy.

Thus, the region's characteristics lend themselves quite well to the further development of a service-driven economy. Realizing this and incorporating it into a vision and a strategy leads to a set of perceptions about the region's economy that are quite different from some that have been widely held. Some examples of these perceptions are set forth below.

- The UP is not remote. It sits astride a key North American trade corridor with close proximity to inter-modal linkages.

- The UP climate and physical environment offer not only tourism opportunities but a logical setting for research, product or service development and testing relating to cold-weather technology, energy conservation, wind power, wildlife and habitat management, environmental testing and remediation, and recreation equipment.

- Technology allows the region to be less dependent on forces beyond local control such as cyclical extractive industries or government budget pressures and better able to realize its future based on what its people want it to become.

- The key to capturing value added in a globally competitive, service-dominated economy is managing intellectual endeavors and linking related service outputs to the production process, rather than just capturing more of the value added in the physical production process.

- Existing firms and institutions in the Upper Peninsula are the repositories of key intellectual resources that can be unbundled from their traditional product or service production and used to develop new niches as the drive for efficiency causes more firms to outsource more functions.

- The skills and technology developed to cope with government environmental regulation are a source of strength in the future, not merely a cost burden to be endured.

The rationale for a vision which focuses on a service-driven economy can be summarized by a quote from Brian Quinn, one of the world's leading experts on the ingredients of business-firm excellence in the emerging economy:

> *With rare exceptions, the economical producing power of a modern corporation lies more in its intellectual and service capabilities than in its hard assets. . . . Similarly, the value of most products and services depends primarily on the development of knowledge-based intangibles, like technological know-how, product design, marketing presentation, understanding of customers, personal creativity, and innovation. Generating these effectively in turn depends more on managing the company's intellectual resources than on directing the physical actions of its people or the deployment of its tangible assets.*

A Sense of Place: Michigan's Upper Peninsula

Virtually, all public and private enterprises—including most successful corporations—are becoming dominantly repositories and coordinators of intellect, i.e., "knowledge based" or "intelligent enterprises." Intellect and services create value-added. The capacity to manage human intellect—and to transform intellectual output into a service or group of services embodied in a product—is fast becoming the critical executive skill of this era.[2]

Formulating a Strategy

The scope of this essay does not permit the full development of a potential strategy for seizing the opportunities identified above. While several strategies might work, certain ingredients would be essential to all of them and can be identified here.

First and foremost, K. I. Sawyer must become the site of the Marquette County Airport, and steps should be taken to plan its evolution into a truly regional airport. Most of the reluctance to take this step, due to concerns about operating costs and whether the relocated airport could pay for itself, are based on a misunderstanding of the role of the airport. Measured only as a place where planes take off and land, few if any airports would be self-supporting. The value of K. I. Sawyer as an airport lies in its capacity to serve as a catalyst for locating other activities in and around the airport, activities for which air transportation and an inter-modal transportation hub are essential. It is the presence of an airport that greatly expands the potential for reuse of K. I. Sawyer and will serve to attract business firms, not the other way around.

Developing a vibrant economic entity around the airport at KIS increases the possibility of its becoming a regional airport. These two factors together would be the key to sufficient traffic increase to bring jet flights and more frequent flights to the area, both of which would serve as further catalysts to economic development.

Second, any strategy necessitates taking maximum advantage of the region's existing intellectual capital. While it is true that we must do a better job of educating our youth and of retaining the best and the brightest in the region, we should not underestimate the magnitude of the pool of intellectual capital already present in the region. While part of the pool consists of faculty in the Upper Peninsula's colleges and universities, much of it is elsewhere. Thus, the pool also is made up of those with technical and research skills in business firms (like new mining technologies, environmentally safe methods of production, environmental remediation, and the production of sophisticated plastics and medical devices) and similar individuals in the public sectors with skills in areas ranging from timber management to wildlife management and environmental regulation. In addition, there is a wide-ranging store of knowledge represented by both those who have retired to the region and those who have migrated here for aesthetic reasons but whose talents currently are underemployed.

Different elements in this pool would be available under quite different terms and conditions and some not at all. The important step from a strategic viewpoint, however, is first to document the identity, location, and characteristics of the constituent parts of this pool of intellectual capital so that the information could be made available as a promotional device in attracting new business. This necessitates conducting an intellectual capital inventory of the region, a methodology for which NMU has begun to design.

The final essential element of strategy is to develop a stronger culture of entrepreneurship in the region. This is not merely a case of having people willing to start new firms. Such a culture involves an attitude of all the players in the community—public officials, bankers, venture capitalists, universities—that values and supports economic risk-taking and new ideas, a culture that spawns new firms which represent not just one more business of a kind already here but also ones which offer new products or services and/or new ways of doing old things. It must be a culture which not only tolerates change but encourages it and accepts the risks associated with it.

Conclusion

Opportunities exist for more rapid economic development of the Upper Peninsula which result from a set of unique conditions and events. They will not come our way again. Seizing these opportunities can significantly change the pace and structure of eonomic growth in the region. These will not be realized without a conscious strategy. Developing such a strategy requires a growth culture, a less risk-averse community leadership, and a clearer understanding and identification of the intellectual resources of the community and the region's real competitive strengths.

NOTES

1   It should be noted that the Northern Michigan University College of Business and the Economic Development Corporation of Marquette County co-sponsored an International Trade Conference in early 1996 which focused on the Upper Peninsula as a trade corridor, but to date, no organization has been formed to develop regional strategies based on the concept.

2   Quinn, John, *Intelligent Enterprise,* The Free Press *(1992).*

A Sense of Place: Michigan's Upper Peninsula

K. I. SAWYER AIR FORCE BASE
William Vandament and the Lake Superior Jobs Coalition
James Collins and John Marshall

Over the last hundred years, presidents of Northern Michigan University have come and gone, leaving a variety of marks on the university and the community. Since 1956, with the arrival of Edgar L. Harden on campus as president, Northern Michigan University has taken on the economic security of the Upper Peninsula as part of its mission. Over the years, various presidents have promoted the university as an engine to help the overall development of the Upper Peninsula and in particular Marquette County. However, in many cases, this role of the president of Northern Michigan University is usually overlooked because it is not directly part of his academic focus, which for many is his main job on campus.

In the 1990s, a situation developed which needed the intervention of some external forces to assist Marquette County in regaining its economic vigor. It was in 1995 that K. I. Sawyer Air Force Base, once a community of ten thousand and a vital economic part of the county, closed its doors. The immediate question was how to put this potentially useful community to best use and replace the economic vitality to the central Upper Peninsula once offered by the Air Force Base.

In order to deal with the problem, a Base Conversion Authority was appointed by the governor, and steps were taken to deal with a massive problem. However, there was a great deal of confusion within the process as the state of Michigan and the Federal government argued over past agreements, and the townships and Marquette County tried to work out an agreement in dealing with governance of the site. The lack of funds and the County's constant struggle with deficits added to the dilemma. As the days and weeks moved ahead, there were delays in decision making and the development of a general plan.

In order to facilitate a solution, a number of agencies and organizations in Marquette County began to work individually and collectively. A joint committee coordinated two business advocacy groups in the County: the Marquette Ambassadors and the Ishpeming-Negaunee Diplomats. Also, Northern Initiatives, Marquette County Economic Development Commission (EDC), Central UP Planning & Development Commission (CUPAD), the Jobs Commission, and the Conversion Authority attended meetings of the Marquette County Board of Commissioners and offered their expert testimony. They were all working to bring about change, but each had its own vision.

Although many people were involved in reactivating the Lake Superior Jobs Coalition, a central player in this development was President William E. Vandament of Northern Michigan University. He infused a degree of organization and leadership into the effort others had been unable to, primarily because of his personality and the crisis situation that existed. Over the years, presidents Harden (1956–1967), Jamrich (1968–1981), and Appleberry all recognized the importance of the Air Force base to the university and could focus on maintaining good personal and institutional relations with the base. President Vandament, however, came into office facing an entirely new situation—a financial crisis brought on by the base's closure that needed quick and direct action.

The focal organization became the Lake Superior Jobs Coalition. This group was first formed around 1982 when Cleveland Cliffs Iron Company faced a decline in iron ore production due to a sluggish national steel industry, and hundreds in the local industry faced unemployment and economic hardship. The Coalition was formed to work with suppliers of CCI, to see what could be done to make the mines more competitive, and to be generally supportive of the iron ore industry. The Coalition achieved some positive results and then all but disbanded when it had served its purpose.

By early 1996, the need became apparent for a private group that could act as an advocate for having Marquette County take responsibility for redeveloping K. I. Sawyer Air Force Base. The idea of reactivating the Lake Superior Jobs Coalition for this purpose arose during a conversation between Reverend Louis Cappo and William Vandament. To his credit, President Vandament saw that the Coalition would need to broaden its base to represent all of the County's interest groups.

President Vandament stepped into the picture to help Marquette County develop an important economic base and to help support the university community. In the past, K. I. Sawyer Air Force Base had been one of the university's important sources of enrollment, and the base's closure could not help but have a significant impact on the university. Vandament's participation in developing new employment on the former base would result in material benefits not only for the community but for Northern Michigan University as well. More jobs would bring new people and the potential for increased enrollment.

As noted earlier, the Ambassadors and Diplomats had already begun efforts on the base conversion. In the spring of 1995, John Marshall, president of Lake Superior & Ishpeming Railroad, was chair of an Ambassador committee, and his counterpart with the Diplomats was

ECONOMY: REDEVELOPMENT OF K. I. SAWYER AFB

Ken Saari of Michigan Gas. The two groups had been formed to collaborate with Federal officials, the Base Conversion Authority, and Marquette County officials in solving problems related to redevelopment of the facility.

President Vandament made a telephone call to Marshall in June 1996. During the ensuing conversation, Vandament mentioned his discussion with Reverend Cappo and asked if Marshall's committee, or at least several members of his committee, and a similar group from the Diplomats would be interested in joining the Lake Superior Jobs Coalition. Subsequently, Vandament made similar contacts with other organizations, in line with his belief that a larger more coordinated group needed to be formed to deal with the complexity of the problem. The immediate response was a powerful "yes" because so many people had been working on the problem, but they were not realizing results due to a lack of coordination. The Jobs Coalition provided that coordination, where one group represented the Marquette County community in trying to advance this initiative.

Reverend Cappo, who originally chaired the Lake Superior Jobs Coalition, continued as its chair, and the two vice co-chairs were Presidents Vandament and Marshall. The members represented business groups and concerns from throughout the County[1] as an *ad hoc* group interested in promoting the welfare of the community at large rather than any particular agenda. The group quickly raised its own funding, facilitating its work when necessary.

On June 30, 1996, the Coalition, through its chair Reverend Cappo, issued a press release announcing that the organization intended to get actively involved in the effort to develop the former K. I. Sawyer Air Force Base. "We recognize that others have been working very hard on this project," Cappo said. He continued:

> *What we hope to bring is support from business, industry, labor and other institutions in our community. We must let our elected officials know that there is public support for bold, positive actions they may take. It's very clear that we have a real opportunity, but we are at a critical point in this process and we need to move forward aggressively as a unified community.*

President Vandament noted that immediate action was needed because of the negotiations with AMR (American) Eagle concerning the maintenance facilities in Marquette County. According to Vandament:

> Our choices are to either lose 150 good jobs, or to retain those jobs and add many more. Although we discuss this issue in terms of jobs, it's important to remember these are real people and families who live here and contribute to our community in many ways. We want these people to be able to continue living and working in Marquette County.

Northern Michigan University's president concluded his remarks by noting that the highest priorities in the summer of 1996 were relocating Marquette County Airport to K. I. Sawyer, reaching an agreement with AMR Eagle on the relocation and expansion of its maintenance operations, and resolving issues concerning local governance which would require County participation.

President Vandament played a very direct role in the Lake Superior Jobs Coalition. One incident in particular demonstrated Vandament's dedication to leadership and action. During the negotiations with AMR Eagle over the maintenance facilities, it was President Vandament along with Reverend Cappo who brought the various parties together to the table for a successful conclusion to the negotiations.

To many, President Vandament acted as the guiding light and primary thrust behind the Coalition. As vice chair, he guided it and provided space and secretarial services. His position as President of Northern Michigan University lent the Coalition a new visibility to Federal and state officials and elected representatives, many of whom Vandament knew personally. Having a person of President Vandament's stature available as an advocate and participant proved to be a critical asset for the Lake Superior Jobs Coalition.

ECONOMY: REDEVELOPMENT OF K. I. SAWYER AFB

Notes

1 Members of the Lakes Superior Jobs Coalition:

H. Richard Anderson	Northern Initiatives	Marquette
Barry Bahrman	West Branch Twp Supervisor	Skandia
Tom Baldini	Int'l Joint Comm US & Canada	Marquette
Rex Buettgenbach	Bresnan Communications	Marquette
Rev. Louis Cappo	St. Peter Cathedral	Marquette
James M. Collins	96th District Court	Marquette
Sam Elder	Elder Agency	Marquette
Dennis Girard	Kendricks, Bordeau P. C.	Marquette
Frank J. Guastella	Red Fox Run Golf Course	Gwinn
Bill Jacobson	Simmons Airlines	Champion
Ron Katers	Snyder Pharmacy	Ishpeming
John Korhonen	City Manager	Ishpeming
Jack LaSalle	MI Bldg & Const Trades Cncil	Marquette
Phyllis Maki	Public Service Garage	Marquette
Frank A. Malette	Escanaba Moving Systems	Gwinn
John F. Marshall	LS&I Railroad	Marquette
Ellwood Mattson	MI Financial Corp (retired)	Marquette
Tom Mogush	WMQT-FM	Ishpeming
Herb Parsons	Mqt Chamber of Commerce	Marquette
Gerald Peterson	City Manager	Marquette
J. M. Pietro	MI Aeronautics Commission	Gwinn
Michael Prokopowicz	Michaels Photography	Gwinn
Bob Raica	Marquette General Hospital	Marquette
Jim Reeves	*The Mining Journal*	Marquette
Don Ryan	Cleveland Cliffs Iron Company	Ishpeming
Ken Saari	Michigan Gas	Negaunee
Walt Sauer	First of America Bank	Marquette
Mike Skytta	MFC First National Bank	Marquette
Chuck Swanson	Swanson & Associates Appraisers	Marquette
Rev. Chuck Tooman	Church of Our Savior	Marquette
Dan Turvey	UP Power Company	Ishpeming
William Vandament	Northern Michigan University	Marquette
Brad Van Sluyters	WLUC-TV	Negaunee

Others on the mailing list for minutes and meeting notices:

Karlyn Rapport	Marquette County Commission	Marquette
Greg Seppanen	Marquette County Commission	Marquette
Lyle Shaw	Financial Consultant	Little Lake
Jay Scherbenske	Mqt County Econ Devt Corp	Negaunee
David Stover	Marquette County Airport	Negaunee

A Sense of Place

Foodways

A Sense of Place: Michigan's Upper Peninsula

SUPERIOR COOK BOOK　　　　　165

PETER WHITE'S PUNCH.

"We'll drink to-night with hearts as light,
To loves' as gay and fleeting,
As bubbles that float on the beaker's brim
And die on the lips while meeting."

Peter White Punch from The Superior Cookbook

FOODWAYS OF THE UPPER PENINSULA

Russell M. Magnaghi

Foodways remain a legacy of the Upper Peninsula's rich ethnic heritage. From the Native Americans to recent Asian immigrants, the past can be found in regional food. Families have and continue to have their own traditions and foods which are produced for a variety of festive occasions. Terms like *rieska, cudighi, bagna cauda, limpa, lutefisk, pasties, boudin,* and *pepperkakor* are but a few which make up the culinary vocabulary of the Upper Peninsula. Here we are interested in the regional foods that are available to the public through commercial outlets, be they restaurants, bakeries, food shops, or specialty stores. The result of this historical experience is a unique Upper Peninsula cuisine in which the ethnic origins of the foods can be lost or absorbed by other ethnic traditions as their own.[1]

Game and fish were important parts of the Native American diet. The Upper Peninsula is home to thousands of deer that are hunted for food by both Native and non-Native people. However, except for special dinners provided by organizations for fund raising purposes, wild game is not sold commercially.

Fish has always been abundant in the streams and lakes of the Upper Peninsula and was also an important ingredient in the Native American diet. Some studies show that as much as 75 percent of the Native diet was based on fish. During the summer months, large fishing camps developed at Sault Sainte Marie, the Straits of Mackinac, Munising, and Keweenaw Bay, to name a few locations. The fish was consumed fresh or smoked for later use.

When the early settlers arrived in the 1840s to seek the minerals of the region, they also found fish in ready supply and made it an important part of their diet. During the winter, when it was difficult to get supplies, housewives lamented the fact that they had cooked whitefish in every imaginable form—in soup, fried, grilled, boiled, roasted, broiled, poached—and they were only a few weeks into the season. The Scandinavians who came in the late nineteenth century were happy to find such a supply of fish, as it always had been an important part of their Old World diets.

Today, fish continues to be part of the regional diet. Both fresh and smoked whitefish and lake trout are found in restaurants and markets. Whitefish is viewed as a Lake Superior delicacy and the high point of a visitor's dining experience. Restaurants like the Vierling in Marquette offer it in *haute cuisine* styles such as almondine, Kensington, piccata, Cajun, and just plain pan fried.

A Sense of Place: Michigan's Upper Peninsula

The Friday fish fry, combining former Catholic dietary practices and use of a local commodity, has become a UP cultural icon. Thousands of people are attracted each week to restaurants, church basements, and VFW posts to eat deep-fried fish along with cole slaw and French-fried potatoes. During Lent, business booms for many establishments. Although dieticians will tell you that for health reasons fish should be served baked, broiled or poached, a "fish poach" will attract few diners.

Berries—blueberries, raspberries, strawberries, thimbleberries—are another regional food whose use goes back to Native American times. Blueberries were an important ingredient in Native diets in fresh and dried form. These berries were first introduced to European tables by the French Jesuit missionaries in the seventeenth century. Berries are an important part of the traditional Nordic diet as well. Since they were readily available in their wild state, the variety of available berries provided an inexpensive and abundant source for jams and jellies to the early immigrants who were trying to husband their meager resources.

During the late summer, hundreds of people throughout the Peninsula head for their favorite berry picking sites to gather their annual supply. In the late nineteenth and early twentieth century, special trains took pickers to locations along the line. During the Depression, hundreds of blueberry pickers descended on Luce County to pick berries for the commercial market. In many ways, berry picking continues as an important social activity for residents of the Peninsula, who at times have to vie for berries with hungry bears.

Strawberries have been developed as a commercial crop, and Chassell remains the "Strawberry Capital of the Upper Peninsula" with a festival held in July. Thimbleberries are a delicacy local to the Peninsula, especially in the woods of the Keweenaw Peninsula. These berries find their way into jams and jellies.

The Cornish pasty is probably the food most identified with the Upper Peninsula. There are heated debates over what constitutes a "traditional" pasty. This free-standing pie is usually composed of diced or ground beef, potatoes, and onions, while the introduction of carrots and rutabagas remains controversial. Jane and Michael Stern write of this controversy in *Real American Food*:

> Serious gastroethnographers distinguish between a true Upper Peninsula Cornish pasty, made with cubes of steak, and a Finnish-style UP pasty, made with ground beef and pork. Further debate swirls around issues such as whether the dough should be made with lard or suet; and the filling—with or without rutabaga; and the crimp of the crust—at the top or along the side edge. (Stern, 236)

Foodways: The Upper Peninsula

The pasty was introduced to the area in the 1840s by Cornish miners as a hearty food which could easily be taken into the mines. Over a century and a half after its introduction, it is a food which has been accepted by everyone, and only in the Upper Peninsula can the designation "Pasty Shop" be found in the Yellow Pages. Pasties are sold fresh or frozen from pasty shops which dot the countryside from Ironwood to St. Ignace. As with the many Upper Peninsula foods, it has become so popular with visitors that it is shipped throughout the country as well.

Breads, cookies, and pastries cross ethnic lines. During the first part of the twentieth century, the Italian bakeries found in many central and western Upper Peninsula communities produced hundreds of loaves of bread a week. Italian households needed frequent deliveries, and in the winter bread was delivered in charcoal-heated sleds. Over the years the demand for "real" Italian bread declined, and today Schinderle's Italian Maid Bakery in Iron Mountain and Bread of Life Bakery in Bessemer remain among the few still producing traditional bread. On their shelves can be found Italian cookies, *biscotti, pizelle, cialde, torchetti,* and *grissini*.

Saffron buns and bread from England, limpa bread, ginger cookies, cardamom bread, and other delights from Scandinavia are also found throughout the Peninsula. Angeli's Bakery, Babycakes, and the Huron Mountain Bread Company in Marquette all boast varied inventories of bakery goods, offering such specialty breads as *baguettes*, saffron buns, *challah, focaccia,* and *cornetti*. The Trenary Bakery offers a variety of bakery goods but is best known for its cinnamon toast of Finnish origin. The gigantic cinnamon buns of the Hill Top Cafe in L'Anse became legendary with the local public years before such huge buns became popular elsewhere.

The Upper Peninsula proved to be an ideal location for the development of dairies. Immigrants working in the mines or woods found that they could augment their diets and bring in some spare cash by keeping dairy cattle. They also found that, as in Wisconsin, the climate was right for cheese production. Italian immigrants in Iron Mountain developed Stella brand, with its famous grated parmesan cheese and national market. *Juustoa,* or "squeaky cheese," has been popular with Finns and non-Finns as well. Today locally produced juustoa can be found in grocery coolers. Traditionally, this cheese was produced with unpasteurized milk. Local cheese companies produce a variety of cheeses, but cheese curds remain a popular item. John Jilbert, with his Rudyard plant, is one of the largest cheese manufacturers in the UP.

A SENSE OF PLACE: MICHIGAN'S UPPER PENINSULA

Meat products and in particular sausage are another varied category of Upper Peninsula foods. During the early days of the immigrant experience, following Old Country traditions, families would slaughter a hog in the fall. Every part of the animal was used. Before refrigerators, large crockery containers were used to store the meat. Filled with pieces of meat and sausage, the containers were covered with melted lard that kept the air and spoilage from the meat products. All through the winter months, pieces of pork and sausage were fished out of the lard and prepared for the table.

For years, as late as the 1970s, Piedmontese immigrants, Italian-Americans, and even non-Italians would gather at a farm in Boot Jack in the Copper Country to continue the fall tradition of sausage making. On the appointed day, dozens of men would gather and spend the day socializing, and under the watchful eyes of "Jaco" Succa the men processed the meat, ground, blended, and stuffed sausage. This community event saw hundreds of pounds of *sautissa*, a Piedmontese breakfast-style pork sausage, stored away for the coming winter.

The original recipes have migrated with the sons and grandsons of immigrants from the household and ethnic meat shops to supermarkets. This is what happened to Erspalmer's and Trolla's sausage recipes from Hurley, Wisconsin that have entered Gogebic County. Swedish potato sausage can be found at church sales and in markets. Head cheese or Swedish *sylte* is found in many stores because it is an all-ethnic food, enjoyed not only by Swedes but by Italians, French Canadians, and others as well. The Italian *cudighi* originating in Negaunee has become synonymous with sausage. In the Lombard dialect north Italians brought to Negaunee, *cotechino* was a fresh garlic pork sausage laced with *coténna* or pork rind, which lent a special flavor and consistency. Over the years a recipe more agreeable to the American palate has replaced the original. This modified cudighi is now a common UP food. *Sautissa*, still sold in Gogebic County, can be cured like a salami or boiled as a fresh sausage. *Supressa*, a cured meat, is still commercially made in the Upper Peninsula and is available to aficionados of Italian food.

Italian dry salami was another north Italian product that was originally made by families and cured by hanging in damp cellars. This food item is no longer produced in the Upper Peninsula but can be found at Reinerio's across the Wisconsin border in Pence. Immigrants from Abruzzi in east central Italy introduced porchetta or porketta to Iron Mountain. This is a pork roast seasoned with dill, fennel, garlic, and red peppers and slowly oven roasted. One of the few places which still makes traditional porketta is Bimbo's Wine Press in Iron Mountain. Every Tuesday, a side of pig is prepared, roasted overnight, and served with freshly baked Schinderle's crusty rolls on Wednesday afternoon. The treat continues to be available until it runs out, and the process is resumed the following Tuesday. For those who cannot get to Iron Mountain, small porkettas can be found in markets throughout most of the Peninsula.

Within the region, a number of meat and sausage factories continue to produce a variety of ethnic and non-ethnic products. In Caspian, Otto's Favorite makes a sliced and formed steak. Vollwerth's in Hancock continues to produce ethnic sausages such as Finnish ring bologna or *maakara*, ring blood sausage or Polish *kiska*, German braunschweiger, Swedish potato rings, and Polish sausage or *kielbasa*. For those who wish to make their own sausage, Aldo's in Champion has packets of dry ingredients for Italian sausage and pepperoni and jerky cure on grocery shelves.

The pork pie or *tourtière* was a favorite with French Canadians especially during the Christmas holidays. Ground pork seasoned with spices is baked in a pie shell. This product is available at various locations in Escanaba and at Lawry's in Marquette and Ishpeming.

In the markets, a number of canned and frozen goods can be found. From Canada come two foods which were traditional to the Upper Peninsula: Habitant brand traditional French Canadian pea soup can be found in many stores. Those seeking boned salted codfish, referred to by Italians as *baccalà*, will find it in little wooden boxes from Nova Scotia. The most complete offering of Finnish and Scandinavian goods is found at Touch of Finland in Marquette and includes sweet goods from the Old Country. Sometimes locally produced pickled herring and Italian antipasto can be found in local stores. The Paul J. Baroni Company in Calumet produces spaghetti sauces, frozen pizzas, and ravioli. In Ishpeming, Ralph's Italian Delicatessen and in Marquette, the Italian Place & New York Deli and Esperanto World Groceries and Deli all provide customers with culinary experiences.

Upper Peninsula thirsts have been quenched with a variety of libations over the years, with the most common being beer and wine. There is evidence that currant wine was discussed as a production possibility in 1834 by Henry Schoolcraft at Sault Sainte Marie. Although wine grapes are not native to the UP, southern and eastern Europeans had them shipped in from California and New York by rail. Usually families made two hundred gallons of red wine annually for their own use. The sale of wine in immigrant boarding houses greatly augmented a family's yearly income.

An offshoot of wine making was pioneered by Italians—the production of *grappa*. Once the wine had been made, the grape skins were recycled, fermented with sugar for a few days, and the finished product was distilled. The result was a clear and extremely potent liquor. During Prohibition, immigrants who did not understand or appreciate the irksome Volstead Act grew rich on the production and sale of alcohol. In Chicago, liquor from Raymbault Town, a suburb of Calumet, was considered the best on the market. In Iron County the story goes that, since Prohibition, there is more copper in the ground (from distilleries) than there ever was iron!

Since the mid-twentieth century, local wine production has dramatically declined, due to a drop in prices and the death of immigrants who enjoyed the production and consumption of their homemade wine. Some individuals produce fruit wines, but, except for Italian-Canadians in Sault Sainte Marie, little grape wine is produced in the North Country.

The coming of German immigrants after 1848 saw the introduction of beer making. Every large community had its brewery and in some cases beer gardens which were popular in the summer. The Ruppe family in the Copper Country was the last commercial brewer producing Bosch and Sauna beer. In the 1990s, micro-breweries with their restaurants have replaced the old breweries around the Peninsula.

A number of alcoholic drinks have been popular and in some cases legendary in the Upper Peninsula. Author John Voelker popularized the whiskey old-fashioned. Popular experience shows that the quality of the old-fashioned improves the closer one gets to Ishpeming. A little known drink, the Anaconda—made of lemon juice, maple syrup and whiskey or gin—was a favorite at the Beach Inn (1900 to 1950) in Munising. Peter White punch has been made privately but has never become a popular commercial drink. It was first made to celebrate the semi-centennial of opening the Soo canal in 1905. Peter White actually found the recipe in an old trunk from Middletown, Connecticut dating from 1737 (See recipe on page 104.). The drink itself is quite potent with ingredients—ranging from sugar, juices and English tea to several varieties of rums, brandy, chartreuse, and champagne—that make it expensive to concoct and might help explain its limited popularity.

Many plants were introduced to the Upper Peninsula with the coming of the French and later in the nineteenth century with the arrival of European immigrants. The potatoes and peas that French fur traders and missionaries brought during the seventeenth century have become important staples of the region. Native Americans found both plants important additions to their diets. Immigrants introduced seeds from the Old Country. The Blemhuber family first introduced a variety of fruit trees to the central Upper Peninsula. John

Foodways: The Upper Peninsula

Bergdahl, a farmer in Skandia, first developed an apple orchard in 1886, and some ninety years later the twelve acres were still producing fourteen varieties of apples. In 1914, a group spearheaded by V. S. Hillyer developed a large orchard which eventually consisted of some 4,800 fruit-bearing trees, including not only apple but cherry, plum, and pear as well. Apples proved to be the most hearty and are still found growing in orchards in a variety of locations, providing juice for cider and the ingredients for pies and other apple-related products.

Native foods continue to be gathered. Morels and mushrooms are sought after as valuable additions to any meal. Native Americans used maple sugar as an important nutritious part of their diets, mixing it into a variety of foods and drinks. The production of maple sugar could be considered one of the first industrial activities in the region. Records show that government trading posts had several tons of maple sugar on hand for trading purposes prior to the War of 1812. Today, for several weeks in the spring, the woods are alive with people tapping the trees and extracting the sap, which is then boiled down and usually made into syrup, although sugar and candies are also made and sold commercially. Honey, a European-introduced product, is produced on a limited basis for commercial purposes at a number of locations in the region.

Finally, a sort of regional culinary abomination celebrating the Green Bay Packers' part in Super Bowl XXXI appeared in Wisconsin and Upper Peninsula Burger King restaurants in January 1997 when they offered the double-everything "Gilbert Burger"—so named for Green Bay Packers defensive tackle Gilbert Brown.

The story of the foodways of the Upper Peninsula has not been exhausted but has merely whetted our appetites. The culinary history of the region is an important ingredient in defining the special identity of Michigan's Upper Peninsula. Searching for materials on local foodways is limited to scattered newspaper and magazine articles. A definitive study has not been developed. In the past, old cookbooks show that few ethnic recipes were included, probably because in the first seventy years of the twentieth century ethnicity—including gastroethnicity—was considered unimportant. Many felt that these foodways would pass away to be replaced by "real American food," but this has not been the case. Recently, Northern Michigan University's Center for Upper Peninsula Studies began developing a foodways collection in order to preserve an important part of our rich heritage and make it available to the public as well. A select bibliography on Upper Peninsula foodways follows.

Notes

[1] "Immigrant food" refers to food in its native state unacculturated by the American experience, while "ethnic food" refers to foreign food that has been altered by its foreign experience.

BIBLIOGRAPHY

[Anaconda and the Beach Inn] *Mining Journal* (04/01/1990).

Cooking with Our Ancestors. Iron County: The Junior Historical Society, 1974.

Dorson, Richard M. *Bloodstoppers and Bearwalkers: Folk Tradition of the Upper Peninsula*. Cambridge: Harvard University Press, 1956.

"Double Your Pleasure with the 'Gilbert Burger,'" *Mining Journal* (01/19/1997).

Eberly, Carol, ed. *Our Michigan: Ethnic Tales and Recipes*. East Lansing: Eberly Press, 1979.

Harris, Margaret B. "A Cook's Tour of the UP; Some Dishes That Are Divine," *Development Bureau News* (05/01/1932).

Kowlaski, Jake. "UP Food: A Taste of History," *Mining Journal* (11/10/1996).

_____. "The Hilltop," *Mining Journal* (04/05/1997).

Lockwood, William G. and Yvonne. "The Cornish Pasty in Northern Michigan," in *Michigan Folklife Reader*. C. Kurt Dewhurst and Yvonne R. Lockwood, eds. East Lansing: Michigan State University Press, 1986, pp. 359–74.

———. "Cudighi on Michigan's Iron Range," paper presented at "Forged from Iron: Industry, Society and Culture on Michigan's Iron Range," September 20–23, 1994, Negaunee.

Magnaghi, Russell M. "The Blemhubers: Farmers Extraordinaire," *Preview* 5:8 (August 1985): 22, 24–25.

———. "The Jesuits in the Lake Superior Country," *Inland Seas* 41:3 (Fall 1985): 190–203.

———. "Blueberry Picking," *Harlow's Wooden Man* 25:3 (Summer 1989): 6.

McEachern, Steve. "Something Fishy," *Mining Journal* (02/15/1993).

Meier, Cy. "Finnish Recipes for St. Urho's Day," *Upper Peninsula Sunday Times* (03/09/1980).

Merinoff, Linda. *The Savory Sausage: A Culinary Tour around the World.* New York: Poseidon Press, 1987.

Palemske, Jill. "UP Boasts Variety of Ethnic Foods," *Mining Journal* (07/01/1976).

[Peter White Punch] *Mining Journal* (04/18/1905).

Reinbold, George W. *Italian Cheese Varieties.* New York: Chas. Pfizer & Co., 1963.

Root, Waverly and Richard de Rochemont. *Eating in America: A History.* New York: William Morrow & Company, 1976.

Stern, Jane and Michael. *Real American Food.* New York: Alfred Knopf, 1986.

"Tasty Pasty in Michigan, A Cornish Delicacy Is Given a Finnish Flavor," *Natural History* (January 1980): 101–03.

Williams, Matthew. "The Recipe for Syrup," *Mining Journal* (04/06/1997).

———. "Rite of Spring: Maple Syrup," *Mining Journal* (04/06/1997).

"Pasty Time": Carl Pellonpaa (l) and unidentified fellow miner at the Cliffs Shaft Mine, Ishpeming, ca 1947. Photo courtesy of Superior View Photography, Marquette

The Cornish Pasty
Its History And Lore

Russell T. Magnaghi

The United States has a diverse collection of ethnic and regional foodways, some of which cover the nation and others of which concentrate in specific regions. The Cornish pasty (pronounced *pass-tee*), a self-standing pie made with meat, vegetables, and seasonings, is one of these ethnic foods. It is a popular food primarily in Michigan's Upper Peninsula and Butte, Montana—areas where Cornish miners lived and worked in the nineteenth century. Transplanted migrants from Michigan have also carried the pasty tradition to Grass Valley, California and other locations. In some regions the pasty is commercially produced and available in groceries as a semi-popular fast food.

Over the years a significant body of folklore has developed around the pasty. The term pasty itself is often mispronounced, and some ethnic groups like the Finns say that it is their ethnic food, completely ignoring its traditional origins, while others argue over the ingredients and methods of processing and even eating the food. It is the purpose of this essay to look at the historical origins of the pasty and how it has evolved over the centuries.

Old World Traditions

The simple pasty dish has a lengthy history and has accumulated a lengthy train of lore. The origins of the word go back to the Latin *pastata* which means pasta. It was through the Old French word *paste* that the word entered Middle English as *pastee*.

The concept of the pasty can also be traced back to the time of the Romans, when they sealed meat inside a flour and olive oil paste in order to retain the flavor. In northern Europe, butter and lard replaced the olive oil, and a pastry was developed made of a strong and plastic dough that could be made into a free-standing pie.

This concept of the pasty was rapidly accepted in the British Isles. The Anglo-Saxons first developed *haggis*, later commonly associated with the Scots. Originally haggis was a sheep stomach stuffed with meat and cereal and boiled. Other cooks went on and took flour mixed with shredded sheep suet and water to create a stiff dough. This was called Sussex and Kentish suet pudding or Norfolk dumpling. Meat or fish was encased in such a suet crust, wrapped in a cloth and boiled. The result was a hearty and nourishing meal. Such expediency naturally led to the Cornish pasty, consisting of meat and potatoes and, at one time, meat and cereal.

So it was that by the eleventh century the Anglo-Saxons had created a solid, yeomanlike fare, their national cuisine consisting of meat, bread, cheese, puddings, and pies. The famous Bayeux Tapestry recounts the Norman Conquest of 1066 when William the Conqueror successfully invaded England. One set of scenes on the tapestry shows a dinner in England. As food historian Maggie Black notes of the Tapestry scene, "The last scene shows the 'top brass' at table, tucking in to what appears to be steaks (*entrecôtes*), round flat breads and perhaps chicken pasties."

The use of the term pasty or pastee goes back to approximately 1300. In *The Land of Cokayne* it is mentioned: *"Al of pasteiis beb be walles, Of fleis, of fisse, and rich meat."* Records of the city of London dated 1301 list Richard, son of Gregory, as a "pastemakere." At the same time, "Bred an chese, butere and milk, Pastees and flaunes" was written in *Havelok the Dane*. As food historian, William E. Mead writes in *The English Medieval Feast*:

> *In preparing meats for the table the medieval cooks made great use of pastry. Innumerable recipes prescribe that the meat or fish or the fruit or the custard is to be placed in what is picturesquely termed a coffin.*

The reason for cooking food in pastries stemmed from the fact that food "cooked more satisfactorily" in a crust rather than being stewed over a fire.

By the late fourteenth century, the pie and pasty maker had taken his place along with the baker and waferer in medieval Britain. Unfortunately, there were constant problems over the centuries with maintaining quality among these bakers and pasty makers, as evidenced by official ordinances and literary notes. Conditions so deteriorated among medieval cooks and pie makers by 1378 that Richard II issued a special ordinance regulating the prices charged by London cooks and pie makers for their roasted and baked meats. At the time, the cost of a capon baked in a pasty was eight pence, and the best hen cost five pence. If the customer provided his own bird, the charge "for the paste, fire and trouble upon the capon" was one and a half pence and for a goose only two pence.

At that time, there were four types of bread vendors in London who had their shops or stalls in Bread Street. Municipal ordinances regulated their activity. One of the types was the pie baker or their *regraters* who sold filled pastries—ready-to-eat pies of fruit, meat, fish or poultry that would be comparable to the pasty.

The ordinances did not seem to deter unscrupulous bakers. In 1562, the public was warned to "Beware of ... pies and pasticrustes and all vunleuned [unleavened] breade." Some twenty years later, a health warning was given in *Haven Health:* "Hard crusts and Pasticrusts, doe engender adust choller." Furthermore, during the fourteenth and fifteenth centuries, there were several regulations issued by the government to prevent cooks and pie makers from using peppery and spicy recipes to conceal the use of tainted meat.

Chaucer's *The Canterbury Tales* is filled with descriptions of food in the fourteenth century. In the cook's Prologue written around 1386, mention is made of pasties. The Host noted in the tale that the cook, Roger, had drained the gravy of many a stale pasty along with selling twice-heated meat pies in his fly-infested cook shop. Thus, the public concern for poor-quality pasties found its way into the literature of the time. The Franklin in Chaucer's group who kept such a grandiose table probably served double-sized, two-crust pies at home. On the road, however, he would have preferred smaller ones, like Lombard chicken pasties, consisting of sliced chicken, eggs, pepper, ginger, and rashers of bacon. Another popular medieval pasty was made of mushrooms and cheese and seasoned with black pepper and dry mustard powder.

Little is known about the quality of the pastry used for pasties and pies at this time. The medieval cook or housewife learned pastry making by word of mouth. Contemporary cookbooks do not usually mention pastry recipes, merely that the paste should be of "strong dough." This was especially true for pasties or standing pies for larger birds. Cheaper rye or coarse wheat flour was necessary and approved by pasty or pie makers and their customers. In 1393, two recipes for chicken and mushroom pasties appeared in *Le Menagier de Paris* which found their way to England. These recipes do not discuss the pastry, only the ingredients. In the modern version of the recipe, the author points out that either tart shells could be used or the ingredients placed in a "sort of turnover." It was also noted that pasties were served at a dinner with roasts and boiled meats during the Middle Ages.

Over the centuries, a variety of ingredients went into the pasty, which was produced in a variety of sizes. Small tarts and pasties were common. "Chewettes" were filled with pork and chicken on a meat day and turbot, haddock, codling, or hake on a fish day. "Darioles" containing egg yolks, and cream mixed with wine, spices, minced dates, and strawberries were forerunners of minced pies. At times, little pasties were made and fried in lard instead of being baked in the oven. In medieval times, the *pety pernolloys* or *pety pernauntes* were usually fried. The dough or paste was made of "fair flour," saffron, sugar, and salt; and the filling included pieces of bone marrow, egg yolks, dried fruit and spices. In the fifteenth century, these little fried pasties were filled with pulped pork or veal, formed, and called "hats." On fish days, the pastry for the "hats" included almond milk, and the filling was composed of fish liver and saffron.

Fish was a common ingredient for pasties, especially on fish Friday and other days. In 1525, it was noted that pasties made of salmon, trout, and eel were common. Porpoise, "the venison of fish day" as Anne Wilson calls it, was a common filling for the pasty along with spices. When fish Friday was dropped during the reign of Elizabeth I in the seventeenth century, so went porpoise and other fish pasties.

The popularity of the venison pasty in England goes back to the medieval period as well. The meat was marinated overnight in "meare sauce" which was made of "vinegar, small drink and salt." Furthermore, it was highly seasoned. Those centuries back, Gervase Markham wrote:

> *And if to your meare sauce you add a little turnsole, and therein steep beef, or ram-mutton, you may also in the same manner take the first for red deer venison, and the latter for fallow, and a very good judgement shall not be able to say otherwise, than that it is of itself perfect venison, both in taste, colour, and the manner of cutting.*

An original recipe from *Two Fifteenth Century Cookery Books* provides us with a spicy venison pasty meal:

> *Take haunches of venison, parboil it in fair water and salt. Then take fair paste and lay thereon the venison cut in pieces as thou wilt have it, and cast under it and above it powder of ginger, or pepper and salt mixed together. And set them in an oven and let them bake till they be enough* [done].

The pasty appears in three of William Shakespeare's plays with a variety of meanings. In *Titus Andronicus,* written in the late 1580s, Titus states at one point, "And make two pasties on your shameful heads." In *The Merry Wives of Windsor,* probably first presented in 1597, Anne Page offers the guests "a hot venison pasty. . . ." Parolles, a follower of Bertram, Count of Rossilion, in *All's Well That Ends Well,* which dates from 1602 or 1603, states, "I will confess what I know without constraint; if ye pinch me like a pasty, I can say no more." So we have heads being made into pasties, the consumption of the popular venison pasty, and reference made to the pinch or crimp made in pasty preparation.

Problems with counterfeiting pasty meat was common. After Samuel Pepys and his wife attended a dinner on January 6, 1660, he wrote that the dinner was good, only "the venison pasty was palpable beef, which was not handsome."

FOODWAYS: THE CORNISH PASTY

Over the years, the variety of English pasties remained a constant. Writing in 1776 Thomas Pennant wrote of dining on goat meat in Wales:

> *The meat of a splayed goat of six or seven years is reckoned the best; being generally very sweet and fat. This makes an excellent pasty; goes under the name of rock venison, and is little inferior to that of the deer. Thus nature provides even on the tops of high and craggy mountains, not only necessaries, but delicacies for the inhabitants.*

The ingredients which went into the pasty were as varied as the people who made them. Around 1839, game pasties were written about, and in 1880, whortleberry pasties were mentioned. In 1972, K. Stewart in his *Times Cookery Book* described chicken liver and bacon pasties, and *Butte's Heritage Cookbook* edited by Jean McGrath in 1976 described not only traditional Cornish pasties but under "Butte Pastes with Variations" listed the use of left-over roast, ground round, chicken, elk, venison, and even an egg pasty!

The Pasty in Cornwall

Although the pasty was and continues to be eaten throughout the United Kingdom, it is best known as coming from Cornwall, the most southwestern county of England. The traditional land of the pasty is eighty miles in length with the Atlantic Ocean on the north and west, the English Channel to the south, and the Tamar River separating it from the neighboring county of Devonshire to the east. For centuries the Cornish people have been miners. Since the prehistoric era they mined tin, and later copper was the important mineral. Of all of the foods made by the Cornish, the pasty remains supreme, eaten at lunch, at tea, and for supper. The Cornish pasty is usually made of meat, but the filling can be made of a variety of ingredients. As Upper Peninsula historian Mac Frimodig wrote:

> *There were mackerel pies, pilchard pies, conger pies, bream pies, ram pies, muggety pies, curlew pies, taty pies, lammy pies, leek pies, and herby pies. There was even a variation of the pilchard pie called the "starry-gazy" in which sardines were introduced to their final resting place in a vertical position so that their heads protruded through the top crust, enabling them to watch their own last rites.*

The variety of fillings is so great that there is an old Cornish saying: "The Devil is afraid to come into Cornwall, for fear of being baked in a pasty."

Until relatively recent times, fish and sometimes birds formed the staple diet of the Cornish poor. In 1591, Thomas Celey of St. Ives protested the impressment of fishermen into the navy. "If the men do not continue their fishing, the country round will miss their best relief. The country is poor, and there is little flesh and less butter or cheese." This scarcity of food was created by government regulations and poor transportation and did not need the additional loss of essential fishermen. The situation became so bad that the people relied on song birds for food and also ate seals.

By the eighteenth century there was not much improvement in the food situation. In 1776, it was noted that laborers provided their families with potatoes or turnips or leeks or pepper grass that, when available, were rolled up in a black barley crust and baked under the ashes. Now and then milk was available, but these people had not had red meat in three months. Despite this diet, the children were healthy and happy.

"Lammy pasties" made from stillborn or overlaid lambs were once a favorite feast day dish of a parish in the vicinity of Penzance. The tale is told in 1883 of a visiting clergyman who entered the church on the feast day and, seeing the large congregation, decided to present a lengthy sermon. When it looked as if the sermon would never end and the congregation would not get to their lamb pasties, an older fellow rose and addressed the preacher, "Sir, 'tes a braa fine sarmon, and I'm sure we're much obliged to 'ee for 'un, but the lammy pasties 'es gettin' cold, and we can't stay any longer!" With that, the congregation followed the gent out of the church.

Adrian Bailey in *The Cooking of the British Isles* has written, "These [pasty] recipes remain in the rural areas of Cornwall not only because of the stubborn inflexibility of the people but because the food exactly suits the demands of the open-air life and the tastes it inspires."

The Pasty Comes to America

Poor economic conditions forced over a hundred thousand Cornish people to leave their homeland and seek a better life in the United States beginning in the nineteenth century. As a result the tradition of the pasty, along with saffron buns or cakes, was brought to the United States by the Cornish miners. At first the Cornish miners were attracted to the iron mines of Pennsylvania and New Jersey, or they prospected in Virginia and Maryland. These early arrivals found mining jobs and wrote to their relatives and friends who followed them. As early as 1830 they began to migrate to the lead mining region of southwestern Wisconsin and into neighboring Iowa and Illinois. The center of their activity in the Upper Mississippi Valley was Mineral Point, Wisconsin, where the Wisconsin State Historical Society maintains a state park honoring the Cornish heritage and the pasty. By 1850, there were as many as six thousand Cornish immigrants living

Foodways: The Cornish Pasty

in Grant County, Iowa and Lafayette, Wisconsin and another three thousand in Dubuque, Iowa and Jo Daviess County in northwestern Illinois. Many became miners, while others engaged in farming.

With the discovery of copper and iron deposits in Michigan's Upper Peninsula in the late 1840s, Cornish miners were attracted northward from the lead mining region. Because of their experience in the Old Country, Cornish miners were considered the leading mining experts in the world, and at that time this knowledge was essential to the American mining industry. In northern Michigan, mining was the only occupation open to the Cornish, as farming was out of the question given the poor soil and harsh climate. A few Cornish women worked as dressmakers, milliners, and school teachers, while widows sometimes kept boarding houses.

The California Gold Rush which started in 1848 sent hundreds of Cornish miners to the Far West to seek their fortunes. Grass Valley, California attracted many Cornish miners, while others moved to other locations on the Pacific Coast where mining was expanding. These early arrivals were followed by still others. In 1866, a devastating slump in Cornish copper mining intensified the ongoing migration. In the early 1880s, the rich copper fields in Butte, Montana were opened and developed. Throughout the Far West, Cornish miners were constantly moving to "keenlier lodes" in western Nevada on the Comstock Lode and then to gold strikes in British Columbia, South Dakota, and Arizona. Many miners who spent a few successful years in the American mining industry returned to Cornwall or Wisconsin where they could purchase farmland and live like squires. Cornish immigrants continued to come to the United States up to the 1920s. When opportunities in the mining industry declined at this time, Cornish miners found new jobs in the Detroit automobile industry and elsewhere.

The Pasty in Legend

Over the years, the pasty has entered local legend and more; what follows are a number of colorful stories related to the pasty, its preparation, and consumption.

In terms of the origins of the pasty, tradition says that arsenic in the mines rusted the lunch pails of the Cornish miners. As a result, the wives protected the lunch by covering the bottom of the pail with flour and water, and then someone added a top crust.

At first, if a Cornish miner did not want to carry his lunch pail to work, he placed the hot pasty under his shirt to take the chill off his chest on the way to work. By lunch time, because of the physical activity working in the mine, the miner was warm and sweaty, and the pasty in his shirt was ready to eat!

One winter when Jenny Phillips tried to stretch her food budget, she scrimped on the beef and pork for her husband's pasties. His immediate reaction upon returning home was, "Jenny, let's be having a little more mayt in me pasty and not so much turmit and tatey—me stummick's no bloody root cellar, y'know."

Folklorist Richard Dorson noted that just about any ingredients could be used in the pasty: traditional items (round steak, potatoes, turnips, rutabaga, suet, and onions); seedless raisins with rice and butter; kidneys with bacon strips and shaved potato chips or dates; berries, eggs, or liver; but never beans. In a Colorado mining town, a Chinese cook once made the mistake of putting beans in his pasties. When a Cousin Jack[1] discovered the intrusion of beans in his beloved pasty, he gently "bounced" the cook from the peak of Silver Mountain to the valley below.

Another story is told of a newly married Cousin Jack whose wife, Cousin Jenny,[1] had not yet mastered the art of pasty making. When he returned home from the mine after his first home-made pasty, he complained sorrowfully: "Damme, when I got down the shaft the pasty was all busted up in the pail. Damme, mother, make a pasty you could 'eave it down the shaft and 'it a 'undred feet down, and it wouldn't bust."

The lore associated with the pasty continues. Some say that the little pie must stand up to the miners' surroundings as an indication of its quality. In 1906 J. H. Harris wrote in *Cornish Saints and Sinners,* "When small a pasty is a snack; when large it's a meal." Concerning a degree of secrecy connected with the making of pasties and the ingredients, there appeared in *Time* magazine the following: "Cornwall is as protective about its pasties as Devon is about its cream" (12/28/1966). When traveling food authors Jane and Michael Stern discussed pasty making with Nancy Lawry in Ishpeming, Michigan, they had to report, "Although Nancy happily told us everything that goes into one of her renowned pasties, she could not provide exact measurements. 'That's a kinda touchy subject up here,' she said. 'Pasties are our reputation, and I'd be worried if someone else got a hold of just how we do it.'"

The Purist and the Pasty

The Cornish are concerned about what constitutes a real Cornish pasty. As a result, there are pasty purists in a community who have constantly regulated the proper pasty preparation and consumption. Bitter controversies have developed over what the exact ingredients

Foodways: The Cornish Pasty

should be, how it should be held when eaten, and even whether or not the meat should be diced or sliced or whether or not hamburger should be used.

The simple pasty can be made made using a variety of ingredients and techniques, and herein lies the debate as to what constitutes a traditional pasty. The crust is made with suet, lard, or butter, water, and flour. The meat can consist of pork and/or beef, but then a decision has to be made whether it is cubed, diced, or ground. Can hamburger or sausage be used? The primary vegetable ingredients, which can be diced or sliced, are turnips, onions, and potatoes. The inclusion of rutabagas or carrots reopens the controversy, as does the question of how much meat or potatoes should be used. Sometimes a small amount of parsley is added for flavor. The recipes change with every cook consulted, and, as a result, there is no standard pasty recipe.

Ethnicity has further affected the pasty. The Cornish introduced the pasty, but it is claimed by other nationalities and has become a bit of a universal food. Many Finns in the Upper Peninsula consider it their own national food and argue that its origins were in Finland and not Cornwall. In Butte, Montana an "Irish" pasty has developed over the years. Croatians, Irish, and Italians all enjoy the pasty. Whatever their national origin, many men in the Upper Peninsula will swear that "nobody can bake a pasty like my wife."

As a result there have been changes. Potatoes have gained a dominant role, and turnips have given way to finely-ground carrots. Diced or chunk meat is sparse in many pasties, and even hamburger has been introduced.

The question of gravy or sauce is critical. One Slavic chef has been known to inject a garlicky sauce through the posterior of the pasty. In the Upper Peninsula, the use of gravy is considered barbaric by many, while it is traditionally used in Butte, Montana. In some Upper Peninsula restaurants, pasties are cut horizontally before freezing, and then they are heated on a grill. The use of catsup on pasties in the UP would be considered strange elsewhere.

The Negaunee mining historian of Cornish heritage, Frank Mathews, had his own way of eating the pasty. He insisted that the pasty should be eaten on end so the juices can drain down to the last bite. For him this was dessert. Then there is the question of what utensils are to be used to eat it. The purists say it must be eaten with the aid of knives and forks.

A Sense of Place: Michigan's Upper Peninsula

The Pasty on the Move

The traditional pasty, saffron cake or buns, and heavy "caker" were the common foods of the Cornish. Outside of the Chinese, the Cornish were one of the few immigrant groups whose food became a staple fare in the various centers to which Cornish immigrants migrated.

The pasty is the most important and well-known food brought by the Cornish and is closely associated with mining. It provided not only food for the miners underground but a wealth of legend and color to the Cornish story in America. Today it continues to be eaten at various locations throughout the United States. One of its problems is that it provided a substantial meals for miners but today can be considered a bit too heavy for some people.

In the Midwest, pasty production is a cottage industry in a number of communities. As the market expands so does the production, and, as a result, machines have been introduced in pasty preparation. Purists in the business insist that automation destroys the true pasty and its ethnicity, but obviously this is highly debatable.

In Michigan, the pasty is produced at many locations in both the Upper and Lower Peninsulas. From St. Ignace on the east and stretching across the Upper Peninsula to Gogebic County on the west, communities have their pasty bakeries, restaurants, and specialty shops. In the 1960s, local chambers of commerce like that in Marquette promoted the idea of making May 24 official "Pasty Day." Probably Upper Peninsula telephone books are some of the few in the country that have "Pasties-Meat Pies" listed.

One of the earliest pasty shops in the Marquette area was Madelyne's Pasties, which opened in the 1950s and then in 1965 moved to Ishpeming. They were the first to fast freeze pasties for shipment. For years they were one of the largest producers, but they ceased production in 1981. Lawry's Pasties first opened in Ishpeming and later opened branches in Marquette and Harvey. In 1966, Roger Lawry converted forty tons of potatoes, nine tons of vegetables, four tons of lard, twelve tons of flour, and fifteen tons of strip steak into enough pasties to stretch five miles laid end to end. In the late 1980s, Nancy Lawry told the Sterns that she started every morning making pasties from scratch and by the end of the day had produced as many as two to four hundred. One Fourth of July she set a single-day record with seven hundred pasties. Beginning in the 1980s, Lawry's appeared in *Roadside Food and Good Food* by Jane and Michael Stern, which is a guide to good regional food. These gourmets were thoroughly impressed with Lawry's pasty: "You understand their

Foodways: The Cornish Pasty

[pasties'] popularity in the cold north woods when you take possession of a Lawry's pasty. Just to hold this big piece of food imparts a feeling of security." Although the Lawrys guard their recipe, the Sterns created one which appeared in their *Real American Food*.

OPEN WIDE

The largest pasty ever recorded, this monster was made by Northern Michigan University students on October 20, 1978. Baked in an outdoor oven, it included 250 lb of beef, 400 lb of potatoes, 75 lb of carrots, and 25 lb of onions, all wrapped into 250 lb of dough.
(photo courtesy of the Marquette Mining Journal)

Papa Paul's Pasties is located in downtown Marquette and operates a factory that sells wholesale to restaurants in Sault Sainte Marie and elsewhere in the Upper Peninsula and in Rhinelander and Shawano in neighboring Wisconsin. In Marquette there is Jean Kay's Pasties, and pasties are on the menu of Northern Michigan University. Small hors d'œuvre pasties are served at receptions on campus and elsewhere. Throughout the Upper Peninsula in communities like St. Ignace, Escanaba, Iron Mountain, Rapid River, Laurium, and Ironwood pasties are sold.

From the Lower Peninsula city of Flint, pasties are produced and sold throughout Michigan including the Upper Peninsula and in the Chicago area under the UP Brand. In downtown Traverse City, there is Cousin Jenny's Cornish Pasties. In Birmingham, a Detroit suburb, Ackroyd's Scottish Bakery sells a variety of Celtic bakery goods including a light crusted pasty.

The center of the pasty in Wisconsin is Mineral Point in the southwestern corner of the state. Here in the former lead mining region with its Cornish heritage, the pasty remains king. Elsewhere in the state, however, pasties are produced commercially, as in Menomonee Falls, a suburb of Milwaukee.

In the Far West, the pasty thrives in a variety of locations. In the vicinity of Butte, Montana, the pasty is part of the local cuisine. Shops making and selling them are common, and they appear on local restaurant menus. The biggest difference in their consumption is that more than likely they will be served with gravy. Upper Peninsula pasty purists cringe at the mere thought of ruining a delicious pasty with gravy, while they will not hesitate to douse it with catsup; but don't tell that to the Butte purist. Grass Valley, California is also a minor center of pasty cuisine.

Aficionados have spread the pasty beyond the confines of the Midwest. The pasty has been found in Florida and other locations where Michiginians are found during the winter months and in California malls.

Recent investigations into the ethnic history of Mexico show that the pasty even found its way into that nation. The city of Pachuca in the state of Hidalgo, some seventy-five miles northeast of Mexico City, has a long silver-mining history. As a matter of fact, today much of Mexico's silver production comes from the vicinity of Pachuca.

During the nineteenth century, Cornish miners settled in the area at Real del Monte and introduced Mexicans to soccer and the pasty. Today neighborhood restaurants in Pachuca carry *pastes* on their menus. Here, too, the traditional pasty has undergone a change, as these are filled with chile, meats, moles, and other Mexican-style adaptations.

Mainstream America frequently uses foodways as a factor in identifying ethnic and regional character. This is certainly true of the humble pasty. Despite its folklore and arguments over what constitutes the "best" pasty, the little meat pie is one of the local ethnic foods which has become closely associated with the Upper Peninsula and helps to give the region its special identity.

Note

[1] "Cousin Jack" and "Cousin Jenny" were nicknames for males and females from Cornwall.

BIBLIOGRAPHY

Anderson, James M. and Iva A. Smith, eds. *Ethnic Groups in Michigan.* vol. 2 *The Peoples of Michigan.* Detroit: Ethnos Press, 1983.

Bailey, Adrian. *The Cooking of the British Isles.* New York: Time-Life Books, 1969.

Black, Maggie. *The Medieval Cookbook.* New York: Thames and Hudson, Inc., 1992.

Cosman, Madeleine Pelner. *Fabulous Feasts: Medieval Cookery and Ceremony.* New York: George Braziller, 1976.

Dorson, Richard. *Blood-Stoppers and Bear Walkers: Folk Traditions of the Upper Peninsula.* Cambridge: Harvard University Press, 1952.

Frimodig, David Mac. "...With Mayt, Turmit, and Tatey." *Michigan Natural Resources Magazine.* January–February 1971), 22.

Hieatt, Constance B. and Sharon Butler. *Pleyn Delit: Medieval Cookery for Modern Cooks.* Toronto: University of Toronto Press, 1976.

Jenkin, Alfred K.H. *Cornwall and Its People.* New York: A. M. Kelley, 1970.

McGrath, Jean, ed. *Butte's Heritage Cookbook.* Butte, MT: Butter Silver Bow Bi-Centennial Commission, 1976.

Marquette *Mining Journal,* 05/19/1967.

Mead, William E. *The English Medieval Feast.* New York: Barnes and Noble, 1967.

Riley, Henry T., ed. and tr. *Memorials of London and London Life in the xiiith, xivth and xvth Centuries. Being a Series of Extracts, Local, Social, and Political from the Early Archives of the City of London, A.D. 1276–1419.* London: Longman, Green and Co., 1868.

Rowe, John. *The Hard-Rock Men: Cornish Immigrants and the North American Mining Frontier.* New York: Barnes and Noble, 1974.

Rowse, A.L. *The Cousin Jacks: The Cornish in America.* New York: Charles Scribner's Sons, 1969.

Stern, Jane and Michael. *Real American Food.* New York: Alfred A. Knopf, 1986.

———. *Road Food and Good Food.* New York: Alfred A. Knopf, 1986.

Todd, Arthur C. *The Cornish Miner in America.* Glandale, Calif.: Clark, 1967.

Wilson, C. Anne. *Food and Drink in Britain from the Stone Age to Recent Times.* New York: Barnes and Noble, 1974.

A Sense of Place

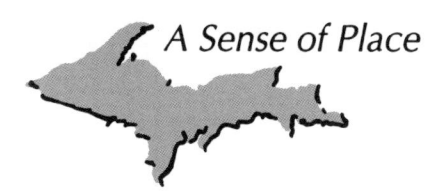

Literature

*John Voelker, wearing one of his many striped shirts, writing on the legal-sized, yellow-lined notebook paper which so characterized his handwritten work. No date.
(Reprint courtesy of the Northern Michigan University Archives.)*

Anatomy of a Murder
From Fact to Fiction to Film

Leonard G. Heldreth

At about 12:30 a.m. on Thursday, July 31, 1952, Lieutenant Coleman A. Peterson of the United States Army walked into the Lumberjack Tavern in Big Bay, Michigan. In his left hand was a loaded 9 mm German Luger. Without saying a word to anyone, he walked decisively to the bar, pushed aside two men standing there, and began to fire. Maurice K. Chenoweth, known as Mike, the owner of the bar and a former Michigan state policeman, was standing in front of the cash register. The first bullet struck him in the neck, and without uttering a word he began to slide down behind the bar. Peterson leaned over the bar and fired the remaining five shots into Chenoweth's body as it lay on the floor; one shot went through the heart, two hit the abdomen, and two hit the shoulder. Then, Peterson turned, left the bar, walked back to Perkins Trailer Park where he lived with his wife, and gave himself up to Special Deputy Fred Marsh, who was a caretaker at the park.[1]

Thus began the most famous murder case to occur in Michigan's Upper Peninsula, a case which would be reshaped into Robert Traver's best seller, *Anatomy of a Murder,* and into Otto Preminger's film of the same name. Yet with each reshaping of the initial events, certain details were modified; characters were added, eliminated or modified; and liberties were taken with the facts to provide better entertainment. To understand how these many changes occurred and why, it is necessary to begin at the beginning, with the murder as it was reported in contemporary accounts.

The shooting was the climax of a series of events that had begun earlier that evening. Lieutenant Peterson, thirty-eight, and his wife Charlotte, forty-two, had been living in Perkins Trailer Park for about a week, for Peterson had been transferred to the area to serve with the anti-aircraft artillery unit stationed in Big Bay. Mrs. Peterson left for the tavern (the area's social center) that evening after dinner, and her husband, who had lain down for a nap, told her he would meet her there later. During the time she was at the tavern, she was seen to kick off her shoes, play shuffle board, and drink four shots of whiskey and water. During the shuffleboard games, the owner and manager of the tavern, Mike Chenoweth, had been quite attentive and had told Mrs. Peterson that it was not safe for her to walk back to her trailer about half a mile away, because bears had been seen around. When she left the tavern, she found Chenoweth waiting outside for her in his car with the engine running. He insisted on driving her home, and she and her dog George, a Labrador mix, got into the car. When they arrived at the gate to the trailer park, the gate was locked, but Chenoweth said he knew another road which entered the trailer park from the back and drove off onto a dirt road leading into the bush on Country Road 550. There, as she later recounted, he stopped the car and attacked her, bruising her neck and beating on her legs before tearing her skirt, ripping off her panties, and raping her. When the dog tried to come between them, he pushed the dog out of the car.

After the rape, when Mrs. Peterson was only semi-conscious, Chenoweth apparently put the dog back into the car and drove back to the trailer park main gate. There, when Mrs. Peterson let the dog out and started to get out, Chenoweth began to assault her again, but she broke free screaming, and with the dog holding a flashlight in its mouth, she managed to escape through a hole in the fence as Chenoweth kicked at her. She ran to her trailer where, hysterical and bruised, she told her husband what had happened and swore on a rosary that Chenoweth had raped her. Over half an hour passed from the time she reached the trailer until Lieutenant Peterson picked up his pistol and walked to the Lumberjack Tavern where he shot Mike Chenoweth.

Peterson was taken into custody by the state police, driven to Marquette, and charged with murder. He and Mrs. Peterson engaged as their defense lawyer John D. Voelker, a former prosecuting attorney who had lost the last county election and gone back into private practice. The trial began on Monday, September 15, 1952, and the jury reached its verdict a week later on Monday, September 22. They declared Peterson "not guilty" by reason of temporary insanity. Three days later, two examining physicians declared Peterson was now sane, and he was released from custody. Thus ends the official record of the murder trial.

The defense attorney, John D. Voelker, forty-nine, was also a writer; and during fourteen of the preceding sixteen years, when he had served as prosecuting attorney, he had published a number of articles, including a piece of detective work that argued that Hemingway had actually written about the Fox River instead of the Big Two-Hearted River in his short story of that name. He had also published an article on nuclear warfare in *The Saturday Review of Literature*,[2] an article on his classmate Glenn Seaborg, and several articles on fishing. Writing under the name of Robert Traver (Traver being his mother's maiden name), he had published his first book, *Trouble Shooter*, in 1943. Other books followed: *Danny and the Boys* in 1951 and *Small Town D.A.* in 1954. The latter book was apparently one of the reasons Governor G. Mennen Williams named Voelker to the Michigan Supreme Court, and he was sworn in on January 1, 1957.[3]

LITERATURE: ANATOMY OF A MURDER

After the Peterson trial, Voelker began writing his novel, basing much of the courtroom drama directly on the trial transcripts, and produced a manuscript of 840 pages written in green felt-tipped pen on a yellow legal pad. On January 6, 1958, *Anatomy of a Murder*, which had been rejected by three publishers, was finally brought out by St. Martin's Press under the name of Robert Traver and was phenomenally successful. The Book-of-the-Month Club chose it as a main selection, and in a trade edition it remained on the national best-seller list for sixty-five weeks. Plans were made to turn the novel into a play, and a number of film directors seemed interested in the property.

What steps had Voelker taken to achieve such success? First, he had carefully preserved the most interesting characters and dramatic moments from the trial transcripts, including nearly verbatim dialogue. In the novel, Judge Weaver makes the following statement regarding a murder trial to attorney Paul Beigler (Voelker's surrogate in the novel):

> *The field is a most interesting one. It so far supersedes and renders inconsequential both stage and screen productions, and the best products of the novelists, by sheer force of accumulated actual experience, as to make outpourings of the imagination pale and wilt by factual contrast.... Whenever there is a jury trial there is neighborhood interest, reputations at stake, serious liability, and often even future life involved...* (245–246).

Robert Traver evidently believed the words he put in his character's mouth, for he transfers most of the events of the original trial to the pages of his novel, changing only the names. In an interview during the filming of the movie, Voelker remarked, "Of course, there are real people who can be compared to the characters in the book, but this was creative fiction of the highest order because I changed their names" *(Mining Journal,* 5/12/59). Thus Mike Chenoweth becomes Barney Quill, Coleman and Charlotte Peterson become Frederic and Laura Manion, John Voelker becomes Paul Beigler, and so forth, down to the smallest character.

Much of the dialogue corresponds almost verbatim with the newspaper records of the trial, as the following examples illustrate. In the original trial Marsh, the caretaker of the trailer park, said that Charlotte Peterson said to him, "Look what Mike has done to me!" and he told the court, "I saw a mess. Her face was beaten and bruised" *(Mining Journal,* 9/17/52). In the novel, Mrs. Manion says, "Look what Barney did to me," and Lemon (the name given to the Marsh character in the novel), says, "She—she was a mess" (265).

In a similar fashion, Police Lieutenant Spratto made the following statement during the actual trial: "I said, 'Lieutenant, where's the gun?' He pointed to the gun on the table and said, 'I'll get it for you.' But, Lieutenant Wixom said, 'No, I'll get it'" *(Mining Journal, 9/17/52)*. In the novel, Lientenant Drago says, "I asked the Lieutenant where the gun was and he pointed at a table and said he would get it, but I said no and instead got it myself" (284–85).

A parallel pattern appears in the testimony of Lieutenant Peterson. In the newspaper accounts of the trial, Peterson, under questioning from the defense attorney, made the following statement about his war experiences: "Quite often when ten of us got back from a patrol, we'd have ten different stories." Under prodding from the prosecutor, Peterson told about an incident in Korea "when he and some eight other men had a 'half-track' in their support. There were about eight men wounded, and when they were evacuated there were eight different stories as to what had happened" *(Mining Journal, 9/20/52)*.

In the novel, Lieutenant Manion says, "Well, quite often after an action had been completed and we got back to talk it over, if there were ten survivors, there'd be ten different stories of what happened." Under further questioning, Manion tells the following account: "I recall one incident in Korea. One of my half-tracks was supporting the infantry. I had eight men in this action, and a commie mortar round dropped in and wounded all eight. I happened to be far enough away to see what happened without getting wounded.... all of them told a different story" (349).

In the trial, Dr. Petty says, "This is the condition I've seen in men who have come back from combat and in men during combat. Some of the most remarkable heroics take place in this state, as well as some of the worst cowardices" *(Mining Journal, 9/20/52)*. In the novel Dr. Matthew Smith says, "This is a condition that I have seen and discussed with men who experienced it during combat .... Some of the most remarkable heroics take place in this state, as well as some of the most remarkable cowardice" (363). And so on—the parallel examples could be multiplied many times.

Sometimes Traver amplifies an incident in the courtroom which the newspaper has glossed over. In the newspaper accounts, reference is made to "a temporary delay in the trial, when a minor disturbance took place among the audience in the courtroom during which time the jury was excused" *(Mining Journal, 9/19/52)*. In the novel, a mentally deranged veteran in the audience rises to his feet, stammers, and tells the jury to let the defendant go.[4]

In at least one place, Traver rewrites the account to make Paul Beigler, his alter ego, look better than he did in the actual trial. In the trial account, "When Prosecuting Attorney Edmund J. Thomas asked Spratto what Peterson said, Defense Attorney John D. Voelker objected, asking if he had been informed of his constitutional rights." After comments from the judge, Voelker withdrew his objection (*Mining Journal* 9/17/52). But in the novel, when the same question is asked, Traver writes, "The Judge glanced quickly at me and I shook my head. I could have objected on the grounds that it had not yet been shown that the police had first warned the lieutenant of his constitutional rights, including his right not to talk. But I did not object because I was morally certain that Julian had indeed warned my man, he always did" (284).

In addition to re-naming the principals, Voelker also changed the names of places: Big Bay becomes Thunder Bay; the Lumberjack Tavern becomes the Thunder Bay Inn; Ishpeming, Michigan, becomes Iron City; and so forth.

In addition to the names, a few of the details were changed. Instead of the shuffleboard played by Charlotte Peterson, Laura Manion plays pinball at the tavern the night of the attack. Charlotte Peterson's dog is changed from a Labrador mix to a small terrier, perhaps to emphasize that the dog could not have protected Mrs. Manion.[5] Of the bullets that struck Quill in the novel, none hit him in the throat as they did Chenoweth. In the novel, the sanity hearing for Manion is held the same night for better dramatic unity, whereas in the real trial, the sanity hearing was held three days later.

For all that he appropriated from the accounts of the original trial, Voelker added the essential ingredients to make the story an effective narrative: several new and memorable characters, a romantic subplot, and a first person point of view. Among the significant characters added are Maida, Beigler's secretary, who seems to be a mixture of several people whom Voelker knew. Also added is Parnell McCarthy, the hard-drinking aide to Beigler who switches to orange soda early in the novel.

Although the character of Paul Beigler is clearly Voelker's surrogate in the novel, Beigler differs substantially in his circumstances from Voelker. While the author and his character share a love for good whiskey, strong Italian cigars, and trout fishing, Beigler is a bachelor while Voelker was very much a family man with a wife and three daughters.

The murdered innkeeper in the novel, Barney Quill, also differs in marital status from Mike Chenoweth, the original victim. The two share physical characteristics, both are former state policemen, and both are accused of the same crime. Quill, however, is divorced in the novel, with his wife and daughter living in Wisconsin; in the actual situation, Chenoweth's wife and daughter lived with him in Big Bay.

Making Beigler a bachelor and Chenoweth a divorced man enables Voelker to introduce a character named Mary Pilant, who is Barney Quill's friend and perhaps mistress and who inspires romantic feelings in the lawyer Paul Beigler. Mary has fallen in love with a local army officer, and jealousy has caused Barney Quill to hate the army, drink too much, and perhaps rape Laura Manion as a method of striking back at the organization. The novel also emphasizes that Quill's will leaves the tavern to Mary.

The only evidence in the news stories at the time to indicate anything unusual was going on with Mike Chenoweth was that the bartender at the Lumberjack Tavern said Chenoweth had been drinking more than usual and acting strange for about two weeks; further, he said Mrs. Chenoweth had asked him to lock up three of Chenoweth's pistols. No further discussion of this situation occurs in the newspaper accounts of the time.

By adding the Pilant character, Voelker was able to add a subplot which provided a reason for Quill's rape of Laura Manion. Further, it provided a romantic interest for the hero and ended the novel on a positive note with Beigler going off to have dinner with Mary. Mary Pilant, who seems to have been created wholly by Voelker, would become a major character by the time the screenplay was finished.

The entire tone of the novel was determined by Voelker's choosing to tell the story through the first person narration of Paul Beigler, the trial lawyer. Voelker's manuscripts of other works indicate his interest in point of view, for he changes point of view in rough drafts to see what sort of effect such a change would have on the narrative. In Paul Beigler, Voelker creates a knowledgeable, sympathetic character who comments on everything from the architecture of the court house to the status of trout fishing in the Upper Peninsula. Telling the story through Beigler's eyes also imposes a unity on the account and a framing device that gives the story depth and detail. Like Beigler, the reader does not know the truth of the situation, and the reader shares the suspense while at the same time being privileged to Beigler's knowledge of the law. Through making these changes in plot and character and unifying the material with an attractive point of view, Voelker created a very readable novel from a trial that would otherwise have been forgotten.

LITERATURE: ANATOMY OF A MURDER

Otto Preminger, who would ultimately direct the film version of *Anatomy of a Murder*, first heard about the book in August of 1957, six months before it was published, when his story editor, Tom Ryan, read the manuscript and sent Preminger a favorable report. Preminger was in France filming *Bonjour Tristesse*, and before he could act, the stage and screen rights were acquired by someone else. After returning to the United States, Preminger read the novel and was impressed by its intense reality and its vivid picture of the law, qualities which reminded him of his days as a law student. An article in a trade newspaper indicated that the sale of the screen rights had not been completed, so he checked further into the matter to find out that, indeed, the rights had not been assigned. Through various legal maneuvers and the settling of three lawsuits involving the theatrical rights, Preminger finally acquired the film rights to the novel from Voelker in 1958 for $150,000 and 5 percent of the gross revenue of the film.

At the time he began pre-production plans for *Anatomy of a Murder*, Preminger had been producing films with his own company, Carlyle Productions, for five years. Born in Vienna in 1906, he had come to the United States in 1935 and become a citizen in 1943, signing a contract the same year with Twentieth Century-Fox as a producer-director. His first major work as a director was *Laura* (1944), and he followed that with films such as *Forever Amber* (1947), *The Fan* (1949—an adaptation of Oscar Wilde's *Lady Windemere's Fan*), and *Where the Sidewalk Ends* (1953). He also played the Nazi commander in *Stalag 17*, released during the same year.

In 1953, he left Fox and formed Carlyle Productions to produce *The Moon is Blue*. Considered very daring because of its subject and use of the word "virgin," this film was denied a seal by the Motion Picture Producers Association of America (MPPAA) and declared off limits by many religious organizations. By current standards, the film is extremely tame; racier dialogue and more sexual innuendoes occur in almost any current prime time television comedy.

This conflict was only the first of several between Preminger and American censorship.

Carmen Jones, an adaptation of Bizet's opera transferred to the southern states with a black cast, followed in 1954, with *The Court Martial of Billy Mitchell* in 1955. Preminger clashed with the MPPAA again in 1955 when he released *The Man with the Golden Arm*, because its subject matter was drug addiction, a topic off-limits for motion pictures of the time. In 1957, he adapted George Barnard Shaw's *Saint Joan* and cast Jean Seaberg, an unknown, as Joan; the following year he starred her in his next film, *Bonjour Tristesse*.

A Sense of Place: Michigan's Upper Peninsula

After acquiring the rights to *Anatomy of a Murder,* Preminger hired Wendell Mayes to write the script and worked closely with the writer to shape a screenplay that pleased both of them. When Preminger got the opportunity to direct, he took Mayes to Hollywood with him, where he directed during the day while Mayes wrote, and then they conferred at night. In the spring of 1958, Preminger came to the Upper Peninsula to visit Voelker and decided at that time to shoot all the exteriors on location; on a later visit in January of 1959, he decided to shoot the entire film on location.

On January 15, 1959, James Stewart and Lana Turner were announced as the stars of the film, but Turner quit the part in early March, charging that it was "impossible to deal with his [Preminger's] unpredictable temper." Preminger replied that the dispute was over costumes; Lana Turner wanted to be dressed glamorously while Preminger wanted her to dress realistically to fit the documentary style in which he hoped to make the movie. Preminger announced, "I'll get an unknown and make her a new Lana Turner," but twelve hours later he signed Lee Remick, described in the press release as a "sensational stage and screen actress."

At twenty-three Remick might have seemed a bit young for the part of Laura Manion, whom the book described as forty-one but still extremely attractive. As it turned out, the change in age became less important because her husband was also made younger in the film. Remick had debuted in *A Face in the Crowd* (1957) playing a majorette and had played in *The Long Hot Summer* (1958) and *These Thousand Hills* (1959); she arrived in the UP on March 22 with her seven-week-old daughter.

Eve Arden was recommended by her agent for the part of Maida, Paul Beigler's secretary. While Arden had acted in a number of films, including *Stage Door* (1937), *Cover Girl* (1944), *Mildred Pierce* (1945), and *We're Not Married* (1952), she was best known for her television series, *Our Miss Brooks,* which ran from 1952 to 1955. The part of Mitchell Lockwich, the prosecuting attorney, was originally announced to be played by James Daly, but he was replaced by Brooks West, Eve Arden's husband. Ben Gazarra was signed to play Lieutenant Frederic Manion, the defendant, and Arthur O'Connell played Parnell McCarthy. George C. Scott, who played the assistant to the prosecuting attorney, was hired by Preminger after two interviews, although Preminger had never seen him act.

The casting that most fascinated Preminger was hiring Joseph Welch, the Boston attorney who had become famous from his part in the Army-McCarthy hearings. *Anatomy of a Murder* was Welch's film debut, and Preminger was so eager to have him that he gave Welch one of the highest salaries in the film and further sweetened the pot by casting Mrs. Welch as a juror. Preminger's ploy paid off, however, because he received far more publicity from the casting of Welch than he could have bought with Welch's salary.

For the part of Mary Pilant, Preminger had planned to cast "an as yet unknown aspiring actress," but his final choice was Kathryn Grant, wife of Bing Crosby. Lloyd LeVasseur, County Clerk of Marquette, was cast as Clovis Pigeon, the county clerk—an appropriate choice, since Pigeon was originally modeled on LeVasseur and Voelker said that LeVasseur had been rehearsing the part for twenty-three years. Other cast members included Royal Beale as Sheriff Max Battisford (replacing Emile Meyer, who was injured in an auto accident three days before shooting was to begin), Murray Hamilton as Alphonse Parquette, and Orson Bean as Dr. Matthew Smith, psychiatrist.

On January 21, the Marquette County Board of Supervisors gave permission to use the courthouse, and later they agreed to let the courtroom be painted with the understanding it would be repainted to the original color. The new color was a rosy tan because the original light color would appear too light in the film. Other changes to the courthouse included bracing the second floor to support the heavy movie equipment and adding further ventilation to deal with the heat generated by the equipment.

While the film makers attempted to use existing structures such as the courthouse, Voelker's home, the Ishpeming Railroad depot, the sheriff's office, and a local hospital, some construction was necessary. A hot dog stand was constructed near the lake, theoretically to take advantage of the natural beauty of the shoreline, but the scene was set at the end of Washington Street in front of what was hardly an object of natural beauty—the old coal loading facility, which operates throughout the scene. A twenty-by-forty-foot, single-story addition was added to the Big Bay Inn as well as a new sign, and a beauty parlor was constructed in an empty building in Michigamme.

Over three hundred Marquette residents tried out for parts as extras, and about a hundred and sixty were selected for bit parts. The casting director tried to pick women who were middle-aged or older and retired or elderly men, because he felt these were the types that would be hanging around a courthouse. The extras were to be paid ten dollars per day and fifteen if they used their cars. Despite some complaining at the start of filming and some requests for fifteen dollars as standard pay, most of the extras seemed satisfied with their pay and would probably have played the parts for nothing.

A Sense of Place: Michigan's Upper Peninsula

The arrival of the major cast members on March 22 was filmed and later broadcast on *The Ed Sullivan Show* on March 30. Shooting began on March 23 and proceeded almost exactly on schedule. The courtroom scenes were filmed first over a period of about four weeks, with a break on April 20 for filming two scenes at the train depot in Ishpeming, where Arthur O'Connell greeted Orson Bean while a hired train chugged away at a hundred dollars an hour. O'Connell had caught a virus in New York and had been hospitalized at Bell Memorial Hospital during the week.

By April 24, the courtroom scenes were finished except for some hall shots, and filming moved to St. Mary's Hospital, then to the county jail, and then on to Big Bay. During pre-production Preminger had said he wanted to film at the Lumberjack Tavern "in the interest of realism and authenticity," and early publicity argued that the filming in the Lumberjack Tavern would be the first time scenes of a murder were actually filmed at the site of the murder. Thus, even though the new addition to the Big Bay Inn was used for the exterior shots, the interior shots were filmed at the Lumberjack.

On May 2, Duke Ellington arrived to work on the film score and to lead the band that played in the road house. Filming continued at Voelker's former home in Ishpeming, at the Carnegie Public Library, and at Nault's Bar, despite an early May snowstorm. Then the crew moved to the Mt. Shasta Lodge, which functions as a road house in the film, and to two days of shooting in Michigamme for street scenes and a beauty parlor sequence. By May 15, almost exactly on schedule, shooting was completed, and a mass exodus began.

Some interesting facts and trivia about the film included its projected budget of two million dollars (dirt cheap by today's standards), of which over half a million was expected to remain in the Marquette County area. *Anatomy of a Murder* was also the first film handled entirely on location during production, including even the film editing. It also used more dulling spray up to that time than any other film—over thirty cans—because of the polished woodwork in the courthouse that reflected into the cameras. The dog who appeared in the film was actually two dogs, Snuffy and Danny, cairn terriers trained by Bob Blair, who also trained the cats in *Bell, Book, and Candle*. James Stewart used John Voelker's rods and lures in the film and smoked the short black, imported Italian cigars that Voelker and his hero smoke. Voelker asserted the cigars were "not as bad as they appear to be; they are infinitely worse."

As most films do, *Anatomy of a Murder* played loose with the architecture of the area. In one scene, Stewart and O'Connell are going through books in a law library. Welch comes down the corridor and peeks into the room, sees the two, smiles, turns, and leaves. The "law library," which was fabricated in the Ishpeming Carnegie Public Library, was composed of law books moved there from Northern Michigan College; and when Welch walked down the hall at the court house and appeared to peek in, he actually looked into the men's room. Creative editing connected the two scenes.

As with any transformation of a long novel into a screenplay, many details were inevitably changed, from the introduction of Duke Ellington's band to the increased emphasis on Maida, Eve Arden's part. As with any screenplay adapted from a novel written in first person, much of the point of view was lost. The most significant change in the structure of the film was the enlargement and refinement of the character of Mary Pilant, played by Kathryn Grant. In the film, she becomes the illegitimate daughter of Barney Quill rather than his mistress and thus a more suitable romantic prospect for Beigler, played by Jimmy Stewart. It is interesting that in an interview during the filming, Voelker said, "There will be no last-minute witnesses, no sitting on the lap of those testifying, no finger pointing in third degree. That's corn, pure corn, and all lawyers who see trial movies recognize this" (*Mining Journal* 4/16/59). Nonetheless, in the film version, Mary Pilant is presented as a surprise (some would say "last-minute") witness at the end of the trial; she finds Laura Manion's lost panties in a clothes chute in the Thunder Bay Inn and thus establishes beyond a doubt that Quill committed the rape of Laura Manion. Thus, Mary in the film symbolically gives up her loyalty to her dead father in favor of her support for Paul Beigler, setting the stage for further romantic involvement after the film ends.

In mid-April, the Michigan Week Group selected *Anatomy of a Murder* as Michigan's "Product of the Year," and on Monday, May 11, a testimonial dinner was held at the Negaunee Memorial Gymnasium. The food was decidedly local; the menu began with "Michigan Apple Juice Cocktail" and included "Baked Michigan Potatoes *en foil*, Buttered Michigan Peas, and Michigan Peach Melba Salad" with "Michigan Cherry Pie." Various awards and citations were given— including one to Stewart for enduring Voelker's cigars. At the dinner, Preminger announced that the world premier of the film would be held simultaneously in Marquette and Ishpeming on Monday, June 29, John Voelker's fifty-sixth birthday. Proceeds from the premier would go to Bay Cliff Health Camp for physically handicapped children. Ticket prices were ten dollars, seven-fifty, and five dollars, with a dollar being considered the admission charge and the rest a contribution to Bay Cliff. It was not to happen quite that way, however.

In March, the Bay Cliff Board had received notice that the health camp was ten thousand dollars in debt, but the Board decided to open in June as usual and hope that somehow the debt could be paid. On the last night of shooting in Big Bay, Willard Cohodas asked Voelker if he could secure a copy of the film to raise funds for the camp, and Voelker indicated his approval as long as he did not have to be involved with the project. Cohodas contacted Colombia Pictures' Ishpeming office in the Mather Inn and found out the world premier was scheduled for the Michigan Theatre in Detroit; he asked then if Marquette could have the World Preview. After some negotiations over a period of days, Colombia agreed to provide one print of the film, which was to be advertised as the World Preview on June 29.

The preview at the two theaters was a sell out–889 tickets–and to raise extra money, Cohodas arranged for a birthday dinner for Voelker on the same night and sold tickets to that. As Mr. Cohodas relates the story in information sent to the Marquette County Historical Society, "Just before the show started in Ishpeming, I went up on the stage with Max Reynolds, treasurer for Bay Cliff, and handed him a check for ten thousand dollars, which is exactly what we raised from the ticket sale and the birthday dinner. That kept Bay Cliff Health Camp going and it has been going ever since!"[6] The film started at 7:30 pm in Ishpeming and 8:00 pm in Marquette; as a reel finished in Ishpeming, it was taken to Marquette to be shown there. The Detroit premier on July 2 was held as a benefit for the United Nations Association.

Critical response to the film at the time of its release was good. James Stewart received the Volvi Cup for best performance of the year at the twentieth international Venice Film Festival, and *Anatomy of a Murder* received four Oscar nominations: Best Picture, Best Actor (Stewart), and Best Supporting Actor (Scott and O'Connell).

Not everyone was impressed with the film and its designation as Michigan Product of the Year. The Reverend Paul Ward wrote to the *Mining Journal* to attack the award and to label *Anatomy of a Murder* "one of the most immoral books to be published in recent years" because it showed a lawyer more interested in having his client acquitted than in seeing justice done. "That a Michigan Supreme Court Justice should be the author is about unbelievable."

A few people wrote in to agree with Ward, but reaction to the film was generally positive. A Milwaukee review noted, "If Miss Remick hasn't been recognized as a star previously, this vehicle should make her one," and George C. Scott was "exceptionally impressive." But the film was referred to as "an earthy movie," and reviews noted,

LITERATURE: ANATOMY OF A MURDER

"Some eyebrows were lifted by the frank dialogue included in the courtroom scenes." In Chicago, the police commissioner ruled certain phrases in dialogue to be obscene and immoral and denied permission for the film to be shown until the words were taken out, but he was overruled by the courts. In a July 13 article, NEA Staff Correspondent Erskine Johnson asked if there would be "amusement in 1979 about today's eyebrow-lifting 'Anatomy of a Murder' dialogue." It is clear that even Mr. Johnson had no idea how far the language barriers would fall in twenty years.

The Chenoweth/Quill murder case came back into a real courtroom in July of 1960 when Mrs. Hazel A. Wheeler, the forty-seven-year-old widow of Mike Chenoweth, filed a nine million dollar lawsuit against Dell Publishing Company and Columbia Pictures claiming invasion of privacy. Joining her in the suit was her eighteen-year-old daughter, Terry Ann Chenoweth. In April 1962, a United States Appeals court upheld the lower court's ruling that the suit be dismissed; the discussion indicated that, while identification of Mrs. Chenoweth was possible, her privacy was not invaded, since it was obvious the author had made the character different from the actual individual.

Today the film is still quite suspenseful and amusing, and it maintains its feeling of authenticity. The acting remains strong, with Stewart, Remick, and Scott as the standouts; and Ellington's score works, perhaps better than it seemed to at the time. If the film has a fault, it is Preminger's rather static direction. Preminger likes the long shot—a scene running for more than three minutes—often with camera movement, such as pans or dolly shots. Such a technique for assembling a film, often referred to as *mise-en-scene* editing, contrasts with the *montage* technique of assembling a film from a number of short shots, usually with little camera movement in the individual shots. On the positive side, the *mise-en-scene* method gives actors time to build their emotions and the scene. Preminger felt that he gained a vitality in the film from such scenes, and he further tried to film the scenes in chronological order to help the actors keep a better sense of the action. He planned the film carefully and often shot from only one angle rather than shooting from a number of angles and then picking the best one in the cutting room. When this approach works, it often helps the actors perform more effectively and gives a smoother continuity to the action than would a lot of short, choppy shots. On the negative side, this technique can lead to a stagy quality that causes the narrative to look more like a filmed play and less like a movie than the *montage* method, which tends more to exploit the film medium. Often, the choice is simply a personal one, and Preminger chose the method he preferred.

A Sense of Place: Michigan's Upper Peninsula

Nevertheless, the film could have been more intense if Preminger had been more daring in the staging of some scenes, in the editing, and in the film exposition. The camera work is sometimes static, and the visuals of the film are often predictable. This quality is less apparent in *Anatomy of a Murder* than it is in some of Preminger's other films such as *Saint Joan*, but it still exists and somewhat detracts from the film. *Anatomy of a Murder* is a solid film, but it lacks the original edge or style that a top-flight director—a Hitchcock, a Ford, a Houston, or even a De Palma—might have given it. Voelker's novel, through its point of view, characterization, and use of setting, has a depth that the film lacks; it has an original voice and a verbal style that give it that edge. The subject material, however, carries the film along over any awkward spots, and overall it is first-rate entertainment. In retrospect, it is clear that even in a novel and film so closely based on actual experience, modifications of character and of plot seem to be necessary to give the audience what the writers and directors think they want.

In this case, Voelker and Preminger were probably right to make the changes in plot and character, just as Voelker was right to use the circumstances and language of the actual trial to give the account an authenticity that would have been hard to imitate, and Preminger chose to shoot the film on location to preserve that authenticity. Together, the improved dramatic structure, especially of the novel, and the realism made an unbeatable combination; and Traver's book and Preminger's movie, now popular for forty years, will undoubtedly continue to attract new readers and viewers.

John Voelker resigned from the Michigan Supreme Court at the end of 1959 because, as he said, "while other lawyers may write my opinions, they can scarcely write my books. It is as simple as that." He continued to live in and write interesting articles and books about Michigan's Upper Peninsula until his death from a heart attack on March 18, 1991. The books he left include *Troubleshooter* (1943), *Danny and the Boys* (1951), *Small Town D.A.* (1954), *Anatomy of a Murder* (1957), *Trout Madness* (1960), *The People Versus Kirk* (1961), *Hornstein's Boy* (1962), *Anatomy of a Fisherman* (1965), *Laughing Whitefish* (1965), *Jealous Mistress* (1967), and *Trout Magic* (1974). What is not clear is why none of Voelker's other novels have been as popular as *Anatomy of a Murder* and why none of them have been made into films. It is about time the UP was put to good use again as a sound stage, this time with more outdoor sets. Has anybody sent Stanley Kubrick a copy of *Laughing Whitefish*?

LITERATURE: ANATOMY OF A MURDER

Notes

1. All information concerning the murder is taken from articles in the Marquette, Michigan *Mining Journal* and from trial testimony. Where no specific source is cited, as in most instances, the sources agree on what happened. The disagreement was less about *what* happened than about *why* it happened. References to the novel are to the Twenty-fifth Anniversary Edition (New York: St. Martin's Press, 1983.)

2. In "Blueprint for Survival" (7/13/46), Voelker advocated "that the heartland of any country waging aggressive atomic warfare shall be instantly destroyed by counter atomic attack." This theory of Mutually Assured Destruction (MAD) became the defense stance which served as official United States policy from the late forties until the fall of the Soviet Union. How much Voelker's articulation of this doctrine, in a nationally circulated and highly respected journal, affected the formulation of government policy is uncertain.

3. One of Governor Williams' aides read the book and sent a note to the governor that said, "He's your man."

4. A Marquette resident identified for me the individual involved and verified that the scene had occurred during the trial just as Voelker described it.

5. When an earlier version of this article was published in the first issue of the *Marquette Monthly*, John Voelker wrote to me (green felt pen on yellow legal pad) and indicated that he remembered the dog as a small one; yet the front page picture in the *Mining Journal* of the Petersons and their dog shows a black Labrador-sized animal.

6. In the original version of this article, I indicated that Bay Cliff received nine thousand dollars from the premier of the film, drawing my information from newspaper accounts and other sources; Mr. Cohodas correctly pointed out that the film showing was the world preview and said that the error in the donation, wrongly reported by sources at the time, had proliferated through the later accounts. I'm glad to set the record straight.

A Sense of Place: Michigan's Upper Peninsula

The Story

John VandeZande

In a tiny town whose name's been changed and hasn't been the same since I met a man who told me the story. As far as the town talking about him, he said, he wasn't bothered by that. Weren't they always talking about someone: Mrs. J's son who said he was her brother because, as the town thought it well knew, she had no real husband and he no father he could put an earthly name to; Mr. M's money which was more than theirs and so being didn't they have it that he had stolen it from his sister by writing her out of the will somehow, Mr. L's "condition" which, didn't they say, was nobody's fault but his own, he being what he was? No, if they talked about him, and he thought he knew for a fact that they did, he was not bothered by it because he had the story and they didn't. It was as simple as that.

Some years before their little town had been made famous in a way which had changed their lives by someone having written a book about it. The book had been a best seller and even though the man didn't read he knew what that meant. That is, he had found out what that meant. The town's name had been changed from what it had always been to what it was in the book because before the book it had never had a name that anybody knew and what good is a name if nobody knows it, they said. Then the movie people had come and had made a movie about it, the book. For three months the movie people were in their little town, eating in their one restaurant, sleeping in their one hotel, both of whose names had been changed from what they had always been to what they were in the book. A sign outside the town on the same post below the sign which said what the town's name had been changed to said to sleep in the hotel and to eat in the restaurant whose names were now what they were in the book. For three months the movie people were there with their trucks and cranes and lights and cameras and, since the story had happened sometime before the book had been written about it, and even longer before they had made the movie about it, old cars and trucks and extras in older clothes which were made to go up their town's quiet tree-lined streets and stop and then go back again by the director who would call for "Action" and then the whole thing would go again—not the way it was, the way it was in the book. Ever since then the man had been saying that it was all wrong. That it was not that way! Not that it was not that way, but that it was not that way, what they said, what they were saying to total strangers who continued to come to town long after the movie had been made, not to see the movie, nor to hear the story (not about the movie but about the way it was) but to see where the movie had been made (parts of which they later heard had been omitted or changed, but no matter); some had read the book (not him for he didn't read, but no matter, he knew what the story was) and all of them said that they knew what it was, but they didn't. He did. He told me. He didn't tell me that he had told them; only they told me that. He told me that there was no talking to them.

As it was he didn't tell me, it was on tape, a big beige going-to-fuchsia chrome-trimmed leatherette-covered reel-to-reel tape recorder, given to him by the one who had been the lawyer in the movie, who had been the lawyer in the book (he had to trust them on that one; he hadn't read the book) who was the lawyer in the story, the way it was, which was what he said he wanted to talk to me about. Not actually talk because he had been talking for years, he said, and he was afraid that the talking wouldn't last, but listen to, the two of us, so that we could see it the way it was, which was what he said he wanted to talk to me about. I had gone to the little town (a pretty little town, really, small, compact, "no more than a wide spot in the road," my grandfather would have said, tucked against the base of a series of hills which crisscrossed against a pale blue sky) to see where the movie had been made and when I arrived I looked for the bar where the man in the movie had been shot. I had gone to the hotel where the bar had been in the movie, but when I got there the man on the stone steps sitting in front of the open empty door like a guard (behind him, in my mind's eye, I saw the movie's ghostly figures standing about and looking down at where the man had lain) told me that it was not here, that the bar was not in the hotel (I was taken by how much he reminded me of Chester Morris in the old Boston Blackie movies, not that he looked like Chester Morris, Morris was, as you know, shorter, darker, with that straight back black hair: this man was taller, thinner, with sandy colored hair, but his voice was like Morris' in the old Boston Blackie films, crisp, clear, sure about what the facts were or if he wasn't you knew he would be and so would you before the movie was over) but that it was down the street, the movie only made it look that way. That is, they had shot the movie making it look as if the man who had shot the bartender in the bar had gone into the hotel and after they had gotten it on film, they had moved their cameras and actors and extras and crew down the street to the bar and had shot the rest of that part of the story there. He told me that the people in town who had read the book had said that it was not that way in the book but that, no matter, he knew how it really was.

He told me that if I wanted to hear it the way it was that I could come to his house where the whole story was on the tape recorder machine given to him by the one who was the lawyer in the movie.

Literature: The Story

The tape recorder, he told me, was in the court scene the way it was in the movie, not, from what they had told him, the way it had been in the book, but that, no matter, it was his now and what difference did it make if it was in the book as long as it was in the movie and the one who was the lawyer in the movie who was the lawyer in the book who looked nothing like the real lawyer had given it to him. He said that he never looked a gift horse in the mouth. I told him that I don't either. I don't.

That night the two of us sat in his little house and watched and listened to the tape on the recorder go around so that we could see and hear the story in order to see it the way it was, the real story, he said, not the story on those reels of film which everybody who came to town had seen, but the story on these reels, the real story. Later that same night in the bar down the street they told me that he told the recorder the same story every day and then erased it and then told it again, but that the story never changed, that he told it the same way every time and really didn't need a tape recorder at all. They said that when he was still talking to them that he had told them that what he said into the recorder and what it said back to him did not sound the same, that the voice was not his voice and that, as it was so far, it could not be trusted. Maybe the next time... Anyway, they said, the tape recorder never was in the book, but that he was harmless enough. He just didn't know the story.

Earlier that night, in the dark of his little house, the tape recorder on the floor between us, the two of us sat, his expression flushed and hopeful, mine cocked and seriously quizzical, and listened to the voice, sure, clear, easily confident, which sounded like Chester Morris in the old Boston Blackie films, as he and I sought out the story's bright beginnings in the dim ravellings of its end. As we got it that night, it seems that there were these two men...

A Sense of Place: Michigan's Upper Peninsula

Three Poems

SONG

Philip Legler

Brother of air I breathe,
Brother of the wind, of storms,
Brother of the Wendigo
Trampling the tops of pines,
Thunder in the topmost branches,
Brother of water, of rain,
Brother of Lake Superior, of fishes,
Of fishermen in boats with heavy nets
And of the loon and the cry of the loon,
Brother of streams and rivers,
Brother of the hawk, stooping,
Brother of logs, brother of fire
And campfires and stories in the night
Old as Cassiopeia above the bay,
As fog closing over morning,
Brother of the Copper Country,
Of Mandan, Delaware, Phoenix, Mohawk,
Brother of the Keweenaw,
Of the bear and the deer,
Brother of the snake and raccoon,
Brother of earth, hands into the dirt,
Brother of mines and miners
And of the ghosts of mines and miners,
Brother of rock and cemeteries,
Brother of fallen leaves, of snow,
Brother of geese flying.

HOW TO KEEP WARM

Philip Legler

Winter is here again, deep snow
covering the grass. In the snowfield
now, once daisies even in late fall,
the wind blows me backwards, facing
the slough. Up to my crotch in snow,
I turn back, thinking of snowshoes,
how I will walk out the way a man

gives himself up to it, leaving his
tracks behind. The tracks that pad
back to camp remember. Like the night-
fire dead in the fireplace, I had not
thought of it until it was gone. Overhead a gull dips, searching for food.
How to keep warm! In town they pack

rooms, snow tunnels in the yards.
Weeks ago when the cold began, we kept
our hands inside your coat pockets,
soft as the nests squirrels build to
survive. They have stored their acorns.
The ice on the slough builds ten inches
thick and stops, blocked, at the lake,
ice-caps jutting up. And so I turn,
retracing my steps as I've done all along.

LITERATURE: THREE POEMS

IN FRONT OF OUR HOUSES

Philip Legler

It's hard to rent
in Marquette, Michigan; any day
the city's a buying place where most of us
believe we've settled
down, held by our monthly payments,
stais and dry-docked beside
lake and horizon.

The Mining Journal
arrives, washing the waves in closer,
two ships over the weekend to our front steps,
naming the vessel arrivals,
John Dykstra and *Sparrow's Point*
listing tomorrow's docking
at which harbor.

In winter, ship-
wrecked hunks of ice push up the beaches,
and downtown parking meters like frozen buoys
lean against buildings.
Winter is six months here; we need
our comfortable, high-priced
anchored houses.

But summer nights
we follow in the wake of cars
moving slow as boats drifting by the ore dock,
and those in the bay
where small craft warnings are up, tied
only to their sunset
still reflections.

At the upper harbor
quiet as dusk a ship is leaving,
its lights darkening the waves and windshields
tracing a gull
riding his shadow beyond the lighthouse.
In what deep hold are we stowed
away tonight?

The lake submerges
the city behind us like an island.
Even in front of our houses, owned by the bank,
the neighborhood lawns,
well kept, that stop at our streets at morning,
carry us out like boats
to Canada.

A Sense of Place: Michigan's Upper Peninsula

A Sense of Place

Environment

Living Farther North
A Year's Cycle
Lillian Marks Heldreth

SPRING: The Northern Migration

Geese flying south are a melancholy sight, for summer seems to travel away with them, but geese flying north bring brightness. One spring I was privileged to witness the spring flight from a grandstand position.

Our cabin is located at the south end of a mile-long inland lake that is too small to harbor large goose flocks overnight. However, Witch Lake and Chief Lake, only a few miles to the south, have ample accommodations for avian travelers.

We arrived at camp one evening in April, just at twilight. The air was alive with the song of spring peepers backing up the encore of a wood thrush. Somewhere in the background, I thought I heard the "quonk!" of a goose or two.

I slept soundly that night, but sometime toward morning, as my sleep lightened, I could hear the sound of many people talking loudly. Surely there weren't enough people on the lake yet for a party. Whoever they were, I wished they would shut up so I could get back to sleep. By six o'clock I gave up and sat up. As I came to full consciousness, I realized that the talkers were avian, not human.

I went outside. The conversationalists were invisible, but their sound drew nearer, moving up from the southeast. In a few moments I saw them flying directly overhead. The low sun shone through their great flight feathers, and, reflecting from the lake, colored their white breasts rose. Having just left their bed and breakfasts to the south, they were low, maybe twenty or thirty feet up. I could clearly see the lead goose calling, and I could tell which goose answered; I could hear the windy whir of their powerful wings.

I had never seen so large a flock before; behind the leader, the sides of the V waved back so far that the point seemed to be passing the north end of the lake even as the trailing individuals flew over the cabin. The flock was about a mile long on each side.

Scarcely had the calls of that flock died away to the north when the first calls of the next one sounded from the south. For three hours the flocks streamed by, no more than ten or fifteen minutes apart. To get some idea of the numbers, I counted one wing of one flock until I got to one hundred; seeing how far one hundred geese reached at that height, I could estimate how many in a flock. Almost none of them were smaller than a hundred; the average was about five hundred, and several flocks numbered a thousand or more. I kept re-checking my estimation because I could not believe I saw so many.

The north end of Marsh Lake seemed to signal a choice-point. Upon reaching it, about half the flocks veered off to the northwest; the other half went northeast. Also near that point, an updraft was rising. The geese that turned northeast went right over it, each bird being lifted as if it were flying over a little hill. The effect was a bobble in the goose-skein that seemed to move along it, like a ripple in a shaken jump-rope.

I watched geese until my neck got sore from looking up; I marveled at the beauty and numbers of the birds; I wondered what guided them on their journey of thousands of miles. How did their small brains hold a map of the continent? How did they learn to fly in a formation which lets each goose take advantage of the lift generated by the goose in front, like cars slipstreaming behind tractor trailers? The lead goose lacks that advantage, so they trade off periodically, passing the responsibility and extra effort around.

Then there was the little matter of generating that lift in the first place. The previous fall, my colleague John VandeZande brought me some fresh, undamaged flight feathers from a goose that had been killed by an owl. Each feather was a perfect airfoil; when I moved one through the air, it tried to lift out of my hand. The shafts of the feathers were round only at the very base; farther up they were flattened into a long, tapering rectangle, more efficient, and stronger. In the vanes, each tiny spicule was precisely angled to do its individual lifting job on that particular feather in that exact position on that wing. Great design is characterized by elegance and economy. You could not find anything, anywhere, to equal the complex simplicity of those feathers.

Watching the geese fly, knowing the perfection of their equipment and navigation, I realized why I value wilderness, and why I hate to see any living species disappear forever. The geese fly as part of the great web of life that is our planet; they fly with the wind and rain and fog. They must travel with the weather, not against it.

For a few hours that morning, I had witnessed one of the great movements of the web, the swing of the sun and the seasons bringing the geese back to the north. I had heard their voices, talking across the whole of the sky that I could see. Glad of the gift, I went inside to pancakes and the conversation of my family.

Environment: Living Farther North

SUMMER: Staying Put

This is the twenty-third summer I have spent in this town beside the inland sea. And that is the longest I have stayed in one place in the fifty-five years of my existence. Friends have left, moving to exciting places like California or Colorado, to historic towns in the East, or to Minneapolis or Washington DC—places warmer, more civilized, or more sophisticated than the Upper Peninsula. As they prepared to leave, I somewhat wistfully shared their excitement, tempted by the thought of a new life, a different ambiance.

But as I sit on the front porch with my morning coffee, I realize that, for me, envy of my nomadic friends is only momentary. I have no real desire to trade places with them.

For the first eighteen years of my life, my family seldom occupied the same house for as long as a year, and five years was the longest time we ever spent in the same town. I attended three different schools during first grade and a total of ten before I graduated from high school. I was a perpetual outsider, always the new kid on the block, the loneliness of my only-child status compounded by my lack of any stable peer group. Some people fear the solitude of forests; I love the woods, but fear large rooms full of socializing strangers.

When we first moved to Marquette, it was but another in a long succession of strange places. It even looked like other towns I have known well. And the place had one geographic distinction that was highly annoying. All my life I had looked at maps that showed Lake Superior at the top, to the North. But for most of the city of Marquette, Lake Superior is to the *east*. I, who normally possess a fairly accurate sense of direction, tended to get hopelessly lost when people said "go east," because in my skewed view, the lake was still at the top of my mental map. As a result, I would head south, ninety degrees off course. Knowing the names of the streets, like East Hewitt or South Front, didn't work, either, because I orient by sight, not abstract names.

Two or three years went by, and the children were born before I got the map of Marquette and vicinity properly fixed in my mind. By the time we moved to our present location some twenty-one years ago, I was comfortable with the fact that our house faced an east-west street. Maybe my own internal magnetic fields had to re-align themselves, but they have been steady ever since. In this place we have lived, and our sons have grown from toddlers to young men. I walked them across the street and half a block west to kindergarten; I watched them take themselves to first grade, second grade. From the front gate, I could see them go into the Parkview building.

One icy February day I raced to the school in answer to a call from the principal. Terrence had fallen on the only ice-free pavement in town and had broken his collar bone. By that time I had the route from our house to the Emergency Room memorized, nor have I had a chance to forget it in later years. The boys had pretty much grown through the wrecked bicycle stage when, late one night, Terrence woke us up.

"Mom! Dad! Grandmamma really doesn't feel good. You'd better get up!"

My mother was feeling very ill indeed. In seconds we had her wrapped in coats and in the car, and once again I headed north on Pine, then west on Magnetic, while the family alerted the Emergency Room staff. All night I waited, pacing floors that I had paced when Terrence knocked himself out by flipping his walker at the age of one.

I sat on chairs that I occupied when Randall swallowed shoe de-icer a year later, remembering the ear infections, mashed fingers, and major cuts that had brought me and the boys through these doors so often. And I saw the smile of recognition on my mother's face when her family physician walked in at three in the morning, to reassure her that the cardiologist was excellent and that she was in good hands.

"In good hands" is a good way to describe what it is like to spend this many years in the same small city. I almost never stop at the grocery store without seeing at least one of my friends. If I happen to strike up a conversation with a clerk I've never seen before, it is likely that soon we will mention someone we both know. These days, I am less likely to be held up by inability to find the merchandise I want and more likely to be delayed by extended visits in the aisles of Econo Foods or ShopKo.

Lately my friends have started talking about retirement communities, condos in Florida, and spas by the ocean. "You have to start planning now," they say. I say that maybe they do, but as for me, I don't wish to go anywhere. Lake Superior is on the right on my mental map, and my longtime friends are at the top. I'm staying put; thank you very much.

Environment: Living Farther North

FALL: Ghost Month

October is a haunted month, when the season makes its turn from warm to cold, from harvest to winter, from life to death. The autumnal equinox has passed. From now until almost Christmas the nights will be longer than the days. We shall know more darkness than light.

October is the trickster, the coyote-month, the month of deceptions, when children dress like demons, and the weather takes sudden turns for the worse or better without warning. The day after the fall storm that took the *Edmund Fitzgerald,* we had air like spring, so still that Lake Superior looked innocent as a farm pond.

Last October, on one of those calm, hazy days, my spouse and I threw a few supplies in the car and took off for camp. By the time we got there, Marsh Lake was reflecting purple thunderheads, but the air was still warm.

In the yard, our shaggy gray dog ran in excited circles, chasing the wind. Drops began to patter on the roof. A blaze of lightening shimmered the scene. The dog jumped straight up with a yap of surprise. She was on the ground again, dazed, when a mighty crack of thunder vibrated the porch floor. I called her inside before another flash could send its charge through her feet. Poor dog — the ground had never bitten her before.

The storm was as brief as it had been violent. By the time supper was over, the three of us could go walking in the autumn twilight, smelling dead leaves and damp earth. Bunching and releasing like some spring-loaded toy, the dog bounded ahead through the strange warm evening.

Something chittered and chattered in the dark. We stopped, listened to the dry, shuffling sound. What thing approached from the dying swamp? Only the last two leaves on an aspen tree, scratching out the death rattle of summer.

We wandered back to the cabin, where we carried fresh cups of coffee to our lawn chairs. Darkness was almost full. Across the lake tamaracks glimmered, golden ghosts, the last trees to hold any color.

I relish not only the beauty of October, but also her mystery, her sense of oncoming night. On the last day of the month, according to the ancients, the Summer Queen yields her place to Winter's King. Queen Life gives way to King Death as the year's balance swings, yet he is not the ultimate winner, nor she the ultimate loser. Each is the other's essential complement.

A Sense of Place: Michigan's Upper Peninsula

During October they dance together, she clad in fall sunshine, he shrouded in snow squalls and icy rain.

The storm now past, Summer stepped a final solo. Lulled by her temporary peace, we dawdled over our coffee. The tamaracks faded to black as the Big Dipper brightened. Just at the edge of hearing, somebody's dog barked, paused, and kept on barking. A fish plopped. The beaver, making a late-season grocery run, startled us with a smack of her tail. Our dog crunched a steak bone. For a while, natural sounds were drowned by the whine of a distant logging operation, but even that eventually ceased.

In the stillness, I thought I could hear molecules of air colliding with a faint, high hum.

Suddenly to the south rose a shrill chorus of yips, answered by fainter yips to the north. Against that background rose a longer note, wailing like a treble siren. It shivered, fell, and rose again. Clear and wild and far, that sound chilled the night, holding us suspended, without breath.

"Coyote," I said.

"Yep," confirmed the man beside me.

In the past ten years we had spent many evenings listening to the lake and woods, but never before had we heard that particular song. I strained my ears, but no more music came.

October settled her night around us. We folded the lawn chairs, collected the coffee cups. Tomorrow the weather might be too cold for lawn-sitting. Best to batten the hatches, call in our dog.

It had been an eventful evening. October's excitement comes from her very unpredictability. The peak color may be early this year, or late. And in the last moments between summer and winter, we may hear voices from the edges of our world, coyotes or maybe even wolves, reminding us that despite the intrusion of concrete, the great dance is still danced at the year's turn, on the lakes, in the swamps, in the woods.

Environment: Living Farther North

WINTER: Drawing Trees

On one of the last mild days of November, my partner and I were ending our afternoon walk around Presque Isle, passing Charlie Kawbawgam's grave on our way to the parking lot. The sun had just set, leaving a band of winter red across the western sky.

Against that glow, leafless branches of maples and birches made a tracery of black lace, stark in the twilight, and through that network shone a new moon. Leaning on my staff, I stood in silence. I had been lamenting the passing of summer, but here was a beauty no summer landscape could show, the intricate skeletal structures of trees.

For several minutes I studied those patterns, the intertwinings of twigs, the heavy dark line of the ore dock, the water shining below. Then the sunset faded and we walked on, but as we drove home past the power plant and Shiras Point, I thought about my life's love affair with winter trees.

Of course it started in childhood. Sometimes in winter my father would take me along when he went hunting on the old family farm. That place, choked in forest growth, always looked different in winter when the leaves were gone. The contours of the mountains, swathed in summer in layers of green, were suddenly revealed, steep and sharp, highlighted by snow. Against those slopes the trunks of trees stood out in deep shades of black, blue, or purple, depending on the angle of the light. And all around me would be a profound winter silence, broken only by the rattling of oak leaves still clinging to their branches. I would stand and gaze until I nearly froze, caught in that spell of melancholy peace.

Those scenes left a strong impression that manifests itself in one of my commonest habitual behaviors.

Because I have trouble staying awake during long meetings, I have become an inveterate doodler. I don't concentrate on these drawings; they just arise from somewhere inside. Ten or fifteen minutes into a faculty meeting, I start searching for the right pen among several in my purse. It must be black, preferably very fine-pointed, with ink that flows freely but does not blot. Pen now in hand, I start to take notes: "Exec. thinks new curriculum good solution to the problem of..." and then my hand wanders to the left-hand top margin of the page.

The pen-point describes a vertical arc, and another facing it, the outer dimensions of trunk flaring into roots at the bottom and branches at the top. Then the pen moves faster, adding branches, then twigs. I never know what this particular tree will look like. It grows in silhouette, quirky, its patterns repeated over and over but never quite the same. Long before the computer people discovered them, my fingers were drawing fractals; for fractal geometry describes the growth of branches, twigs, and stems.

If the meeting is long and boring, my first tree will soon be joined by another and another, as my mind leaves the airless room to meditate on the frilly forms of birches, the knotty limbs of oaks, the upright feathers of tamaracks. Winter trees define themselves by the totality of their shapes, not by the simple signatures of leaves.

Soon the collection of trees will delineate a landscape of hills, their forms traced in the overlapping lines of many small trees.

I suppose that what I love most about winter landscapes is their revealing nature. Spring, summer and fall drape the contours of the earth in veils of differing colors, smoothing out hollows and covering rocks. Only in winter can I trace the meandering patterns of streams down mountainsides or appreciate the humped forms of the Upper Peninsula's granite hills.

I like to drive out the Forrestville Road and park above the bridge. Standing there, I can look out over the valley of the Dead River as it meanders darkly through the snowy flats, tracing its way around islands and over riffles. The trees follow it, birches white on white, cedars and white pines the only touches of winter green. I listen to the wind and watch until the scene is as surely imprinted on my mind as the cold air is upon my face.

I drive away, back to the offices and classrooms and meetings. I forget the flowing river, until during the dullest part of some committee's deliberations, my hand wanders away from my notes and begins to trace the outlines of a birch tree.

Then I am once more a part of the natural pattern of winter, drawing myself into that mystical lacework of trees.

Fly Fishing in the Upper Peninsula

Earl Hilton

It is a good thing that Norman Maclean's *A River Runs Through It* featured fly fishing in Montana and not in the Upper Peninsula of Michigan. The great popularity of the novel has brought hordes of people to fly fish in Montana. Even though many of them are probably more concerned with making a fashion statement than with serious fishing, they do crowd the rivers.

Howell Rains's, *Fly Fishing Through the Midlife Crisis* concentrates on fishing in western and southern waters. John Gierach, author of such works as *Sex, Death, and Fly Fishing*, also favors western streams.

Writers have celebrated Upper Peninsula streams without attracting large numbers of fisher persons from outside the area. Our own John Voelker, writing under the name of Robert Traver, has produced such volumes of fishing lore as *Trout Madness* and *Trout Magic*. Earlier, in Ernest Hemingway's *In Our Time* (1925), the name of an Upper Peninsula river furnished the title of what is probably the classic fishing story of all time, "Big Two-Hearted River."

In Part One of that story, young Nick Adams leaves the train at Seney and walks the tracks to a pool in a river where he admires a large trout holding steady in the current. Then he shoulders his pack, walks a relatively short distance to a suitable site, sets up his tent, cooks and eats supper, and goes to sleep without remembering the things he is apparently trying to avoid remembering.

In Part Two, Nick has a two-hearted experience. He loses a beautiful trout but catches two satisfactory ones in a lovely meadow stretch. Then he returns to camp, having decided not to face the deep, dark, tangled water of the cedar swamp.

It is worth noting that in 1995 a fly fisher from Illinois walked the track from Seney to a nearby river and there caught a trout of respectable size. The fly he used was an Elk Hair Caddis. The river he fished was the West Branch of the Fox. Therein lies a problem that has been troubling literary critics and fly fishers since 1925. Nick could not have walked from Seney to the Big Two Hearted River (no hyphen in the name on the state maps) in one afternoon.

Before we turn to the question of what river Nick fished, though, there is another difficulty. Nick used live bait—grasshoppers. However, he used fly fishing equipment and technique, so we can provisionally accept him as a fly fisher.

A Sense of Place: Michigan's Upper Peninsula

John Voelker had guessed that Hemingway named his story as he did in order to protect the *really* great stream Hemingway favored—the Escanaba.

After teaching a summer term at Northern Michigan University and becoming intrigued by the mystery, Sheridan Baker of the University of Michigan's English Department has offered a more convincing explanation. In an essay in the *Michigan Alumnus Quarterly* (February, 1959), he suggests that the river Nick fished is a fictional river created by Hemingway and drawing on memories of many rivers. Then, for his title, Hemingway chose the name of a real Upper Peninsula river that carried the symbolic weight he wished.

So the Upper Peninsula has one river that has gained literary fame, although fame has somehow not drawn the crowds of would-be fly fishers who have descended upon Montana. The Big Two Hearted remains a productive stream. It has not been as over-developed or as over-fished as Voelker declares in *Trout Magic*. By now, some other streams here have suffered more. Possibly one reason it has escaped with as little damage as it has is that Hemingway's story attracts more students of literature than seasoned fly fishers. Some years back, a professor of English from Louisiana State University came to teach a summer term at Northern Michigan University and brought with him instructions from other members of the staff at LSU to bring back samples of the sweet fern Nick smells in the story.

Rivers other than the Big Two Hearted bear names that stir the imagination and excite curiosity. Consider the Black, which Nick remembers fishing; the Yellow Dog and its tributary Big Pup Creek; the Dead; and the Laughing Whitefish. *Lake Superior Place Names* by Bernard Peters, formerly of Northern Michigan University's Geography Department, gives the sources of many of those names.

No list is likely to include the names of all the rivers and major creeks in the peninsula that produce trout, but here is a handful of them that have trout in at least a part of their length: the Black; the Presque Isle; the Ontonagon, with all its branches; the Net; the Paint; the Fence; two streams flowing into two of the Great Lakes, both bearing the name of Sturgeon; the Huron; the Yellow Dog; and the Salmon Trout. In Marquette's immediate vicinity are the Dead, the Chocolay, and the Carp; and a short way to the south is the Escanaba, with its East, Middle, Big, and Little West Branches. Farther east lie the Whitefish and the Laughing Whitefish; the Hurricane; Mosquito; Sucker; Slapneck; the Fox, with West and East Branches; the Driggs; Indian; and Tahquamenon. Every veteran Upper Peninsula fisher person will think of one or more omitted here.

Environment: Fly Fishing

There are many more smaller streams, some of them branches of the major rivers. Many of these are open enough to be fished with flies. Even streams too small to appear on Geological Survey maps are worth exploring. They may open into pools wide enough to be fished if the fisher is careful and skilled. In the long run, beaver dams injure trout streams by causing sediment to settle and the water to warm, but in the shorter run they may hold fine trout. None of these streams is as famous as England's Test, New York's Neversink, Pennsylvania's Yellow Breeches, Montana's Madison, or even the lower peninsula's Au Sable, but each furnishes a favorite piece of water—a home stretch for at least a handful of fly fishers. Consider John Voelker's lifelong attachment to the Escanaba and its tributaries, including Uncle Tom's pond and its outlet.

Sporting goods stores sell guides to Michigan streams. These can be helpful, but for the beginner or someone moving into the peninsula, the best bet for finding good spots is to first find an experienced local fly fisher and then use charm, subtle bribery, or whatever it takes to get his advice and perhaps his company.

As fishing pressure increases, more and more stretches of water once open to all are fenced and posted, but land owners here are generally not as fierce in protecting their streams as are owners in some western states. It is still not too difficult to find places to practice fishing and even to catch a few. The state has bought some stretches and set them aside as public access. Also, much of the Upper Peninsula is public land—state or federal forests or parks. This land is open for fishing, although the fisher may have to walk some distance, since some roads have been closed to protect endangered species of plants or animals. In the northern part of Marquette County, several trout lakes have been purposely left accessible only by hiking trails. Other large areas in the peninsula are held by timber or power companies. With some restrictions, these are also usually open to fishing.

Old logging roads lead to some promising water. Four-wheel-drive vehicles with high clearance are safer for these. There are stories of fishers who brush over their tire tracks when they turn onto such roads.

One of the better ways to reach stretches of river away from any road, and therefore usually less fished, is by canoe. Fishers can find canoe rentals near almost every stream that is big enough to launch in. The Michigan Department of Natural Resources will furnish a guide to canoe streams in the state, and experienced local fly fishers will know of some not included in the guide. On some of the smaller ones, it is wise to carry a saw to clear the way through occasional tangles of alder brush.

A Sense of Place: Michigan's Upper Peninsula

The trout you will find in these streams are Eastern Brook Trout, Rainbow Trout, Brown Trout, and a very few crosses between Brookies and Lake Trout called Splake. We do not have the Golden or the Cutthroat. In some streams or ponds you will find two or three species together. In the warmer water of the larger streams, you may find Browns, sometimes large Browns. Brookies prefer the smaller, colder, and least polluted streams.

An occasional trout of over thirty inches is caught in Upper Peninsula water, but not often. Most of those record trout are what are called *coasters*—trout living in Lake Superior or Lake Michigan but coming upstream to spawn. Similarly, it is not often that a fisher comes upon a pool boiling with rises, to use one of the most overworked clichés of sports reporting. One evening in August of 1995, a fly fisher caught and released thirty trout running up to twenty inches in the lower reaches of one of our larger rivers. A beginner should not expect to repeat that experience. In general, our trout do not grow as large as those of New Zealand, Wyoming, or Montana.

Our trout do have, however, one great advantage over western trout; they often taste better. Crayfish thrive in some of our limestone-based streams and ponds. Fresh water shrimp grow in others. Trout feeding on these develop yellow, pink, or orange flesh and a special flavor. Those from seven to nine inches are best. Larger ones may be more fun to catch and a good size for broiling, but they are likely to be coarser.

If it were possible to say just which fly to use to attract trout, fishing would be a science rather than an art and an obsession. Some fishers try to make it a science by becoming entomologists, learning all the life stages of all the insects inhabiting Upper Peninsula streams and in which season they appear.

Others rely on the usual popular flies—but with some special favorites specific to this area. The Michigan Hopper will save the fisher the effort Hemingway's Nick Adams expended catching live grasshoppers. It also keeps the record for using only flies clean. Of course, it will not interest trout in heavily wooded areas where real grasshoppers do not appear, and it will not interest them before grasshoppers hatch. Here, as elsewhere, many use the Coachman or the Royal Coachman. It has been said that more trout are caught on those flies than on any others, largely because more fishers fish with them more of the time.

The Betty McNault originated in Colorado but is probably more popular here. One man from Marquette has used Bettys he tied himself to catch trout in Iceland and Spain and salmon in Ireland.

Environment: Fly Fishing

This fly has the advantage of being fishable either on the surface, where it effectively imitates the mayfly, or beneath, where it passes for a minnow—at least to the unsophisticated trout. Such national favorites as the Adams and the Cahill are useful here. The Caddis works well in the spring but also later in the season. The Professor is useful in the wet fly version, and some fishers have good luck with the Grizzly King. Bucktails do well also. The Humpy often catches trout late in the season. The Stonefly Nymph can be deadly in certain streams in August and September.

In general, without being an expert in the field of insects, one can try to match the hatch. That is, see what is in the air and on the water and what the trout are taking down, and then look through the fly box for something of the same general shape, color, and size. A refinement on this sometimes practiced is to cut open the first trout caught, and examine the contents of its stomach.

If nothing seems to be hatching, and there are no rises, fishers can try their favorite flies and enjoy casting whether or not they get a response. They may also try a gaudy attractor fly, or perhaps a large streamer on the grounds that trout find more of their food under water than on the surface. When nothing else brings a response, one fisher puts on a large, fluorescent orange fly. Sometimes trout hit it, although it resembles nothing eaten by trout that men know of. One theory holds that trout hit such flies from sheer annoyance. Another holds that trout know many things that men and women who fish for them do not know. A final note on flies: Do not expect to see the large mayflies in May in the Upper Peninsula. Look for them in late July and August.

In certain circumstances, some trout will strike at spent matches, used chewing gum, and cigarette stubs. Baby trout often rise to the first snowflakes of winter. One of the charms of trout is their sheer unpredictability.

The depth one should fish a wet fly, streamer, or nymph is another problem fishers in the Upper Peninsula, like fishers everywhere else, must deal with. Trout lie at different depths during different seasons, in different weather, and at different times of day. In very warm weather, for example, larger trout may lie at the bottom of deeper pools where they may (or may not) be tempted by weighted flies.

In the Upper Peninsula, cold weather is more likely than hot weather to be a problem. John Voelker, who has reported on fishing in almost all parts of the peninsula under almost all possible conditions, tells of casting across ice at the edges of streams to reach open water in the center. Most veteran fishers here can recall fishing during falling snow on some opening days.

Again, as in other areas where trout are found, the fisher must learn to read the water—usually smaller waters than in Montana or Wyoming. But here, too, fishers learn to guess where in the stream trout may lie: in inlets or outlets of quiet pools; in riffles, bends, or rapids; in the underwater structures of fallen logs where they are fond of hiding; among the water lilies where they may tangle leaders; in the undercut banks; or beneath overhanging grass or brush.

It is useful here to know what species lives in any stretch of river. Browns may lie in fast current, but Brookies prefer quieter water, perhaps just to the side of a current entering a pool.

The variety of such scenes is nearly endless. Combine the beauty and variety of the water with the beauty and unpredictability of the trout and you will have a glimpse of the grip that fly fishing for trout holds on so many of us.

The pressure on our streams is less than the pressure on streams either to the east or to the west, but it is great enough to cause concern for the preservation of our streams and our trout. The Department of Natural Resources has limited one section of the Escanaba to artificial lures only, with a minimum length of ten inches and a creel limit of five.

Another section of the Escanaba has been set aside for artificial flies only, with an unwritten agreement by those who fish it to release all trout. Anyone keeping a trout from that water would be ostracized at the least.

Although the catch-and-release philosophy is gaining ground here as elsewhere, not all fishers agree with it. Some argue that it is cruel to hook and injure a trout unless the fisher is going to eat it. Others reply that if the trout were given a choice, they would take life with a sore lip. Rangers along the Yellowstone River can tell you the average number of times the Cutthroat is caught and released each season.

Compromise is possible. Many fishers feel justified in keeping a few while releasing the rest. Some, who are fond of the flavor of Brook Trout, make a point of releasing Browns and Rainbows.

Fishers who find themselves approaching the limit they have set for themselves can still get in an afternoon's or evening's fishing without going over their limit by releasing trout, exploring other stretches of river, or trying different flies.

Environment: Fly Fishing

Older fishers, who find it is becoming difficult to tie on small flies or to keep their footing on loose, slippery stones in fast water, often practice a form of recreation that keeps them in touch with rivers and trout without harming either. They watch trout. They find a place beside a promising bend or pool and try to make out the well-camouflaged trout, sand color over sand bottom, almost black in water darkened by conifer roots. They can see them sometimes when the light is right. And they can see the trout when they move, when they rise for an insect, or when they take a nymph or minnow beneath the surface.

For some fishers in the Upper Peninsula, the attachment to trout and streams does not end with the passage of the mid-life crisis or with old age. At the point where the Little West Branch Road touches the main Escanaba stands a stained plank held up by two posts. On it is inscribed a man's name, the dates of his birth and death, and the message, "Gone fishing." Presumably the man's ashes have floated down the river, exciting the curiosity of large Brown Trout.

A Sense of Place: Michigan's Upper Peninsula

Upper Peninsula Summer Camps
An Historical Look at Their Place in Our Lives and Nature

Jon L. Saari

Camp is a place where nature—including our own human nature—is not an enemy to be tamed.

Upper Peninsula camps are part of a regional "woods culture" that combines human and natural elements; indeed the camps reflect the efforts of their creators to make a home in nature. In some natural landscapes, such as Federal wilderness areas, national policy-makers have determined that all remaining human traces, from roads to structures, should be eliminated; humans are guests who enter and leave these spaces, ideally, without a trace. In areas developed as human habitats, on the other hand, the landscape has been transformed by human action, whether by cutting forests or filling in wetlands, in order to create cities, towns, and farms; nature is designed into the cultural landscape as parks, boulevards, gardens, and landscaping. At camp, nature still depends on human sufferance, but the control is light and delight is taken in lakes and woods on their own terms. Camp stakes out a middle ground; it embodies an attitude towards nature different from awe or conquest.

The family summer camp is one among several types of camps found in the Upper Peninsula. A forerunner would certainly be the Grand Camps of the urban well-to-do who had already established vacation homes in the Upper Peninsula in the late nineteenth century; examples are the fifty "cabins" designed by architects and built for members of the Huron Mountain Club on the Pine River in northern Marquette County or the McCormick log building complex that once existed at White Deer Lake (Rydholm 1989: 242–243, 265–267, 278–280, 301–307, 358–363, 439–440, 477, 593–595, 596–654). Such camps engaged whole families in leisure activities, and the later middle-class family camps may be thought of as scaled-down versions of the Grand Camps. The family summer camp is also related to the earlier camps used by local men as bases for hunting, fishing, and winter trapping, often for their own survival. In the logging era of the First Great Cutover of the Upper Peninsula (1880 to 1920), many of these camps were the abodes of squatters on company land who simply cut down trees and made primitive log dwellings. The life and times of these colorful backwoods shackers and homesteaders is celebrated in John Voelker's book *Danny and the Boys* (1951), which is set in the region north of Ishpeming, Michigan. Many camps in this same area have recently found their chronicler in William P. Bjork, whose 1996 book, *The Camps UP North: A History in the Woods,* discusses forty-seven hunting camps built in northern Marquette County between 1880 and 1910. Only a few of these original camps have survived into the present.

A Sense of Place: Michigan's Upper Peninsula

In a long term perspective, the various types of camps shade into one another. A homestead cabin or rural log house that once housed a family can become a summer camp a generation or two later. A lumber camp may be abandoned for a time and then reinhabited and fixed up by hunting parties or squatters. A place built as a family summer camp may become a hunting camp used primarily by menfolk in the fall months, or a hunting camp may become more of a summer camp a generation later. The very word *camp*, however, sets some limits and should guide our thinking about camps in general. A camp, in its extended meaning beyond a military encampment, is "the temporary quarters, often in tents or cabins, of nomads, Gypsies, detainees, travellers, holiday-makers, Scouts, Guides, etc" (*The New Shorter Oxford English Dictionary*). The Upper Peninsula usage, peculiar to this region, is a logical extension of this idea, except that the word *camp* is attached to a different list of historical characters: the temporary quarters of lumberjacks (lumber camps), of woods workers and their families in the early 1900s (cordwood camps), of fishers, trappers, and other hunters (hunting and fishing camps), of vacationing families in the turn-of-the-century tenting era (tenting camps), and of local townspeople who simply wanted, and want, a place away from home (summer camps). In the last example, it is the coming and going from town to camp that justifies the usage of the word *camp* more than the structures that are there, which might as easily be called cabins, cottages, shacks, second homes, or summer houses—as indeed they are in other parts of the country. In the Upper Peninsula (as well as apparently in Maine and the Adirondack Mountains), all such structures that are used as temporary and seasonal quarters are routinely called *camps*.

Six Markers of the Family Summer Camp, with a Finnish-American Touch

The family summer camp may be said to have its own niche within the camp tradition of the Upper Peninsula. I have identified six markers or characteristics, only one or two of which (numbers four and five) are distinctive of the Finnish (and "wannabe" Finnish) variant of the family summer camp.

1. Seasonal usage during the summer months

Summer camps were, and are, not intended for year-round residence. Heating sources are minimal, sometimes only an open fireplace but occasionally wood-burning cooking stoves or oil or gas burners. Walls, ceilings, and floors are seldom insulated. May through October define the months of potential use, with June, July, and August as the prime months. Seasonal hunting and fishing camps are also intended for part-time use, but have a different rhythm of

Environment: Summer Camps

usage. The 1995 log of one such camp in northern Marquette County yields a picture of usage pegged to the hunting and fishing seasons, with the largest number of visits occurring in May, September, October, and November (Bjork Interview and log). What follows is a list of the specific dates when the camp was used:

January 22–23
February 19
March 10, 18–19
April 18–20, 29
May 4–7, 10, 13–14 [May is the opening month of fishing season]
June 9 [June is the height of the bug season]
July 25–27
August 5–12, 27
September 2, 5, 12, 16–17 [work bee to open camp]
September 20, 22–30 [goose hunting season]
October 1, 3–6, 9–10, 12, 20–21, 27
November 2, 4, 8–11, 13–30 [deer hunting season]
December [no visits]

Hunting camps require a good heating source—usually woodburning stoves—and can, as the log shows, be used in deep winter, although sparingly. A camp may be winterized and still be a camp, as long as it is used seasonally and occasionally, but once it is a year-round residence, it ceases to be a camp in a functional sense.

2. Family participation, including women and children

The family summer camp is not male-dominated; this is the principal distinction that sets it off from a fishing or hunting camp. It is open to the whole family, and its reach often includes an extended family of aunts, uncles, and cousins as well as parents, brothers, and sisters across several generations. The main determinants of belonging are interest and family membership. Ownership is usually by a number of people related by blood or marriage, with the intention of perpetuating the ownership of the camp within the family. A camp thus becomes tied into a family, both legally as property and psychologically as a property in common, whether or not all extended family members are listed on the deed. Neighbors and friends can be important in the life of a family camp, especially within a lake community embracing numerous family camps, but family relationships are still at the center.

This family orientation can be contrasted with a tradition practiced at a hunting camp north of Ishpeming in Marquette County. The father founded the camp in 1947; it was used initially both as a family summer place and a fall hunting camp. The father passed it on to his three sons, only two of whom were interested or found it practicable to be part of the camp's life. The two sons have in turn added their own children to the deed. But in addition to the legal owners, there are a number of non-owners who participate significantly in the life of the camp and have a traditional right to do so. They were hunting partners of the founder, and they and their descendants can still claim a place at camp. This tradition is enshrined, as it were, in a pecking order at the camp table, a pecking order determined by age and longevity at the camp and not just by family membership and generation. The eldest brother is at the head of the table, but the second brother, who lives further away and gets to camp less often, is preceded at the table by several older non-owners. The youngest boys of eight or nine years sit at the far end of the long table. The order is a hierarchical one that mixes family and friends on an almost equal basis (Bjork Interview).

3. Modest, even humble, scale

The family summer camps that began to be built in the 1920s were not retreats for the wealthy, who had always had second homes in scenic locations, but a new phenomenon—retreats for middle-class and working-class Americans. In the Upper Peninsula during the decades of "camp fever," this sometimes included immigrants who were in their prime earning years, and in the post-WWII years it meant their children. Among the immigrants, it was those who had prospered most in America—shopkeepers, businessmen, professionals—who had the means to consider buying or building a second home. Most immigrants were industrial workers, craftsmen, farmers, or woods workers and had enough to do earning a livelihood to support their large families. For them, buying a house or a farm and then a car were priorities (Jarvenpa 1992: 32–33, 112). But if only better-off immigrants considered having a summer house for their own family, almost all immigrants did acquire the "camp habit" through participating in cooperatively built and maintained camps. Such cooperative enterprises among immigrant Finns, for example, were sponsored by religious, political, or cultural organizations. Pooling their resources and skills, members purchased lake property, put up buildings, and started summer programs for children and youth. Some of these cooperatively run camps, such as leftist-run Mesaba Park near Hibbing, Minnesota, have survived into the present as resorts; but many others eventually collapsed as cooperative ventures and were sold, due to the inability to attract younger members into the fold.

For some immigrants, building camps for others was a means of livelihood, and they may not have had the time, money, or inclination to build one for themselves and their own families. Johannes

Environment: Summer Camps

(John) Osterberg, an immigrant from Finland who moved to Marquette from Brooklyn in 1924, built about thirty-five frame-construction camps for other people along Lakewood Lane in Harvey and along the Chocolay River in Harvey and Green Garden. For Osterberg, a builder by trade, constructing and selling modest camps was a way of earning a living as well as slowly increasing his capital. From about 1930 to the mid-1950s, he bought waterfront lots from Robert E. Blemhuber and others, built camps on the land, and then sold the developed properties. He also built some homes in the city of Marquette and purchased others to fix up. His success in these ventures facilitated his own home ownership, as the family moved progressively from a small house on Crescent Street to larger homes on South Front Street and Ridge Street. "We never had a camp of our own as children," said his daughter Lotta Stewart, "although we often accompanied him to the worksite for outings on weekends and vacations." Eventually Osterberg purchased a camp in addition to the primary residence in town; in fact, he purchased a camp on Lakewood Lane that he had originally built and sold to a friend (Stewart Interview)!

Osterberg's camps included modest structures: a house with three or four rooms and a porch, a fireplace, and sometimes an unattached sauna. Modesty was a hallmark of camp architecture in general, and it was a modesty enforced by limited means as well as ideals of rusticality. Working-class people had more skills and industry than capital, and, once land could be purchased or leased, they set to work to build the camp themselves. Recycling materials was the norm: abandoned or demolished buildings yielded lumber, flooring, windows and doors; an old industrial chimney might provide bricks; railroad ties edged walkways (and in one case even provided the walls for a sauna); and driftwood shored up river banks. Over the years, the camps grew with the family; the main house was renovated, and a kitchen, bathroom, or bedrooms without partitions might be added. Water and waste systems were correspondingly improved. Outbuildings were added over the years so that camp eventually became a complex of buildings: a house, an outhouse, a shed, a sauna, sometimes a garage and boathouse. But despite improvements camp remained camp—a simpler world than the house in the city or town, an unpretentious world where class mattered little, a tolerant "laid back" world where work could be left undone for days without anyone's throwing a fit.

4. A site on or near water

Water was important for all camps, whether lumber camps, hunting camps, or summer camps. For summer camps, water had an additional significance—scenic beauty. At other types of camps, practical concerns dominated, such as water for drinking, for horses, for icing down forest trails, or for making moonshine. A spring, small stream, or swamp might suffice as long as a location was good for other reasons: road access, plentiful game, or abundant trees suitable for log buildings and firewood. A summer camp needs a river, lake, or pond, because the beauty of the setting is a large part of the reason for going there. Beauty, of course, rests in the eyes of observers, but in general it may be said that landscape scenes composed of rivers, lakes, mountains, forests, and meadows seem to captivate the human imagination. The artist Joyce Koskenmaki was astonished that she and her brother, independently, shared a vision of a landscape that they had never seen: large, dark fir trees reflected in the still waters of a lake. She speculated that they shared a genetic memory that pulls humans towards certain landscape preferences (Koskenmaki 1992: 32). While it is difficult to prove such preferences as part of a genetic inheritance, it is less controversial to express the connection in cultural terms; the motif of lakes viewed through trees is powerful in many genres of the visual arts, from landscape painting to nature photography to picture postcards. For Koskenmaki, the cultural connection with Finland through her ancestors was also a visual connection with Finland's lakes and forests.

Water viewed through trees is, of course, the view from many summer camps. Norm Niemi of Wakefield, in redesigning an old resort cabin that he had had transported to a waterfront site on Little Oxbow Lake in Gogebic County, decided to relocate the door to the side away from the lake. "I wanted always to be looking at the lake, never turning my back on it. Without the lake no one would be here." He even designed a mirror so that he could catch the early morning moods of the lake while lying in bed (Niemi Interview)! At Little Shag Lake in southern Marquette County, Emmi Kulkki's family always said they were "going to the lake," not going to camp (Kulkki Interview). The lake was the center and the camps only ornaments along its edges.

5. A sauna near the water

For Finnish-American families, lake or river frontage for the camp was essential for yet another reason—the sauna. This ancient practice of steaming and bathing in a separate wooden building (sauna), preferably on the shores of a lake, was a cultural tradition brought over to North America from Finland. Wherever Finnish immigrants settled, saunas appeared in the cultural landscape as an almost perfect marker of their presence. Where there was a Finn there was a sauna. And while a lake was not always nearby, folk traditions had taught them that nothing refreshes during a hot sauna like a plunge into the cool waters of a lake or river. So when the "camp fever" took hold of certain parts of the Finnish-American community in the 1925 to 1955 period, they purchased or leased land on lakes, basins, and rivers partly to build saunas near the water, even over the water. At Little Shag Lake, the most distinctive cultural element of several older Finnish-American camps is a narrow two-story building on the water's edge, which houses a boathouse below and a sauna above.

6. A recreational pace and purpose different from life in town

A different mind-set rules at camp. There is work, but it is not deadline work, not work governed by the clock. Work at camp is more akin to serious play: brushing out roads and footpaths; hauling, cutting, and stacking firewood; repairing leaks in a low and accessible roof; starting fires in woodstoves and carrying out ashes; adjusting oil lamps; fixing wells, pumps, and septic systems; cleaning out the outhouse or digging a new one; and sweeping away cobwebs and mouse dung that have collected since the last stay at camp. To be sure, upkeep is necessary, but there is control over the pace and timing of work, and none of it is as critical as a sewage backup in the basement in that other home in town or city. Tasks are simpler and can be done by hand with brooms, axes, shovels, and hand tools; and the consequences of not doing them are different. No city government, let alone neighbors, will harass you for not shoveling the snow or mowing the lawn. The eyes of others cannot penetrate so easily into this sanctuary, and when they do they also look differently, expect differently. This, after all, is camp, a place for recreation in the woods and on the water, a place where nature—including our own human nature—is not an enemy to be tamed. A camp owner can be leisurely, even lazy, with a good conscience.

Such is not the case with camps everywhere. Sociologist Judith Huggins Balfe has written about summer houses in New England, where a distinctly different ethos prevails. She argues that the family summer house embodies a Protestant ethic of hard work and selfless devotion to the family. This ethic was practiced by founders whose thrift and smarts established summer houses in the first place; each successive generation reaffirms these values and indeed learns to practice them on site each summer. No loafing on the deck when Grandpa is polishing the windows! Other features of these summer colonies make life within them somewhat rigid and formal. Families may have members from four generations wanting to use the house over the twelve weeks of summer. Because some members live far away, even in other parts of the country, it is necessary to schedule summer visits into precise days and weeks and even require rental fees by members to pay for contracted maintenance and services. The complexity of large multi-generational families, the stern reverence for a traditional work ethic, and the high costs of taxes and upkeep make New England summer houses serious business indeed (Balfe).

One New England minor tradition strikes a different chord. It is the squatter shacks of nineteenth-century Yankee fishermen in certain coastal communities—shacks which are now owned and used as summer places by twentieth-century working class families, especially men. For these menfolk, the shack is an escape from the middle-class expectations of town; maintenance, Balfe notes, is just enough to keep the place from falling down; conveniences are minimum, and the decor is "funky" and playful (Balfe). John Voelker, the Upper Peninsula's best known writer and flyfisherman, would have felt right at home there. His camp on the Sands Plains south of Marquette was constructed of two prefabricated horse barns put up in one week's time. He spread green indoor-outdoor carpet remnants on the grounds amidst old church pews that weathered under the pines. Old wooden cable reels served as tables. Mufflers and other car parts hung from trees on the road into camp, and signs announced chipmunk crossings and touted Voelker's fame as a cribbage player. Nothing was more important than sociability among friends, hard drinking, and trout fishing (Delene). Voelker's conception of camp, while exaggerated, is certainly closer to that of most Upper Peninsula residents than the mainline New England variety is.

Individual Camps and Camp Communities

There is no marker that speaks to summer camps as part of communities where they are located. On this point the diversity is great. Camps that are primarily hunting camps are by necessity set back in the woods, the proverbial cabin on forty acres. Hunting requires access to hunting grounds, whether open public lands, open private lands (such as forests designated CFR or Commercial Forest Reserve), or land of one's own. Such land is often remote, and hunting camps are thus scattered throughout the woods, clearings, and swamp edges where deer abound. Each camp is a world unto itself, where a loyal band of friends and relatives gather for the two weeks of deer camp—a high point of the year anticipated long before and savored long afterwards in memory. Summer camps may also be isolated and remote, especially if they are sited on old homesteads or abandoned farms or along meandering rivers that effectively block off the sounds and sights of neighbors. Yet roads link camps together, and sometimes neighborly hospitality extends to the right to overlook the ever-present "No Trespassing" signs that have become part of backwoods culture in privately owned parts of the Upper Peninsula. Neighbors meet on the roads and sometimes at bridges or public access sites on rivers or at restaurants, stores, and bars in nearby towns. And yet the main motion is back and forth from camp to town, not interacting with others in a community of camps.

One exception to this pattern is summer camps on lakes. There the individual camps are linked together by the water itself. On Little Oxbow Lake in Gogebic County, long evening dinner parties saw friends rowing boats from camp to camp on the lake, eating a course at each site, merriment echoing across the water (Niemi Interview). Shoreline lots of a hundred feet hardly permit effective buffering from neighbors, so a certain civility and awareness of others is encouraged by the lot size. But how much better if the neighbors are old friends and the bond is the sociability of friendship! Summer camp communities in New England are called summer colonies, and some of them date back to the early nineteenth century. They had their origins as religious retreats. Typically held in late summer after the harvest, retreat supporters returned to the same campgrounds year after year, pitching their tents inches apart around a revival center; they eventually purchased the acreage, established associations, and began to build permanent, family-owned cottages (as they are called in New England) on former tenting sites. Large and permanent summer colonies were established in this fashion based upon religious identities— Methodist at Oak Bluffs on Martha's Vineyard, Jewish in the Catskill Mountains, Irish Catholic in the early twentieth century at Spring Lake, New Jersey (Balfe). But summer community identities did not have to be religious; they could also be racial, ethnic, or cultural—indeed a combination of traits, as in the secularized summer houses embodying the Protestant work ethic. Builders and buyers might be individual families, Balfe found, but "they are likely to be attracted to incipient or already developed summer colonies where neighbors will be those with similar social and cultural characteristics..."

A Sense of Place: Michigan's Upper Peninsula

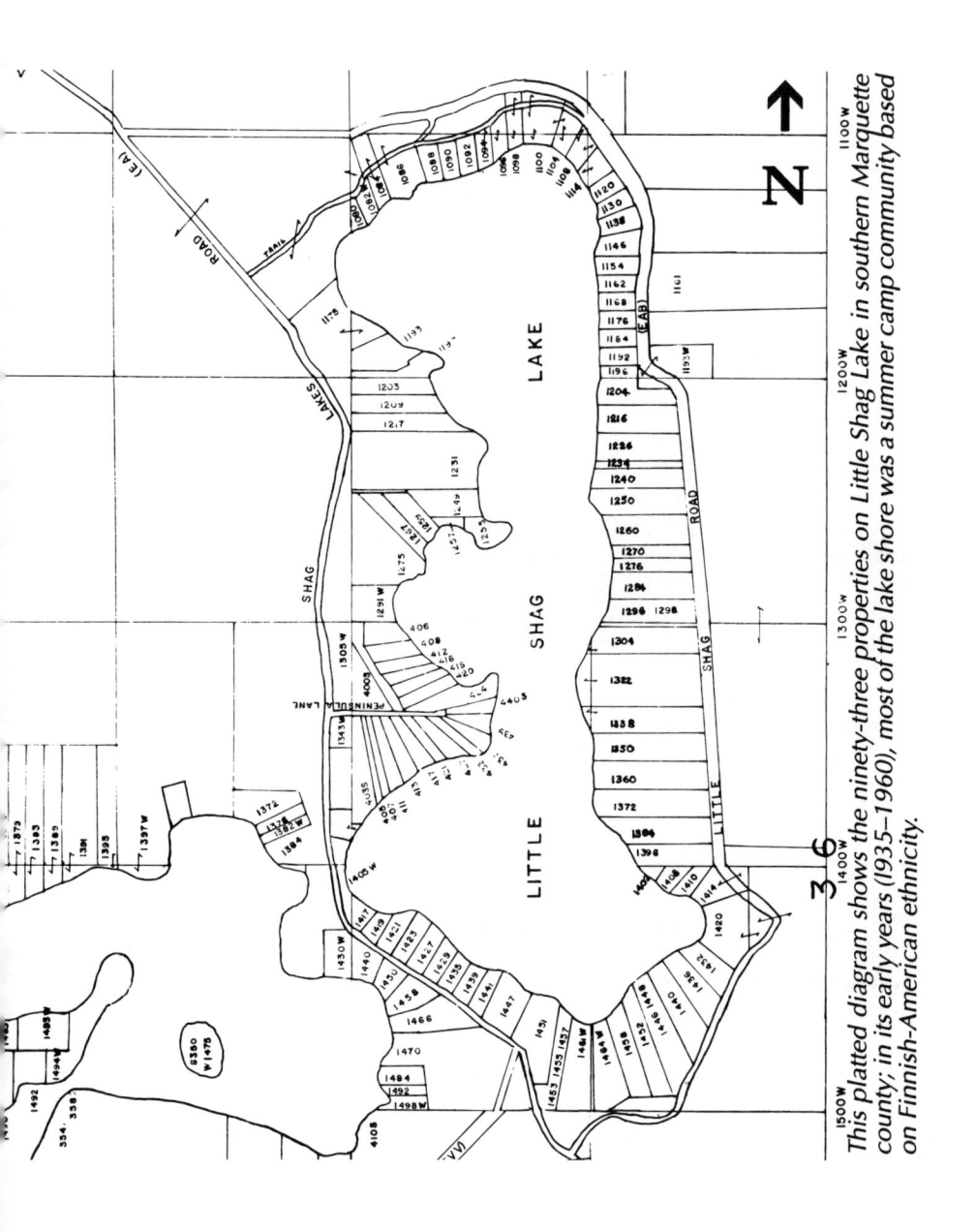

This platted diagram shows the ninety-three properties on Little Shag Lake in southern Marquette county; in its early years (1935–1960), most of the lake shore was a summer camp community based on Finnish-American ethnicity.

Environment: Summer Camps

Little Shag Lake: An Upper Peninsula Summer Camp Community

Little Shag Lake south of Gwinn in Marquette County was a summer camp community almost in the New England sense of a colony of the like-minded. To an extent, it still is in the 1990s, although it has changed from an ethnic-centered community to a lake-centered one. Little Shag Lake was known to some observers in earlier days as "Finn Lake" and to the Finnish immigrants themselves as *Säkkijärvi* (Sack Lake) because of their difficulty in pronouncing the *sh* sound. There is also a well-known Finnish polka with the same name! Located three miles south of the mining communities of Gwinn, Austin, and Princeton, many camps on the lake were built of remnants of company houses torn down in these locations. The first summer camp was started by C. Leander Johnson, a Swedish immigrant who worked as a mine electrician for Cleveland Cliffs and who owned a company house in Gwinn. He bought tax delinquent land in 1926 and two years later had two Finnish log builders from Palmer construct a small log house on the eighty-acre property, tight against the sand bluffs on the east side of the lake. His son, Ture Johnson, remembers that the only other structure on the lake was the shack of a bachelor moonshine maker named Gus Engstrom. It did not take long, however, for a land agent to seize the opportunity to sell lakefront property to prospective summer campers. A Finnish logging contractor from Rock named Walter Selin purchased land on the east and north shores, had lots surveyed, and started selling them around 1930. The buyers were local people within twenty-five to thirty miles, easy driving distance even on the rough dirt roads of those days. Their homes ranged from Sundell to Negaunee, Ishpeming to Rock. Some were immigrant miners, like John Kujala of Negaunee, but most were businessmen and storekeepers. Many were Finnish immigrants who knew each other socially through the Negaunee branch of a Finnish cultural society called the Knights of Kaleva.

By 1935, a predominantly Finnish-American summer community had formed on Little Shag Lake. The sounds of the Finnish language were often heard along the shore on Saturday evenings, the traditional sauna day. One summer camp owner estimated that in the 1950s as many as 80 percent of the camps had saunas. The entire lakeshore was eventually divided into ninety-three lots, with a three-mile circle road along the back perimeter of the camp boundaries. A morning walking group of ten to twenty people still occasionally makes the rounds in summer. Even in the 1990s some neighborly bonds can claim to reach back to the founding generation, linking descendants who have known each other for fifty years or more. But many new faces and new families have appeared in the last ten years. About one-third of the properties have changed hands since

1989, a fact partly related to the closing of K. I. Sawyer Air Force Base near Gwinn. And about one-quarter of the properties have been converted to year-round residences, further complicating a sense of community (Martin Marin Interview). Residents and summer people have different interests and goals, the former wanting more township services, from natural gas pipelines to regular trash pickup, while the latter see their tax assessments rising and resent paying fixed fees for services regardless of use.

In the late 1970s, a group of property owners called the Little Shag Lake Association was created to deal with issues of common concern. The preamble to the bylaws speaks of protecting the water quality of the lake, promoting the well being and rights of all members, and preserving the lake "for posterity with the blessing of God." The first major issue was whether efforts should be made to re-establish the natural drainage system of the lake; the water level at that time was very high and threatening to inundate some of the low-lying homes and camps. No consensus was forthcoming; in fact, a counter group of owners calling itself Lake First organized to oppose what they considered to be artificial manipulation of the lake levels. The Little Shag Lake Association, with the encouragement of the Central Upper Peninsula Planning and Development commission (CUPPAD), has also worked to facilitate land use planning and to increase environmental awareness among its members on such issues as wells, silting, sauna drainage, and lawn fertilizers. But according to George Keskimaki, who was the first President of the Association, there is still too much ignorance and indifference among property owners. He has moved his own sauna back thirty-five feet from the lake and is angered that liberal interpretations of "grandfathering" past practices have allowed other saunas to remain on the lake edge despite two or three changes in ownership. It is an era of increasing conflicts, symbolized by the large Association sign that greets drivers as they approach the lake from the east. Beneath a picture of the lake is a list of property owners in which two long rows of Little Shag Lake Association members are flanked by two short rows of Lake Firsters.

Still, the rise of new environmental conflicts should not be overstated. The common ground among Little Shag Lake property owners (whether within the Association or among Lake Firsters) has become concern for the quality of the lake itself. Zoning and building codes are being enforced in many cases. When two owners undertook a major renovation of their camp recently, they were pressured to install an indoor toilet along with a new kitchen, with state-of-the-art waste water disposal for both. It was farewell to the outhouse. The drainage in their lakeside sauna also had to be rerouted onto land. The state of Michigan has regularly tested the quality of the

ENVIRONMENT: SUMMER CAMPS

Niemi camp on a lake in Gogebic County
Photo courtesy of Christine Saari

Saari camp in a clearing near Kiva in Alger County
Photo courtesy of Christine Saari

water in the lake and judged it to be very good among fully developed lakes of this size. And even the water level, on its own, has come back to a point that most regard as neither too low nor too high.

The changes in the human relationships within the Little Shag Lake summer community have been more dramatic. It is no longer "Finn Lake," because changes in ownership have altered the ethnic pattern; still the east and southeast corners even today are very Finnish-American, with saunas marking practically every camp. Neighbors may well be newcomers, useful in keeping a mutual eye on each other's place, but not people with whom one shares bonds of kinship, ethnicity, or lived history. Generational succession within families has introduced more subtle changes. Most of the old family camps started in the 1930s and 1940s are now into the third and fourth generations. After childhoods in the Upper Peninsula, many of the second generation left the region for war, higher education, and work, and their summer returns resembled occasional pilgrimages from distant places. Retirement has given them the freedom to stay for longer periods; but with primary homes elsewhere (from North Carolina and Florida to Chicago and Minneapolis), with spouses who have their own childhood special places, and with their own children and grandchildren scattered throughout the country, these children of Little Shag Lake do not get to camp as often as they would want to. But that is the very nature of camp: One is always struggling to get there, and the stays are short and therapeutic.

The Maki Camp

So it has been with Bill Maki and his sister Irma. Walking the grounds of their summer camp, Bill touches the shed door where he carved his initials as a fourteen-year-old on the very day that his dad decided to buy this particular camp in 1945. He remarks on the large round stones from Lake Superior that he and his father mortared into terraces to help hold the sand bluff in place. The old boathouse still shelters the two-horse Evinrude that his father got for trolling in the lake decades ago; the bucksaw hanging on the wall, its hand-fitted pieces held in place by a twisted rope, still cuts wood for the sauna stove next door. The camp house itself, like their lives, is a work in progress; there is the original core from the 1930s which they inherited, the bedroom and deck addition of the late 1940s, the running water that arrived in 1986, and finally the renovated kitchen and bathroom from 1993. The furnishings are eclectic: a sitting table in each room, the old commode and wood-paneled radio, wooden chairs and rockers painted white, four landscape paintings reminiscent of Finnish scenes (brought over from the old house in Negaunee after it was sold), photographs of family members and the blizzard of 1938 on display. Their mother they remember sitting at the little white table on the glassed-in porch, quietly watching the lake through the trees. The view she saw was partly shaped by the artistic eye of her photographer husband, who thinned the trees in front of the camp to create a scene pleasing to the human eye.

For Bill and his sister Irma, past and present join together with each stay at camp; ancestral spirits mingle with their own here as at no other place. Bill, like so many of his generation, has been a man on the move—the Navy, then the University of Michigan, then work as a planning engineer in cities throughout the Midwest. The RV parked in the yard, he says, is his tenth home, a home on wheels—certainly a paradox, if not a contradiction. He seems to be searching for a balance that measures life properly and fully, and he knows that camp is an important part of that balancing. He and his wife Vandi are thinking of moving to Marquette for a few years, closer to camp but not replacing camp. To make camp their full-time home would risk losing something valuable, perhaps the very coming and going between city and inland lake, between two different worlds, the one that provides livelihood and cultural stimulation, and the one that nourishes the soul with its relative simplicity and more direct connection with nature. It is an ironic touch that Bill and Irma's Dad, Vaino Maki, in his last years at camp used to insist upon returning each evening to the house in Negaunee for a quiet night of sleep away from "da cang"[the gang] of children and grandchildren.

Where Culture and Nature Intermingle

The summer camp tradition nurtures a particular kind of connection with nature. It is not the nature of the Sublime enshrined in the national parks, replete with waterfalls, grand vistas, beckoning mountain ranges, and roaring rivers where God's presence seems near. Nor is it the nature of the Frontier—trackless, immense, wild, foreboding—where brave men and women tested their mettle (Cronon 1995: 70–81). At summer camp, human beings do not feel dwarfed and somehow cut off from nature, standing on the edge of something awesome. This is a nature where most human beings can learn to be comfortable: an outer edge of thick forest that buffers the road and frames the entryway to the camp clearing; park-like grounds where the trees have been thinned and the vegetation checked; lakes and rivers with inviting beaches and shorelines; small buildings, trailers, and campers that blend into the surroundings; and terraces and walkways that follow the contours of the land. In a word, a nature that is accessible, that stimulates wonder without overwhelming the senses.

The summer camp is middle ground where culture and nature intermingle in a single landscape. It differs, however, from other places that may also be said to occupy the middle ground such as farms, primary homes in rural or wooded subdivisions, or even camps that have been converted into year-round residences. It is different from farms in scale and purpose, for camp has no utilitarian goal or purpose, no connection to livelihood (other than helping pay for itself through occasional woodlot harvest or house rental). It is different from primary year-round residences in quiet neighborhoods because camp, by design, lacks the full and easy access to technological civilization, from garage door openers to city snowplows, from computers to natural gas pipelines, and even in some cases access to electricity and running water. Camp is defined by an experience that is not available in these places, and that is in fact a counterpoint experience: a non-utilitarian immersion in quietude, slowness, and simple pleasures (often related to manual work) in an inviting and captivating natural setting. It remains to be seen if the summer camp will emerge in longer historical perspective as a temporary means of refuge from the hectic pace of twentieth-century urban civilization or as an adaptive model for the well-being of both natural and human communities. Meanwhile, do not wait for the historical verdict to come in. Do yourself and your kids a favor now; build or buy a camp within thirty miles or so of home, and become part of the camp tradition of the Upper Peninsula.

ENVIRONMENT: SUMMER CAMPS

Bibliography

Books, Articles, and Manuscripts

Balfe, Judith Huggins. "Social Structure and Culture" in *Passing It On: The Inheritance and Use of Summer Houses*, ch. 2 (unpublished manuscript).

Bjork, William P. *The Camps UP North: A History In The Woods*. Brimley, Michigan: Birch Tree Enterprises, 1996.

Cronon, William. "The Trouble with Wilderness: or, Getting Back to the Wrong Nature." In *Uncommon Ground: Toward Reinventing Nature*. Ed. William Cronon. New York: Norton, 1995, pp. 69–90.

Delene, Elizabeth. "John D. Voelker" (unpublished manuscript).

Jarvenpa, Aili. Ed. *In Two Cultures: The Stories of Second Generation Finnish-Americans*. St. Cloud, Minnesota: North Star Press, 1992.

Koskenmaki, Joyce. "Are There Forests in Finnish Minds?" *The Finnish American Reporter* 5 #7 (1992), 32.

Rydholm, C. Fred. *Superior Heartland: A Backwoods History*. Marquette, Michigan: privately published by C. Fred Rydholm, 1989.

Traver, Robert. *Danny and the Boys: Being Some Legends of Hungry Hollow*, 1951. 2nd ed. Detroit: Wayne State University Press, 1987.

Oral Interviews (July–September, 1996).

Little Shag Lake, Marquette County, Michigan: Mike Bussone, Ture and Emma Johnson, Ruth Jouppi, George Keskimaki, Emmy Kulkki, Bill and Vandi Maki, Irma Maki, Martin and Lou Marin, Art and Jean Mattson, Ben Perala, Clarence Rivers, Bill Savolainen, Aili Smith.

Little Oxbow Lake, Gogebic County, Michigan: Norm Niemi.

Camp Buck, Marquette County, Michigan: William P. Bjork

Marquette, Michigan: Lotta Stewart

A Sense of Place

Research Collections

A Sense of Place: Michigan's Upper Peninsula

THE EVERETT M. & ELIZABETH B. LOSEY COLLECTION
Inuit and First Nations Art and Other Indigenous Material in the UP

Eileen L. Roberts

Introduction

In 1994, Northern Michigan University became the recipient of a major donation of Inuit (Eskimo) and First Nations (Native Canadian) art. The material had been collected by Everett and Elizabeth Losey, long-term residents of Germfask in Michigan's Upper Peninsula, on their numerous trips into Canada. What had begun as hunting and fishing trips in the late 1960s expanded as research into Canada's rich and diverse past. Motivated by the desire to visit as many of the forts that served as trading posts in the fur trade as possible, they explored Canada from Quebec and Ontario westward into Alberta, then traveled into the Yukon and the Northwest Territories. Their itineraries included trips along the Pacific coast in Alaska's panhandle and British Columbia, continuing southward into Washington and Oregon. As they traveled, they came to appreciate the indigenous cultures of Canada, especially as reflected in the arts and crafts. They purchased objects and artifacts through galleries, museum shops, and native cooperatives, taking advantage when special opportunities arose to buy material directly from the individual who made it. Years of travel continuing into the early 1990s resulted in the formation of a collection impressive in its diversity and quality.

The Loseys lived surrounded by art in their home at Germfask, and it was only after her husband's death that Mrs. Losey very generously donated the greater part of the collection, nearly two hundred objects, to Northern Michigan University. In Fall of 1995, an exhibition of the entire collection was presented in what is now known as the University Art Museum. Since that time, pieces from the collection have been displayed elsewhere on the campus and as part of a multicultural exhibit at the Museum. In accordance with the donor's wishes, the collection will be used as a valuable resource that can be drawn on for a variety of educational purposes over the ensuing years.

Description of the Collection

Based on information provided by the donor, the objects can be classified in terms of the artists or artisans who made them. More than 35 percent of the works are Inuit (Eskimo). Each of the following groups or tribes account for about 10 percent each: Iroquois, Ojibwa, Northwest Coast, Cree, and Dené (Athapaskan). Under 5 percent of the collection is comprised respectively of Micmac and Montagnais objects, with the remaining 5 percent attributable to various other sources. A discussion of select pieces collected from across Canada and into the United States will give some sense of the scope of the collection.

Objects made by the Montagnais and Micmac in the collection are from eastern Quebec and the Maritime Provinces. A small black ash basket (Figure 1) by Margaret Morris from Nova Scotia is a good example of basket weaving made specifically to satisfy the buying public. Prior to beginning the actual basket, a good deal of time and energy is spent harvesting and processing the wood that will provide the splints. The splints are removed from a log in narrow strips that, after being split into half their thickness, are thin enough to be cut with scissors. They are kept damp enough to be pliable and can be soaked in water if necessary just before use. A skilled basket maker knows from experience how to lay out splints of the proper width, length, and number to form the ribs for the basket, beginning from the bottom. Additional splints are then woven above and below alternating ribs. The rib splints are bent upward to begin weaving the sides, with the beginning of one horizontal splint overlapping the preceding one in such a way that they appear continuous. Space is reserved for the insertion of splints that are turned and twisted like ribbon, hence the name "fancy basket," as these are often called. Sweet grass has been woven into the lid, which, when fresh, releases a pleasant aroma whenever the humidity increases.

For centuries, throughout Iroquois country in Canada—southern Quebec and southeast Ontario—one of the staple crops has been corn. Nothing is wasted; in addition to the ears of corn providing a nutritious food supply, the corn husks are used in a variety of ways. Dolls could readily be made for children by folding, twisting, and tying damp corn husks. At times left unadorned, they could also be more or less elaborately dressed to depict adults and children of both genders, standing upright or engaged in traditional activities. It was an easy transition from making such dolls to be enjoyed within the family to their creation for a larger market. The corn husk doll from Ontario illustrated here (Figure 2) is a dancing warrior, an activity the artisan may well have seen at a local pow wow. Feathers that adorn the bustle, headband, and staff have been identified by Professor William Robinson, ornithologist with the University's Department of Biology, as probably being from the striped wood duck. They serve as substitutes for the eagle feathers, which have sacred meaning, that might be worn by an actual dancer.

Research Collections: The Losey Collection

Figure 1. Fancy black ash basket by Margaret Morris
　　　　　Micmac, Nova Scotia
　　　　　LC 94.54 (photo by author)

Figure 2. Corn husk dancer with feather bustle
　　　　　Mohawk, Ontario
　　　　　LC 94.14 (photo by author)

*Figure 3. Birch bark container by M.B.
Ojibwa, Ontario
LC 94.9 (photo by author)*

*Figure 4. Tamarack twig goose decoy
Cree, Ontario
LC 94.23 (photo by author)*

Research Collections: The Losey Collection

Ojibwa tribes are located in Canada throughout a broad area extending across Ontario north of the Great Lakes and westward into the plains provinces. Containers of various sizes, shapes, and functions were traditionally made from birch bark wherever the tree could be found. The birch bark container is a typical example (Figure 3). When sheets of bark are harvested in early spring, the outer layer is light, while the inner bark has a deep rust color. For this container, the white outer bark of the tree has been folded inward. To decorate the container, thin birch bark patterns that can be used repeatedly were arranged on the surface and traced around with a sharp tool. The darker bark was scraped away around the area delineated to reveal the lighter bark below, creating a series of floral and vegetal motifs on the lid and sides. The initials of the maker, "M. B.," appear on one side. Spruce root was used to sew the various parts together, while hide strips provide a hinge for the lid as well as a strap.

Farther north in Quebec and westward into Alberta are regions occupied by the Cree. As a hunting and gathering people whose life depended upon being able to harvest adequate food in a challenging sub-Arctic environment, they long ago developed aides to draw game into accessible locations. The tamarack decoy was just such a device, a traditional hunting tool made to mimic the appearance of a goose (Figure 4). The twigs are neatly trimmed and bound tightly together with cord looped around like stitching. Decoys are made in a variety of sizes, so that, when set out in a marshy region, they have the appearance to a flock flying above of a comfortably resting or feeding family of geese in a safe haven. These decoys have now attracted a wider audience and can even be found advertised as the perfect gift in upscale mail-order catalogues.

In adjacent regions in northwestern Canada are found various bands of Athapaskan-speaking people who call themselves collectively Dené. Because of their proximity to Great Slave Lake in the Northwest Territories, one such group has been named Slave or Slavey. Caribou and moose provide the material used for centuries to make strikingly beautiful outfits, complete with boots or moccasins and gloves. Although the actual making of garments is typically the work of women, given the environment, the necessity of having well-made protective clothing earns them their due respect. The tanned moose hide gloves in the Losey Collection incorporate a variety of different materials: beaver fur, glass beads, felt, rickrack, and cotton cloth (Figure 5). The appliqué work combines two shades of red, orange, green, and black beads stitched on white felt in the shape of a heart, set against the deep brown of the moose hide. Decorated gloves such as these are customarily worn by men, who have as great an appreciation as women for beautifully finished garments. Needless to say, they are also prized as collectibles by the mainstream populace.

The Inuit occupy the Arctic regions of the Northwest Territories and Quebec in the far north. From Sugluk, in northern Quebec, comes the owl carved in a dark gray stone (Figure 6), which has been incised on the bottom with the artist's name—Adam. The owl has been carved in gently rounded curves with incised details describing the eyes, feet, and an overall feather pattern. Stone carving by the Inuit extends back as far as the culture itself, but it was not until the 1950s that the Canadian government financed its development as a means for communities to attain a measure of economic independence in the modern world. The Canadian artist James Houston worked closely with artisans to tie production to art market demands. More recently, artists have begun to assert themselves more strongly. Placing self-expression above the desire for conformity exerted by dealers, they have attained the status of artists, as highly respected as their mainstream counterparts.

RESEARCH COLLECTIONS: THE LOSEY COLLECTION

Figure 5. Moose hide gloves
Slave, Northwest Territories
LC 94.32 (photo by author)

Figure 6. Owl by Adam
Inuit, Quebec
LC 94.S5 (photo by author)

203

A SENSE OF PLACE: MICHIGAN'S UPPER PENINSULA

*Figure 7. Shaman dancer by Vitesha
Yupik, Alaska
LC 94.B3 (photo by author)*

*Figure 8. Miniature bear mask by Wally Cox
Nootka, British Columbia
LC 94.106 (photo by author)*

Research Collections: The Losey Collection

The Loseys extended their travels into Alaska before turning south into British Columbia. They purchased two singular works of art in Alaska, one of which is illustrated here. The shaman dancer by the Yupik artist Vitesha is made from several types of fossil bone varying in color from off-white to browns and grays (Figure 7). In sharp contrast are the red glass beads, used to represent bird beaks attached to the dancing figure's mittens. The Yupik shaman, who acted as a mediator between the human and spirit world, led annual ceremonies held in a communal building where carefully organized singing, dancing, and storytelling took place. The dancing of the shaman was accented by the clicking of the puffin and auklet beaks shaken as the hands moved. These festivals contributed to establishing the proper relationship between humans and animal spirits and to ensuring a successful hunt and survival of the community. When shaman were still active, carving images of them was unnecessary. Now that the modern world has all but eclipsed the ancient one, this artist has been able to suggest the significant role they once played.

Upon their discovery of Northwest Coast art in British Columbia, Elizabeth Losey has said she was immediately attracted to the art of the various tribes that inhabit the region. The miniature bear mask carved by Wally Cox, purchased on Vancouver Island, displays the salient features (Figure 8). The wood, which clearly shows the marks of the carving tools, is accented by black and red paint with white dashes curving around the cheeks from front to side. The crisply painted areas repeat the forms carved into wood, creating a harmonious whole. Fiercely bared teeth lend the mask a ferocity that belies its modest size. Northwest Coast artists have established reputations that have gained them international recognition. While maintaining the stylistic characteristics of traditional art, they have developed art forms that meet the expectations of a sophisticated buying public.

A Sense of Place: Michigan's Upper Peninsula

This survey of material in the Losey Collection only begins to explore what these works can teach us about the people and cultures that produced them. They document how indigenous people have assimilated new materials and techniques to suit their own expressive purposes. They challenge mainstream definitions of art and demand an attention to concerns and meaning that spring from a very different perspective. By enlarging our understanding of native cultures, they provide stepping stones for learning not only about the history and geography of a foreign country, in this case Canada, but also of a set of values and beliefs quite distinct from those of Euro-Canadians and Euro-Americans. Coming from cultures that traditionally do not separate art and life or the secular from the sacred, these contemporary works were made for sale to a larger public. This very fact makes them more accessible to the mainstream, since they mediate a past that is obscure to non-natives, bringing concepts and an æsthetic into a context more familiar to the larger public. It is Mrs. Losey's desire that the collection receive ongoing use in an academic environment. According to the Museum's Director, after the current round of renovations are completed, part of the collection will be displayed continuously on a rotating basis.

Other Collections in Michigan's Upper Peninsula

In many ways, the Losey Collection of indigenous art complements material found in museums at various locations in the Upper Peninsula. Major public and private collections will be briefly described to give some sense of their scope and the method of organization that characterizes them. Details such as street addresses, hours when open, and telephone numbers for many of these museums can be found in the *Traveler's Guide to Native America* listed in the bibliography.

The Marquette County Historical Society Museum in Marquette has a small collection of Native American material that is particularly strong in local history. Display cases present a small but informative selection of Upper Peninsula archæological artifacts documenting the Paleo-Indian through Woodland periods with a good collection of copper artifacts, made from copper probably mined on Isle Royale or in the Keweenaw. The gallery devoted to Marquette County history begins with a diorama showing a traditional Native camp site with typical materials and activities, a diorama that will be redesigned in the near future, complete with audio enhancement. In front of it are displayed objects from the turn of the century to the present time associated with food gathering and processing on the one hand and crafts and culture on the other. The enclosed "Trading Post" documents the fur trade, with items of exchange from indigenous people including pelts, snowshoes, moccasins, and a beaded bag. Thereafter, Native Americans disappear from local history, except for mention of the Chippewa chief who communicated the location of the iron ore deposit in Negaunee that spurred surveying, settlement, and exploitation of the area's natural resources by Euro-Americans.

The Minnetonka Resort's Astor House Historical Museum in Copper Harbor is a private collection of some size. One requests access to the museum at the motel office, then is led to an older out-building to the rear of the property. Antiques for sale, mining memorabilia, a doll and bottle collection, and stray pieces of furniture that may have to be moved to allow perusal of the archæological material, create a somewhat chaotic atmosphere. Stone, bone, and copper artifacts are presented in approximate chronological order in a series of glass display cases. The variety and quantity of stone tools included is impressive, though precisely where the artifacts originated from is not indicated on the labels. Surface finds and those unearthed by road digging and field plowing in the Keweenaw could certainly be expected. That the collector had broad interests, however, is documented by the booklet from the Dickson Mounds in Illinois, Plains Indian post cards, and other miscellaneous material.

A rather eclectic group of indigenous material can be found at the Menominee Range Historical Foundation Museum in Iron Mountain. Donations by members of a single family include curios from Alaska, miscellaneous archæological artifacts, beadwork, and baskets. Given the limited information on the labels, a knowledgeable viewer is best prepared to identify probable sources. One of the most interesting displays presents on-site photographs and artifacts from an excavation conducted in Menominee County at the Pemene Falls site. The Woodland period material includes copper and stone artifacts, and one could only wish for additional information interpreting the site more fully. A more general archæological framework is provided by material displayed at the Menominee County Historical Museum in Menominee, where a small but well organized section on "Indian Culture" presents a representative collection of artifacts arranged chronologically from the Paleo-Indian through Woodland periods. Stone tools of various size, shape, and function; various copper artifacts; pot sherds; and red ocher (powdered hematite or red iron ore) are displayed, any number of artifacts having originated from clearly identified county locations. The remains of two dugout canoes are also local finds. Contact period trade items are displayed, as well as early twentieth-century objects once belonging to a local Menominee Indian family.

One of the finest collections of Native American art in the Upper Peninsula, and perhaps the least known, is found at the tribal college at Brimley. The material is displayed in the Cultural Heritage Center at Bay Mills Community College in a room accessible through the library. Most of the approximately 140 objects (not including prints or books) were donated by a collector from downstate Michigan who had purchased work dating from the mid-nineteenth century through the post-WWII period. Individual donations of regional material bring the collection up to the present. The material is arranged roughly by geographical area, though the limited space available has made necessary a mix in some display cases merely to make everything visible. Just under a third of the items are identified as Great Lakes or, at times, specifically as Chippewa or Potawatomi. Other areas represented include the Northeast (other than Anishinabeg), Great Plains, Southwest, Northwest Coast, and Alaska. A limited number of items also come from Canada. The individual objects are outstanding in their range of materials and techniques, as well as the quality of the work. One would not expect to find such a rich collection outside major downstate institutions, so it is very fortunate to find this material available for public viewing during regular library hours.

The River of History Museum in Sault Sainte Marie is among the Upper Peninsula's newest and technologically most advanced museum. The underlying concept of having the St. Mary's River narrate her history is reflected in the overall design. From the distant geological past through the twentieth century, one walks along the gently curving path of the river while listening to the sounds and voices that explain in the first person the events of time. After coming to understand the life style and world view of the First People, the Anishinabeg, the viewer learns how the French adapted to prevailing customs while pursuing the fur trade. Throughout the ensuing post-contact period, native and non-native history is thoroughly integrated. Explanations of the development of natural resources in the name of progress are balanced with observations on indigenous values and spiritual beliefs relevant today to preserve the natural environment. Historic and contemporary Native American art and crafts are displayed, and historic photographs of the city in one area are complemented by contemporary pow wow photographs in another. The museum's logo of two men side by side paddling a voyageurs canoe, one French, the other Indian, visually communicates the major thrust of the museum—that two cultures working together harmoniously is the only sensible way to travel forward on the river of time.

The Museum of Ojibwa Culture is located in St. Ignace. Operated under the supervision of a city agency, it is a model of cooperation between a public museum and the local tribe—the Sault Sainte Marie Tribe of Chippewa Indians. A significant effort has been made

RESEARCH COLLECTIONS: THE LOSEY COLLECTION

to present a history sensitive to the Native American point of view. Housed in a nineteenth-century church relocated to this site, the display begins with a map presenting the Anishinabeg account of their migration from the Atlantic coast to the juncture of Lakes Huron and Michigan. The Ojibwa cosmos is represented by the "Great Medicine Tree" display. Giving equal emphasis to a scientific approach to the past are the chronologically organized archæological finds, with a limited number of facsimiles such as pottery illustrating the extensive time span the area has been inhabited. Displays demonstrating how indigenous people used local materials—earth, animals, and plants—are included. A section of a lodge has been constructed to display the traditional lifestyle. The video presentation, stressing a sense of community and family values, was produced by the Sault Tribe. Additional displays, creatively organized, document history on the Straits through the seventeenth century. Outside stands a reconstruction of a Huron longhouse based on local archæological excavations. Of the perhaps ten long houses that made up the village at this site, this example, built with a sapling frame covered by elm bark, is quite impressive, measuring some 20 by 120 feet and standing to a height of about twenty feet. The museum grounds are the location of the Sault Tribe's annual Labor Day weekend pow wow, further emphasizing the vitality of indigenous culture in the region.

Also to be found in St. Ignace is the Fort de Buade Museum, named after the seventeenth-century fort built here by the French. This significant private collection of Native American material is displayed in a rather dank space. The first part is devoted to archæological artifacts, primarily stone, organized chronologically from the Paleo-Indian through Woodland periods, though it is unclear how much was collected locally. The second part of the collection displays post-contact material of regional interest, including some quite beautiful beaded objects—full regalia, for example. There is also local historic material of importance: copies of written records, tin type photographs, and other miscellaneous items. Labels are informative but often difficult to read, due to their age and poor lighting conditions.

The Indian Museum on Mackinac Island is presently located on the uppermost floor of the historic Indian Dormitory, operated by the Mackinac Island State Park Commission. The stated theme of the museum is Henry Schoolcraft, who designed and supervised construction of the building in 1838, and Henry Wadsworth Longfellow's poem *Hiawatha*, based on Schoolcraft's writings about Native people inhabiting the Lake Superior region. Couplets from the poem provide the backdrop for a series of displays that are rich in material but rather limited in explanatory text. Objects such as a wooden bowl, war club, moccasins, bandolier bag, flint gun, and iron knives attempt to suggest the context in which Schoolcraft lived and worked. The association with Longfellow's poem is an outdated concept the Park Commission staff intends to remedy. Culturally sensitive objects have already been removed from display, and within a year a survey of this and several other downtown buildings will be completed. Plans include reorganizing and reinterpreting the collection with the assistance of Native American consultants and relocating it elsewhere in the building to make it more accessible to the public.

Conclusion

In 1995, Mrs. Losey gave an additional two objects she had recently purchased to the University, a large Cree twig goose decoy and a porcupine quill box. By so doing, she further indicated the direction the Art Museum might take to document more fully the cultures of North America. Within the original collection are several Ojibwa items from Michigan and Minnesota: a basket, two birch bark containers with quill decoration, and a small porcupine quill box. Since the federally recognized tribes in Michigan are Anishinabeg (Chippewa/Ojibwa, Odawa, and Potowatami), these nations represent the heritage of most Northern Michigan University Native American students. By expanding the collection with local and regional material, we can best establish a partnership with the Native American Studies Center on campus and residents in the surrounding communities. With this goal in mind, the Museum proposed that the Friends of the University Art Museum purchase a major work of art by a local Native American. They welcomed the opportunity, and an exquisite beaded pouch by Linda Cohen of Skandia was added to the collection in Spring 1996. Having established a sense of direction for the University's permanent collection of art, the prospects are good for continuing to build on the firm basis established by the Losey donation.

This survey of collections does not purport to be exhaustive, though it is thorough enough to give a sense of the breadth and diversity of indigenous material available to the public in the Upper Peninsula. When funding is provided, museums generally update displays and interpretations to bring them into line with the highest standards. Increased interest oftens motivates directors and curators to share information and work to support each other's efforts to the greatest extent possible. Northern Michigan University, with its newly organized Center for Upper Peninsula Studies, is in a position to provide leadership to develop cooperation among these institutions, to the benefit of all concerned.

BIBLIOGRAPHY

Allen, Hayward. *The Traveler's Guide to Native America: The Great Lakes Region.* Minocqua: NorthWord Press, 1992.

Brasser, Ted. "Bo'jou, Neejee!": *Profiles of Canadian Indian Art.* Ottawa: National Museum of Man, 1976.

Coe, Ralph. *Lost and Found Traditions: Native American Art 1965–1985.* Ed. Irene Gordon. Seattle-New York: University of Washington Press and The American Federation of Art, 1986.

Fane, Diana, Ira Jacknis, and Lise Breen. *Objects of Myth and Memory: American Indian Art at The Brooklyn Museum.* Seattle-New York: University of Washington Press and The Brooklyn Museum, 1991.

Furst, Peter and Jill. *North American Indian Art.* New York: Rizzoli, 1982.

Penney, David, and George Longfish. *Native American Art.* New York: Hugh Lauter Levin Associates, 1994.

Phillips, Ruth. *Patterns of Power: The Jasper Grant Collection and Great Lakes Indian Art of the Early Nineteenth Century.* Kleinburg, Ontario: The McMichael Canadian Collection, 1984.

Vicent, Gilbert. *Masterpieces of American Indian Art from the Eugene and Clare Thaw Collection.* New York: Harry N. Abrams and The New York State Historical Association, 1995.

A Sense of Place: Michigan's Upper Peninsula

*John D. Voelker Display in the Superior Dome
Marquette, Michigan*

ANATOMY OF A COLLECTION
The John D. Voelker Papers at Northern Michigan University

Heather A. Sorensen
Gayle J. Martinson

High profile court cases often pique public curiosity and interest. In late summer of 1952, the trial of an Army Lieutenant resulted in a 1958 bestseller that thrust Justice John D. Voelker into the spotlight. The novel was made into an Academy Award-nominated movie starring Jimmy Stewart and Lee Remick. Manuscript drafts of this book as well as ten other books, correspondence, legal files, and personal papers were donated to the Central Upper Peninsula and University Archives of Northern Michigan University shortly after Voelker's death. This article describes the life of this unique man, his personal papers, and the impact they have had on the archives and museum efforts of Northern Michigan University. The article also considers possible uses of the collection by researchers interested in Voelker's legal and writing careers as well as his personal life.

The Upper Peninsula of Michigan is a vast, heavily wooded region containing rich copper and iron ore deposits bordered by three of the five Great Lakes. This area has played an important role in America's mining, timber, and shipping industries. Here a unique blend of fiercely independent people (who proudly call themselves "Yoopers") forged lives out of the ore they mined and the lumber they felled.

John Voelker spent the greater part of his life in Ishpeming, Michigan, a key area in the Upper Peninsula's iron ore industry. Born in 1903, John Voelker's life spanned a culturally rich, historic period of the UP. His love of the area and its people is portrayed in his eleven books and numerous articles, many written under the name Robert Traver. These included *Anatomy of a Murder*, the best-selling novel which was made into the blockbuster movie directed by Otto Preminger. Voelker's books range from historical fiction to fly fishing to his personal experiences as Marquette County Prosecutor and reflect his observations of human behavior. Voelker's great love for nature and sense of humor contributed to a unique understanding of the human condition.

Voelker was also a dedicated pack rat. The John D. Voelker Papers comprise an extensive collection of materials documenting various aspects of Voelker's life with a particular focus on his law career, writings, and fishing interests. Spanning a century and some two hundred linear feet of material, this remarkable collection reveals the interplay of Voelker's law career, personal interests, and writings—and provides insight into the man himself.

Literary manuscripts and drafts of his novels, legal case files, and correspondence form the collection's bulk. Correspondence includes communications with family, friends, publishers, fans, fishing enthusiasts, fellow lawyers, literary and entertainment personages, and politicians. Notable correspondents included former Michigan Governor G. Mennen Williams, CBS journalist Charles Kuralt, and film producer Otto Preminger.

The University acquired the Voelker Papers soon after receiving notification that the National Historical Publications and Records Commission (NHPRC) had awarded NMU a grant to establish a regional archives. The offer to donate the papers to Northern Michigan University came at a fortuitous time. The Northern Michigan University Archives had been limping along for years as a child of the History Department. Several dedicated history professors worked tirelessly to get the Archives established with full-time professional staff, facilities, and adequate budget. University administrators, librarians, and history professors discussed acquisition of the Voelker Papers, which coincided with a proposal to NHPRC for a grant to establish an archive for the university and central Upper Peninsula.

Due in part to the attractiveness of acquiring the Voelker Papers, university administrators pledged to continue support of a professional archivist after expiration of the two-year grant period. A new home for the archives within the organizational structure of the university library was also hammered out. Both home and secure staffing were critical in acquiring the NHPRC grant. Likewise, the NHPRC grant award gave the archival program needed prestige and credibility with the university community, which increasingly came to see the importance of the program in preserving the university's records as well as historical materials relating to the central Upper Peninsula. Pieces fell into place when NHPRC start-up monies made the Archives credible and provided the wherewithal for a permanent home for the Archives and the hire of a professional archivist. The university now felt able to accept the Voelker Papers, which it did post haste.

Having acquired the collection, the university established a display room for Voelker's artifacts. The Marquette County Historical Society provided guidance in cataloging artifacts. The History Department offered a class in museum studies which provided a hands-on approach to museum work. In addition, policies were established regarding the museum, gifts, and acquisitions. Showcases and a replication of Voelker's office were set up for display purposes. His personal library, writing desk, fishing rods and flies, cribbage boards, a hunting vest, campaign posters and cards, and other artifacts were

Research Collections: The Voelker Papers

John Voelker in his private law office, Ishpeming, Michigan, circa 1953. The rocking chair is now a part of the Voelker exhibit at Northern Michigan University.
(Reprint courtesy of the Northern Michigan University Archives.)

put on display. In honor of the Voelker exhibit opening, the university held a trout dinner. The evening was highlighted by viewing *Anatomy of an Author,* a film made at Voelker's fishing camp *(Anatomy of an Author 1982).*

Since its opening, over 1500 people have visited the exhibit. Most have been residents of the Marquette area, including former friends, *Anatomy of a Murder* movie extras, and area students. Tourists from as far away as Singapore and Germany have also viewed the exhibit. Spurred by the success of the exhibit and its upcoming 1999 centennial, the university began collecting university and community artifacts towards establishment of a museum and set up an exhibit of Voelker artifacts in the Superior Dome, a regional cultural and sports center.

Voelker received a life teaching certificate from Northern State Normal (now Northern Michigan University) in 1924 and a law degree from the University of Michigan four years later. A rugged outdoorsman, John Voelker also had some charm with the ladies. This was particularly apparent to Grace Taylor, a Chicago native whom he met at a University of Michigan dance and later married in 1930. Voelker established his law career near his wife's Oak Park home. He gave up his position there to return to the Upper Peninsula, telling his wife that it was better to starve in Ishpeming than to wear emeralds in Chicago (VanderVeen 1993:46). Grace Voelker fashioned a life for herself and her three daughters in this Upper Peninsula boom town. In fact, it was Grace Voelker with her indomitable spirit who persevered in donating her husband's papers to Northern Michigan University, even when the university was initially unsure of its ability to receive them.

Voelker's first three books paint a picture of UP life between the two World Wars and the late 1940's. *Troubleshooter, Danny and the Boys,* and *Small Town D.A.* depict UP culture. His *Danny* book humorously describes the circumstances of five bachelor men living in an abandoned logging camp. The other two are collections of stories about the trials of a prosecuting attorney's daily workload. A regional dialect, known as "Yoopanese," is found in all three books. A mixture of Finnish, Cousin Jack (Cornish), French-Canadian, Ojibwe, Irish, Italian, and Scandinavian tongues, the UP has a discernable dialect (Thundy n.d.). Voelker also preserved in writing the dialect known as "Finglish," the mixture of Finnish and English spoken by the UP's Finnish immigrants:

Research Collections: The Voelker Papers

> *'I'll be walking down U. S. cement highway dis morning an' one Fording car come down da road like everting—hit Tauno 'n nass, nass in da bush, Fording car go like hell down cement road—wifty miles hour!' He paused. 'What you goin' do for dat!'*
>
> *'That's pretty tough, Tauno—did you get hurt very bad?'*
>
> *'Holy mokes, Mr. County Lawyer—I yust tell for you—Fording car hit Tauno 'n nass, nass in da bush, Fording car go like hell down cement road—wifty miles hour! What you do for dat!'*
>
> *'Did you get his license number, Tauno?'*
>
> *'Sesus Rist, Mr. County Lawyer! Licings numper! Dats da you bizness get for dat lacings numper!'* (Traver 1943:88-89)

As county prosecutor, Voelker had a front row seat to both human nature and UP culture. Frequently struck with poverty and hard times, UP residents are known for a stubborn, no-nonsense approach to life. This made the job of prosecuting attorney difficult but not without its amusements.

> *During my time as prosecutor—in court and out—I have met scores of these unrepressed personalities whom we call local characters. What these sturdy souls contribute to the color and zest of daily existence cannot be measured. Our small towns are glutted with them. I would not have it otherwise. Sometimes I suspect I am getting to be a character myself...* (Traver 1943:151-152)

After his 1950 political defeat, Voelker returned to private practice, where he was retained as defense lawyer in the case of *People v. Peterson*. Peterson, an army lieutenant, was accused of murdering Mike Chenoweth over the rape of Peterson's wife. The defense entered a plea of insanity, and Peterson was acquitted on the basis of "irresistible impulse" (also known as "dissociative reaction"). It was this case that formed the basis for author Voelker/Traver's next book. *Anatomy of a Murder* (1957) became a best seller and was subsequently made into an Academy Award-nominated movie directed by Otto Preminger and starring Jimmy Stewart, Lee Remick, George C. Scott, Ben Gazzara, and Eve Arden.

Materials and evidence relating to the case and book—including legal files, photographs, court transcripts, and literary drafts—comprise a significant part of the Voelker Papers. The Voelker exhibit also has artifacts relating to the case, including the murder weapon (a German Luger) and bullets recovered from the deceased.

A SENSE OF PLACE: MICHIGAN'S UPPER PENINSULA

Lieutenant Coleman Peterson, Attorney John Voelker, Charlotte Peterson, and "George," 1952. The Peterson case was the one upon which Anatomy of a Murder *was based. "George" carried the flashlight which helped lead Mrs. Peterson back to her trailer the night she was attacked and raped.*
(Reprint courtesy of the Northern Michigan University Archives.)

Research Collections: The Voelker Papers

Anatomy of a Murder became the first major motion picture to be filmed entirely on location. All production work except film processing was done within the Marquette area. This included scenes taken at the county courthouse, the Big Bay Inn, and the Voelker family home in Ishpeming. Movie personnel were soon initiated into local traditions and UP culture. Cast and crew were introduced to Marquette County citizens at the 1959 Suicide Hill Ski Tournament in Ishpeming by Governor G. Mennen Williams. Stars and cast also partook of a local meal, the Cornish meat and potato pie known as the pasty.

Michigan's strong labor tradition became apparent with a dispute over the salary to be paid movie extras. Several local extras quit when the production company stuck to its original salary figure. According to James Merrick, public relations official for Carlyle Productions, it was the first time anything like it had ever happened. Robert E. Anderson, an unemployed iron miner, stated that he received more money from unemployment compensation than he earned in one week as an extra ("Filming of *Anatomy* Resumes..." 1959).

Filming brought changes to the area. The Marquette County Courthouse received a new coat of paint, and the Big Bay Inn received a name change to "Thunder Bay Inn" and a $25,000 building addition, compliments of Hollywood ("Big Bay Citizens..." circa 1959). The Thunder Bay Inn kept its new name (and its free building addition), and, until recently, the bullet holes made by Lieutenant Peterson's gun remained visible. Although the bullet holes are no longer available for viewing, other movie landmarks still exist, including movie stars' signatures on the walls of the Roosevelt Bar in Ishpeming and footprints on a downtown Marquette sidewalk. Wall removal in Voelker's Ishpeming boyhood home was also proposed to facilitate filming. This was one change that did not occur, when a relieved Voelker discovered that he was the victim of a filming crew joke (*"Anatomy* Brings Out Best..." circa 1959).

Movie filming and production were given in-depth coverage by the *Mining Journal* (Marquette's local newspaper), as scarcely a day went by without a front-page report on movie activities. In fact, one reporter was led to comment that "... nothing so exciting has happened in Upper Michigan since Paul Bunyan and his blue ox, Babe, strode through the country" (McIntyre circa 1959). These articles, clipped and saved by Mrs. Voelker, were put into scrapbooks which contain both personal and movie clippings that accumulated during the filming. Scrapbooks as well as several folders of additional clippings and correspondence relating to the movie and friendships which grew out of its making are also a part of the Voelker Papers.

A Sense of Place: Michigan's Upper Peninsula

John and Grace Voelker, and Mrs. Voelker's father, arrive for the Ishpeming, Michigan premiere of Otto Preminger's movie, Anatomy of a Murder. The local premiere was held on Voelker's birthday, June 29, 1959 with the world premiere held three days later in Detroit. (Reprint courtesy of the Northern Michigan University Archives.)

RESEARCH COLLECTIONS: THE VOELKER PAPERS

After five years of hard work, Voelker's perseverance as an author had paid off with success for both the *Anatomy* novel and movie. Good fortune also touched his legal career. In 1958, he was appointed Michigan Supreme Court Justice to fill a vacancy. He then successfully ran for the open position, serving only one year, at which point he retired, stating, "While there are doubtless many others who in my place can write my opinions, for better or worse I'm afraid there are none who can write my books" (Voelker letter to G. Mennen Williams 1959).

Any discussion of John Voelker would be incomplete without mentioning trout. Fishing was a central part of Voelker's life and image. Today, fishing fans come to the Archives to study Voelker's personal journals searching for clues to identify his favorite fishing holes. During his lifetime, fans would write inviting Voelker to fish their favorite spots or, better yet, ask to visit him at Frenchman's Pond, his fishing sanctuary. In fact, this correspondence often tells its own story or illustrates aspects of Voelker's personality and character. This is poignantly so with the unfolding of a friendship that developed between Voelker and a young boy. The boy's father wrote telling Voelker of his son's admiration and asking if it might be possible for them to fish together. Voelker agreed, and the two continued to fish and correspond with each other as the boy grew, went to college, and earned a law degree (Steve Williams Correspondence).

Voelker's passion for fishing permeates his writing, but three of his books (*Trout Madness*, *Anatomy of a Fisherman*, and *Trout Magic*) focus on his adventures with trout. First appearing in *Anatomy of a Fisherman* is Voelker's now-famous essay, "Testament of a Fisherman."

> *I fish because I love to; because I love the environs where trout are found, which are invariably beautiful, and hate the environs where crowds of people are found, which are invariably ugly....* (Traver 1965:10)

Voelker wrote in the winter and fished in the summer. He once remarked that if he had been able to fish for trout in the UP all year, "I would have never written eleven books" (Franklin 1988:4). Ironically, Voelker could not swim well and so rarely waded into fast moving streams and rivers, preferring instead "some quiet brookie pond or isolated beaver flowage... and a fishing platform" (Nault 1990:69).

Voelker's unique personality followed him into the woods. As a matter of fact, it was the only thing that could follow him. When he ventured out to fish or hunt for morel mushrooms, he often parked up to two miles away from the actual location and swept away any tracks that he might have left. (He carried a broom as an essential piece of equipment.) He also used special codes: "The birch buds are as big as squirrel ears" meant that it was time for morels (Noble 1967:12), and opening day of trout season he called "Christmas."

Voelker's interests in nature and the environment suggest specialization areas for the Archives. The Archives intends to focus its collecting efforts on tourism, recreation, natural resource management, environmentalism, economic development, and the arts. Although Voelker had strong feelings for conservation, in later years he felt that he was too old to take an active role. He received many requests for assistance but often declined:

> ... I do not want to get on the political or environmental barricades at this time in my life. I'm damn near 70, I've been fighting bastards all my life, so I think maybe that by now I may be permitted to fish in peace ... I am for what I think you are trying to do but I do not want to get involved. Give 'em Hell—but please let me be. (Voelker Letter to organization, ca. 1972)

Voelker's concern for conservation caused him to be apprehensive about the construction of the Mackinac Bridge that links upper and lower Michigan. Correspondence indicates his concern for the fate of the UP and its environment with bridge construction and use. In his efforts to form a society to "Bomb the Bridge" he wrote:

> One factor in Michigan's favor is that the very inhospitality of the UP to diversified industry is probably a blessing to conservation. That is why I am tempted to form a society to bomb the new bridge. I shudder to think of the stampeding new downstate hordes poised to pour in upon our woods and streams. I only hope that they might be like the average tourist, who would not venture ten yards from the main road to save his life, let alone evacuate his bowels. (Voelker Letter to Leonard, 1955)

Voelker corresponded with several well known and noteworthy people. Former CBS correspondent Charles Kuralt was one. It was he who stated:

> John was really about the nearest thing to a great man I've ever known. He changed my life directly. I was so enchanted by his fly fishing, especially the way he did it, I took up the pursuit myself and have become an enthusiastic fisherman. (Frank 1991:n.p.)

Other notables included film producer Otto Preminger, Boston attorney Joseph N. Welch (Army-McCarthy Hearings, 1954), United States Appellate Court Justice Damon Keith, and fellow UP writer Charles Van Riper (also known as Cully Gage).

Research Collections: The Voelker Papers

Abandoned logging camp located in the Dead River Basin, Marquette County, Michigan, no date. This camp became "Hungry Hollow," the setting of Traver's second book, Danny and the Boys.
(Reprint courtesy of the Northern Michigan University Archives.)

A Sense of Place: Michigan's Upper Peninsula

Although the Voelker Papers are still being archivally processed and organized, patrons have already made use of the materials. In response to patron need, the Archives does allow use of those materials which have been preliminarily sorted. This means that the papers have been initially viewed and have had necessary preservation work done. During the preliminary sort, the papers are also placed in tentative record subseries and folders. To date, researchers have included people conducting background research for movie ventures, professors looking to augment their Michigan author lectures, fishing buddies interested in reliving their adventures, fishing fans in search of secret spots, and fans of the *Anatomy* movie searching for movie trivia. Archivist presentations to university classes and the general public have also focused on the Voelker Papers. In one English graduate seminar, the Archivist was able to use the Voelker Papers to illustrate a lecture on archival collecting and processing procedures.

Once processed, the Voelker Papers will be available to support diverse research interests. The collection should prove invaluable for a variety of research pursuits, including Voelker biographical work, UP topics such as environmentalism, culture and folklore, area or local history, legal court proceedings, and Voelker's literary works. Projected processing completion date is anticipated to be in 1997. Upon completion, a guide to the collection will be published.

In conclusion, the Voelker Collection has given both the archives and museum efforts of the university a necessary boost in development. University commitment to the Archives increased once Grace Voelker donated the collection. With the Voelker artifact collection, key impetus was given to the university's efforts to establish a campus museum, based largely on the success of the Voelker exhibit.

University support of the archival program continues due in part to its recognized responsibility to the Voelker Papers, now a vital part of the University Archives collection. The Voelker Papers have suggested subject directions for archival collecting efforts and have provided the Archives its first major collection in those subject areas.

While it is true that the collection has taken resources and staff time away from necessary archival establishment steps, it has also given the Archives an impressive collection with its own set of immediate patrons. Use of and interest in the John D. Voelker Papers promotes the visibility of the Archives and further enhances the legendary status of John Voelker in Michigan's Upper Peninsula.

Research Collections: The Voelker Papers

BIBLIOGRAPHY

"*Anatomy* Brings Out Best In Prize-Winning Cameraman." ca. 1959. Newsclipping in Movie Scrapbook, 1959. John D. Voelker Papers. Northern Michigan University Archives.

Anatomy of an Author. 1982. Produced by Sue Marx and Directed by Robert Handley. 19 min. Little Red Filmhouse. Videocassette.

"Big Bay Citizens Will Remember Hollywood Visit." ca. 1959. Newsclipping in Movie Scrapbook, 1959. John D. Voelker Papers. Northern Michigan University Archives.

"Filming of *Anatomy* Resumes After Dispute Over Pay for Extras." *Mining Journal* (Marquette, Mich.), March 1950.

Frank, Jennifer E. 1991. "John Voelker: Fisherman Author and Jurist." *Lansing State Journal.* March 20.

Franklin, Dixie. 1988. "Ever the Fisherman." *Michigan Natural Resources Magazine.* 57(2): 4–13.

McIntyre, Dave. ca. 1959. Character Actor in *Anatomy* Tells Impression of UP Newsclipping in Movie Scrapbook, 1959. John D. Voelker Papers. Northern Michigan University Archives.

Nault, Bill. 1990. "A Day to Remember: Fishing with Two of the Nation's Most Celebrated Anglers Was a Heady Experience." *Michigan Out-of-Doors.* 44(2): 66–69.

Noble, William T. 1967. "Voelker: An Anatomy of a Private Life." *Detroit News Sunday Magazine.* June 18: 12–14, 32–35.

Thundy, Zacharias. (n.d.) *Dialect Markers in the Upper Peninsula of Michigan.*

Typescript in the Stewart A. Kingsbury Papers. Northern Michigan University Archives.

Traver, Robert. 1943. *Troubleshooter.* Viking Press.

Traver, Robert. 1964. "Testament of a Fisherman." In Robert Traver, *Anatomy of a Fisherman.* McGraw-Hill. 10.

VanderVeen, Richard III. 1983. "Michigan Profiles: John Donaldson Voelker." *Michigan History Magazine.* (March/April): 46–47.

Voelker, John D. Letter to Dr. Justin W. Leonard, March 28, 1955. "Trout Season, 1955" Folder in Correspondence Series. John D. Voelker Papers. Northern Michigan University.

Voelker, John D. Letter to G. Mennen Williams, Nov. 17, 1959. "Resignation from the Supreme Court" Folder in Correspondence Series. John D. Voelker Papers. Northern Michigan University Archives.

Voelker, John D. Letter to unidentified organization, ca. 1972. Unprocessed Correspondence Files. John D. Voelker Papers. Northern Michigan University Archives.

Williams, Steve, Correspondence (Unprocessed). John D. Voelker Papers. Northern Michigan University Archives.

A Sense of Place

Education

Glenn T. Seaborg

Education for the 21st Century

Glenn T. Seaborg

There is ample evidence that the warning given in 1983 by the National Commission on Excellence in Education, on which I served, is as timely today as it was in 1983. For the sake of our national security and the future of our nation we must take heed. Our report, "A Nation At Risk," opened with these lines:

> *Our nation is at risk. Our once unchallenged preeminence in commerce, industry, science and technological innovation is being overtaken by competitors throughout the world ... the educational foundations of our society are presently being eroded by a rising tide of mediocrity that threatens our very future as a nation and as a people. What was unimaginable a generation ago has begun to occur—others are matching and surpassing our educational attainments.*
>
> *If an unfriendly foreign power had attempted to impose on America the mediocre educational performance that exists today, we might well have viewed it as an act of war. As it stands, we have allowed this to happen to ourselves ... We have, in effect, been committing an act of unthinking, unilateral educational disarmament.*

We all recognize that we live in a rapidly changing, increasingly high-technology world. I have characterized our present age as that of the Third Revolution. The Revolution of Independence gave birth to our nation and established the democratic principles on which our classical concept of equality of opportunity—largely through education—is based. The Industrial Revolution rewarded the American spirit of inventiveness and made us leaders in the world's economy, blessed with an extremely high standard of living. The Third Revolution, the Revolution of Science, has already transformed how we understand our world—through the remarkable expansion of knowledge in a few decades—and is radically altering almost every aspect of our lives. Our response to the challenges of the revolution in science will, quite simply, decide our future. Our most valuable resources are our intelligence and ingenuity. As a nation, we pride ourselves on our history of pioneering new technologies; in the future much will depend not only on that capacity for innovation but also on our general preparedness to participate in the practice and production of those technological advances. The strength of our technological and scientific enterprise will determine our economic well-being, our security and our health and safety.

Science plays a central role in the world of today. Research in basic science leads to advances in applied science and then to widespread practical applications of this acquired knowledge in the derived technology. Incremental scientific advances, as well as major discoveries, result in new technologies of great commercial importance. They can give us entire new industries, as in the case of advances in molecular biology. They can give us whole new ranges of products, as in the case of polymer chemistry. They can revolutionize other technologies and industries, as has been the case for the transistor and the laser.

Basic research leads to the creation of not only new products but also new industrial processes and manufacturing systems. These can greatly increase industrial productivity, reduce costs, and improve the quality of products. For example, advances in microelectronics are aiding the production of automobiles, steel, and many other manufactured goods. Discoveries in biology are influencing the processing and production of pharmaceuticals, foods, and chemicals.

This country cannot afford another generation of students that is ill prepared to respond to the worldwide rapid growth of scientific knowledge and technological power. The nation's future depends on its students.

We must improve general science education for all of our young people (and not only for those who plan to continue their education and become professional scientists, mathematicians or engineers), because we need a large number of scientifically literate, nonprofessional workers with the understanding and skills to manufacture, operate, and repair increasingly complex technological equipment. Future employment opportunities, necessary to replace jobs lost in our declining "smokestack industries," will be in areas requiring technical sophistication and will depend on a workforce endowed with a practice in learning and the flexibility of mind to adapt to a society constantly changing. The old concept of a replaceable worker standing in a production line and doing one thing over and over is obsolete. The workplace demands workers who understand the automated equipment that they use and who can adjust and repair it. They must understand and apply the statistics of quality control and make decisions which require knowledge and judgment. The definition of "basic skills" is changing to include such areas as critical thinking, problem-solving, decision-making, reasoning, teamwork, adaptability, and computer literacy.

We must actively recruit young people from what have been traditionally underrepresented populations—women and minorities.

EDUCATION: FOR THE 21ST CENTURY

Workforce 2000 reported that "White males, thought of only a generation ago as the mainstays of the economy, will comprise only 15 percent of the net addition to the labor force between 1985 and 2000." Nationwide, in 1985, one in five eighteen year olds was African American or Hispanic; in 2010 the ratio will be one in three. As of 1995, minority enrollment in K–12 schools was nearly 59 percent in California alone.

In addition to the need for trained scientists, mathematicians and engineers, and nonprofessional workers with an understanding of complex technological equipment, we need widespread understanding of science among the general population. Support of the critical need for scientific literacy is best expressed by Thomas Jefferson's famous dictum, often quoted and still profoundly true:

> *I know of no safe depository of the ultimate powers of society but the people themselves; and if we think them not enlightened enough to exercise their control with a wholesome discretion, the remedy is not to take it from them but to inform their discretion.*

The vitality of a democracy assumes a certain core of knowledge shared by everyone which serves as a unifying force. I think that the most horrifying example I have heard is that in one survey of adult Americans, only 45 percent—fewer than half—knew whether the Earth travels around the sun or the sun around the Earth! How basic a lack of understanding of the Universe in which we live is this! And these same people will make judgments on the issue of global warming and the commitment our nation will make to solving this potentially disastrous problem? Thirty-six percent of the adults in the same survey believed that boiling radioactive milk would make it safe! Citizens who do not know what radiation is are being asked to judge nuclear power, and citizens who know no chemistry are making decisions about toxic waste. It is fundamental to the effectiveness of our democratic system that our citizens be able to make informed judgments on the more and more complex issues of scientific and technological public policy. Decisions must be made which are of critical importance to our health and safety.

There can be no doubt that scientific literacy, a solid understanding of science and mathematics, is now more important than ever before—and there is irrefutable evidence that the skills of our youth not only are not progressing with the increasing demands but actually are deteriorating at an alarming rate. While our nation's needs for both an educated citizenry and a technologically trained workforce have grown by leaps and bounds, our ability to satisfy those needs has diminished. We must act now to reverse the self-destructive trend.

A SENSE OF PLACE: MICHIGAN'S UPPER PENINSULA

We all have an important stake in the success of our education system, and every part of our society must be involved in meeting the challenge. Education is an investment, not an expense. The Committee for Economic Development reports that each year's class of dropouts costs the nation about $240 billion in crime, welfare, health care, and services. For every dollar spent on education, it costs nine dollars to provide services to dropouts. For example, about 80 percent of all prison inmates are school dropouts, and each inmate costs the nation about $28,000 annually.

There is good news, however. Trends in Scholastic Achievement Test (SAT) scores are not universally discouraging. One positive trend is the narrowing of the gap between minority and non-minority students. Between 1989 and 1995, scores of Mexican-American students rose sixteen points on the verbal and twenty points on the mathematics portions of the SAT. Native American student scores increased nineteen points across the board. African-Americans and Asians also showed gains.

Nationwide, many proposals and programs have been developed by people committed to improving the quality of education in this country and the future prospects of our youth and of our economy.

In September 1989, governors from almost every state in the Union attended the summit conference convened by President Bush in Charlottesville, Virginia. Goal Number Four of the five National Education Goals established at that time relates directly to mathematics and science education: "By the year 2000 United States students will be first in the world in science and mathematics education."

However, the problem we face was illustrated by the report a few years ago of the Committee on Education and Human Resources of the Federal Coordinating Council for Science, Engineering and Technology (FCCSET). This report recommended that we should increase the supply of well-trained science and mathematics teachers. Half of the newly employed teachers of mathematics, science, and English are not qualified to teach these subjects, and fewer than one-third of United States schools have qualified physics teachers. In part as a result of this, 30 percent of our high schools offer no courses in physics, 17 percent offer none in chemistry and 70 percent offer none in earth or space science.

According to the FCCSET Committee report,

> *In the United States today there are 2.3 million public school teachers in grades K–12. The Department of Education estimates that over the next decade we must hire 1.6 million new teachers, or*

an average of 160,000 teachers a year. Yet our primary source of new teachers, college students majoring in education, has fallen 55 percent since 1972. Today we are graduating only about half the teachers we will need to bridge the gap in the future. If it is becoming difficult to recruit teachers, it is even harder to retain them. Twenty percent of new teachers leave during their first year, and more than half leave before the sixth year. We are currently losing thirteen mathematics and science teachers for each one entering the profession.

The task of guiding the intellectual (and often social) development of our young is an all-important one. We must begin to recognize teachers' contributions not only by adequately compensating them for their service, but also by giving them due respect which would motivate them to refine their skills and expand their knowledge to meet future challenges. There are a number of vital new programs and proposals which address this need.

There are many interesting new curriculum development projects. Among the most fascinating to me is an initiative by the American Association for the Advancement of Science (AAAS), Project 2061 (so named to make clear its goal of revolutionizing the teaching of science by the next arrival of Halley's Comet). Its first report, *Science for All Americans* (1989), makes fascinating reading: It represents Phase I (Goals) of the project by attempting to define what basic core of science knowledge should be included in the education of all young Americans. Phase II (Formulation) makes recommendations on new science curricula, instructional materials, testing methods, teacher training, school organization, and educational research and development programs. Phase III (Implementation) will probably take a good deal longer to accomplish, but Project 2061 is well on its way. The project has translated the science literacy goals outlined in its first report into a curriculum design tool, published as *Benchmarks for Science Literacy,* that establishes learning goals for the ends of grades two, five, eight, and twelve. Also in the works are a number of tools to help educators improve their curriculum, improve their own science literacy and effect change in the K–12 education system. Project 2061 plans to merge all of these tools into an interactive multimedia tool to design curricula and serve as a resource.

I would like to conclude by emphasizing the important role that science centers can play in changing the face of education in our country. I will use Northern Michigan University's Glenn T. Seaborg Center for Teaching and Learning Science and Mathematics as an example.

A SENSE OF PLACE: MICHIGAN'S UPPER PENINSULA

The Glenn T. Seaborg Center is an institution committed to enriching the knowledge and understanding of science and mathematics in the general public, particularly students and teachers from preschool through college, in the Upper Peninsula, in the State of Michigan, and beyond. For over a decade the Seaborg Center has dedicated its resources as part of Northern Michigan University to the continuing battle against educational mediocrity.

The Seaborg Center was conceived in the 1980s and became a reality in 1986. As a dynamic educational agency, the Seaborg Center continues today to focus its efforts on three main objectives:

1. To improve the quality of mathematics and science instruction for the benefit of pre-collegiate students through the development of innovative mathematics and science courses and accompanying curriculum materials and teacher training services;

2. To augment the mathematics and science instruction provided by our schools, offering special mathematics and science courses at the Seaborg Center; and

3. To enhance the knowledge, appreciation, and enjoyment of mathematics and science for the general public by providing the community with a mathematics and science center.

The Center has a unique opportunity to demonstrate to all citizens that persons from diverse geographic regions can excel and contribute to the scientific future of our country and the world. The Center is committed to working collaboratively with other agencies to deliver their services efficiently and effectively to all users throughout the Upper Peninsula.

I would like to describe a few of the many programs available through the Center.

The Seaborg Center is a member of the **Michigan Mathematics and Science Centers Network**. These Centers are founded by the state legislature under a statewide plan approved by the Michigan State Board of Education in 1993, and the Seaborg Center became a member of the network the following year. The network supports the efficient coordination of programs and services that benefit schools throughout Michigan. The directors of the centers work cooperatively toward their common goal of improving science and mathematics education in Michigan.

At present, local and intermediate school districts view the centers as essential partners in systematic reform and school improvement. In addition, the centers are a primary vehicle for institutionalizing

EDUCATION: FOR THE 21ST CENTURY

the Michigan Statewide Systemic Initiative, a ten-million-dollar, five-year grant awarded by the National Science Foundation to the State of Michigan in the fall of 1992.

All the centers provide constituent services in six important areas:

* **Leadership** with respect to national and state goals, a shared vision for improving mathematics and science education, and the overall improvement of teaching and learning;

* **Student Services** that improve and enhance mathematics and science education for all K–12 students;

* **Professional Development** that is based on local needs and current research, that is both sequential and systemic, and that strengthens teaching practices;

* **Curriculum support** to develop local curricula incorporating research in teaching and learning as well as national and state recommended standards;

* **Community Involvement** to increase awareness, nurture ownership and leverage resources for innovative, progressive and bold programming in education; and

* **Resource Clearinghouse Services** for collecting and disseminating information, materials and human resources related to science and mathematics.

To meet the State's as well as its own goals, the Seaborg Center provides a broad range of services:

* **The Seaborg Center Fall Conference** brings hundreds of educators annually from throughout the Midwest to hear presenters cover subjects from art to zoology, with topics in mathematics, science, and technology well represented.

* **Graduate Education:** The Seaborg Center, the only Michigan center housing a graduate degree program, is the coordinating department for the university's Master's degree programs in mathematics education and science education. Much of the course work for these two programs is offered in the summer to allow in-service teachers to upgrade their professional levels through intensive summer work and thesis development.

    In addition, each summer the Seaborg Center sponsors credit-conferring courses and workshops in mathematics, the sciences and technology. These supplemental courses are aimed primarily at regional in-service teachers.

- **Applied Academics** has gained a major place in our schools as employers seek applicants with an experience of real-world problems and a background in how to use teamwork approaches to arrive at practical solutions. Through dialogue meetings and new course work, the Seaborg Center brings together interested educators to share ideas and promote initiatives in this field.

- **The Resource Room** is a lending library and work area for teachers and students and the Center's most-used service. The available materials include textbooks, teachers' manuals, classroom manipulatives, and teaching modules. The Resource Room also offers a set of computer work stations on line with the university network and the vast resources of the Internet.

- **The NASA Regional Educators' Resource Center** at the Seaborg Center houses a collection of NASA teaching materials, lesson plans, videos, and posters for distribution to teachers on request. NASA cites the Seaborg Center's collection as one of its best.

As a central part of its mission, the Seaborg Center also offers a full range of programs directly to pre-college students.

- **College for Kids** is a summer program sponsored by the Center. It consists of a series of one-week day sessions for pre-college students. Participants are involved in such exciting, hands-on learning activities as archæology, geology, herpetology, mathematical problem solving, and rocketry.

- **Activity Nights** are special two-hour evening activities for elementary and middle-school students, parents, and teachers. Interested faculty and community members provide hands-on activities as varied as the physics of toys, static electricity, mathematics puzzles, dissecting animal brains, and paper making.

- **Science Olympiad:** the Seaborg Center annually hosts the Upper Peninsula Regional Science Olympiad competition. Middle and high school teams compete in mid-March in a series of science- and mathematics-related events that test ingenuity and critical thinking. Winning teams go on to the Michigan state competition in Lansing.

- **Native American Summer Program:** a two-week residential program held in August which brings fifty Native American middle school students to the campus to help promote future college enrollment.

EDUCATION: FOR THE 21ST CENTURY

* **The Upward Bound Regional Science and Mathematics Center** gives eligible high school students from the Great Lakes states a chance to try college at Northern Michigan University. Each summer, this Seaborg Center-operated program accepts qualified students for six weeks of challenging work in science and mathematics.

* **ASPIRES** is a program offered by the Center which consists of a set of one-hour after-school activities on the campus for students to work with computers or experience some facet of mathematics or science normally unavailable in their classrooms.

* **The Seaborg Summer Academy** provides science and mathematics enrichment for high school students in a college residential setting. One to two weeks in length, the program immerses students in hands-on science and mathematics as they work in university classrooms and labs.

This will give you some idea of the range of services we can make available even to areas as isolated as the Upper Peninsula.

We must work together, employing our considerable resources, to ensure a prosperous future. Whatever the expense of improving science and mathematics education, this is an investment in the future we must make. Excellence is costly. But in the long run, mediocrity costs far more.

A Sense of Place

William & Margery Vandament

A Sense of Place: Michigan's Upper Peninsula

William E. Vandament

WILLIAM E. VANDAMENT
Introduction as Commencement Speaker December 14, 1996
Robert "Buzz" Berube

Members of the Class of 1996, family, friends, faculty, and staff.

When I was asked a few days ago to introduce Dr. Bill Vandament as your commencement speaker, I immediately had an anxiety attack accompanied by leg and lip tremors, a dry mouth and copious sweating. Once I'm able to get over this—which should be in about five minutes—I should be okay!

This introduction is usually done by the Northern Michigan University President, and the only reason we're breaking the tradition today is that NMU's President is the commencement speaker and probably too humble to introduce himself—though that may have been an interesting introduction to hear.

I'm sure each of you has a few heroes—someone you respect or have high regard for—someone you strive to be more like—or someone you'll always listen to for their sage advice. President Bill Vandament is one of my heroes.

He was educated at Illinois's Quincy College and at Southern Illinois University and received a Master's Degree and Ph.D. in psychology from the University of Massachusetts. His distinguished career in higher education led him to the State University of New York at Binghamton, to New York University, to Ohio State University, to the California State University system, and finally to NMU.

He is a native of Hannibal, Missouri, which may explain the similarities between President Bill and Mark Twain, especially his sense of humor—I can't explain his obvious physical similarities to old St. Nick but maybe he can!

I met President Bill in 1991 when he arrived in Marquette with his delightful partner Marge; and, as they say, the rest is history.

President Bill agreed to be our interim president for one year; now he will have stayed six years when his presidency finishes. Along the way he has changed this University significantly. He demands only that we offer a quality education to each and every student at the lowest tuition possible—Last year, as you know, there was no tuition increase! At the same time he insists upon fair pay and benefits for all faculty and staff.

His open and inclusive style of management has allowed our university community to both understand and assume ownership of the problems and successes of this University. This has allowed all of us to use our collective talents to bring this University to the successful position in higher education it enjoys today.

President Bill is the friend we all like to have: He is perceptive, imaginative, hardworking, honest and bright—all this and his legendary *sense of humor!*

I have to share this story with you—about two years ago this university had to cut 2.3 million dollars from its budget to maintain our current tuition levels. Bill—along with faculty, staff, and students—worked hard and made many sacrifices to achieve this goal, and it was painful. Soon afterward the presidential assessment committee met with Bill to discuss his salary. We were paying him as an interim—he was *our* president and the lowest paid University president in the State. Even a $20,000 per year raise would still have left him the lowest paid University president in the state. We made him a reasonable offer, but he flatly refused any raise at all because "the University can't afford it fiscally." As a good committee will do, we reluctantly accepted Bill's advice and we gave him *no* raise.

Our next agenda item concerned extending his contract for two more years. Of course when we suggested this to him, he responded, "Two more years—what—with how little you pay me?"

Dr. W. Ann Reynolds, President of City University of New York, referred to Dr. Vandament as "this quiet, unassuming genius."

I might add the he is worthy of our respect, praise and thanks—maybe even our hero worship.

I would like to present to you—your commencement speaker—the man Marge Vandament allowed to come to Northern Michigan University, a darned good jazz trumpet player and one of my heroes, the president of Northern Michigan University: Dr. Bill Vandament.

WILLIAM E. VANDAMENT
Commencement Address: December 14, 1996

Thank you very much, Dr. Berube, and thanks also to the Board of Control for this generous invitation. I am particularly pleased to speak to you, the graduating class in the fall of 1996. Because Margie and I entered as freshmen at about the same time as most of you, I consider us to be classmates. Some of you have been on the four-year plan, others on a five-, six-, or even seven-year schedule for graduation. I am, of course, on the six-year plan and hope to graduate to retirement in the summer of 1997.

Like some of you, Margie and I didn't intend to be here this long. But we enjoyed ourselves so much that we decided to stay. We hope that your years at NMU have been happy ones as well.

Let me share some of the memories that I have of the last five and a half years. Like you, I was somewhat nervous at first, especially when I heard about an arsenal for student weapons. I had never been at a university that had an arsenal! Then I learned we even had rules about how to carry bows and arrows on campus. Whew! I had not yet learned about the biggest holiday of the year—the opening day of firearm deer season.

We've been through some tough times together, but we have survived.

I remember particularly the winter of 1994–95. With temperatures of minus thirty degrees—in fact, minus seventy degrees with the wind chill factor, we set records that year; but we only missed a couple of days of school. Right?

And what about the winter of 1995–96? Here we had a record snowfall, but that only slowed us down. It did not stop us.

I have vivid memories of many of you trudging through snow to class and to other events on campus. In fact, you students were an inspiration to some of us older folks. You will little realize how your cheerful faces lifted our spirits in the dead of winter or during the long wait for spring. The memory of a smile and a wave from a bundled up NMU student will be with me always.

We faced some hard economic times during the past few years as well. The University had to cut its budgets several times but did try to do it in ways that did not compromise your studies.

Changes in Federal financial aid also cut the Pell Grants to many of you. And so, some of you have had to rely more and more on loans and outside work in order to finish your education. I think those changes have been shortsighted on the part of our Federal officials and people who are concerned only about their personal taxes. More than ever, our country needs an educated population. You have not just benefited *yourselves* by working so hard for a college education; the skills that you have developed will make our country a better place. The investment that the people of Michigan have made in your education has been for the common good. I hope that you will remember that as your income rises in the future. I hope we can count on you to become strong supporters of education for our public betterment.

But you have persevered. And I swear to you that some things at Northern have gotten better while you were here. Let's take parking, for example. Do you realize that we've added 534 additional spaces in the center of campus during your stay here? When I retire, I will probably be known as the university president who loved asphalt. And what about the good ol' Cohodas shuffle? I know I'll never get you to admit it, but the lines are actually shorter now than they were when you came here. You know, things have gotten so peaceful at registration time that last year we took the bulletproof windows out of the cashier's office. Be fair, gang. We're trying.

Well, enough small talk. At a commencement you are supposed to receive a serious lecture. So I will now deliver a short one. But put away the notebooks; this material will not be on the final exam.

I am going to talk about learning to learn, which is why you went to college. There is a simple rule I will repeat often during this review: You *have to know something to learn something.*

Actually, there is much about memory that seems paradoxical. On the one hand, we all know that new information can be elusive— that if we try to take in too much new information at once, we can become confused and actually learn very little. At the same time, we each possess a large file of information that suggests our memories are almost inexhaustible.

Just think of all the facts that you have stored away: the names of all fifty states and many of their capitols, the names and physical characteristics of hundreds of relatives and acquaintances, the names of many professional athletes and their achievements, the melodies and the lyrics of many popular songs, even the birth dates of your closest relatives. The list goes on and on.

William E. Vandament: Commencement Address

Often, you know things that you don't even know you know. Those are things you recall only when prompted by an appropriate clue—and you say, "I knew that." When you think about it, a human being's capacity for memory is truly amazing—almost infinite.

But acquiring *new* information can be a fragile process. Much of the information available in the world around us simply sails right by without our ever recording it. In short, learning new things involves several stages, during which information can become lost and inaccessible to us.

Let's take a look at some of those stages.

First, we'll note that most information in a changing environment is recorded on our senses for only a brief instant. As you sit here today your eyes are taking in a multitude of rapidly changing images; and you are hearing a variety of sounds, sensing many things in the environment such as temperature, humidity, and maybe backside sensations that are unpleasant because you have been sitting so long. For those parts of the environment that change rapidly you will retain most of these sensations only for about a half a second. I repeat: Most sensations stay with you for only half a second and then fade away.

Trust me on this—I don't think you want me to spend a half an hour telling you how I know that. I assure you that it's true.

Look at it this way. If your senses didn't wipe the slate clean very rapidly while the environment was changing, the past and the present would get blurred, and past images or sounds would interfere with new ones. All your visual images would have shadows and the sounds you hear would all have echoes! In short, your senses have been programmed for rapid turnover; otherwise, you'd never be able to keep up with an ever changing world.

So there you are, latching on to some information to give further attention to it, while allowing the rest to evaporate almost literally into thin air. Aside from some information that has biological significance, such as information that tells you that you're hurting or hungry or something like that—you simply do not take note of much of the information bombarding your senses.

What is it that determines which small pieces of information you will hang on to for further attention? Well, in fact, if the new information coming in finds a near match with your previous experiences, you will be more likely to retain it for future processing. If the information does not provide a link to prior experience, you tend to let it pass by.

A Sense of Place: Michigan's Upper Peninsula

Let me provide a simple example of how you can disregard irrelevant information and focus on information that has meaning for you. Imagine yourself at a party, voices buzzing all around you. Suddenly, you hear your name in the distance and immediately pay attention to Sally, who is talking about you. Question: Could you remember anything Sally said before your name? No—obviously your ears were receiving her voice or you would not have heard your name, but you had not retained any of her words until she said something that struck a chord with you—your name.

So, even at this early stage of receiving signals, *you have to know something to learn something.*

Let's talk now about the next stage in retaining information for later recall. The information that stays with you after that first half second moves into an active, short-term process prior to your filing it away for future reference. This is sometimes referred to as the *rehearsal* stage of memory, where one mulls over things. And this rehearsal is important to the process of retaining memories for future use. At this rehearsal stage there are many opportunities for information to get lost. Above all, there is the fact that we can keep track of only a few pieces of unrelated information at any given time.

Here I will note that there seems to be a magical number of seven, plus or minus two, that tells us how much we can keep in our active memory at any given time. The typical telephone number, if you disregard the area code, is seven digits long.

Try a simple experiment today after this program. Choose several series of numbers randomly and ask your friends to repeat these series back to you, varying the length of the series. If you say the numbers in a monotone about one second apart, for example, 4–7–3–2–5, you will find that a series of seven numbers is about all that most people can repeat with accuracy.

With this limited capacity, how then can we later recall thousands of words, sentences, or sometimes even paragraphs? The answer again lies in our past experiences. If, for example, several letters presented to us form a word that we know, we cluster the letters together so that they form merely one piece of information. For example, N–O–R–T–H–E–R–N. (Please forgive the commercial—I couldn't resist it.)

With this kind of clustering, we can remember seven unrelated words as easily as seven unrelated letters. Sometimes, words are presented in phrases or sentences—in other words, in patterns of words that normally go together; and then a whole phrase can become one piece of information to be combined with other bits in our active memory.

Thus, by building on our past learning we now expand our ability to pay attention to larger and larger amounts of information despite the limitations that nature places on us. But what happens in this process if the words that are presented to us are not familiar? If we are unprepared? Well, in the absence of a vocabulary that matches the new situation, we treat each letter as a separate piece of information. If the text or speech is long, we become disorganized and unable to retain information, because we are now dealing with multiple pieces of information rather than the seven pieces that our capacity will allow.

Again, we note that *you have to know something to learn something*.

But beyond this, there is more. Often in learning situations, we are presented with information that is somewhat vague or incomplete. Now, I am certain that our faculty at Northern have always been very clear when they explained things to you. But I can assure you that in real life people can sometimes say things that are not quite logical, and your task will be to interpret what they meant to say rather than what they actually said.

But if we've had enough experience with the subject matter we can fill in the gaps when incomplete information is presented to us. If I were to say "a bird in the hand" and no more, you would all know that I intended to say additionally, "is worth two in the bush." But consider again that you could grasp what the speaker meant *only* if you had the proper experience which helped you fill in the gaps.

Again, *you have to know something to learn something*.

And so the ceremony that we are holding today is called *commencement*. It is called commencement, of course, because it marks not the end of your learning careers but the beginning. While we have focused today on some of the difficulties encountered in learning, there is also a more positive or encouraging lesson to be learned from a study of the way in which our memories work. That lesson can be summarized as follows: The *more you know, the easier it becomes to learn something else.*

Let me assure you that the more you continue to invest in learning about the world, or a job, the easier your efforts to learn will become as you get older. Take it from an old timer, life can get easier if you prepare yourselves while you're young.

A Sense of Place: Michigan's Upper Peninsula

And so I congratulate you today on your achievements. You have made major investments of time, effort, and money to prepare yourselves for the future. Let me assure you those investments have been worthwhile.

You are among a select group of young people in this country. Did you know that less than half of the students who start as freshman actually graduate from college? And the same is true at Northern Michigan University. So if you have friends or family who tweak you about taking five, six or seven years to graduate, you can remind them that less than half the people that you started school with will achieve what you have achieved.

And you are graduating from a premier undergraduate university. In the aggregate, over 90 percent of all your classes have been taught by regular full-time faculty and those faculty nearly all hold the highest degrees that can be earned in their fields. Your faculty and academic departments are well connected with the outside world. I can assure you that our placement rate for graduate and professional schools and for jobs in the workplace is well above that of the typical American university. The majority of programs where specialized accreditation is possible are accredited at NMU. This includes chemistry, speech and hearing, clinical laboratory sciences, social work, music, nursing, technology, and teacher education.

Many of you have taken part in academic enrichment activities such as directed or independent studies, internships, research, cooperative studies or international studies. Several of you have scholarly papers that have been published or presented at professional meetings.

As you will see in the distinguished alumni we have honored today, you are joining a family of Northern Michigan University graduates who have achieved distinction in their fields and maintain close ties to their alma mater. Among the ranks of NMU graduates are a Secretary of the International Monetary Fund, a Chairman of the New York Housing Authority, a U.S. Chairman of the United States Canadian Joint Commission, a President and Publisher of the World Book Encyclopedia, a President of the Airline Pilots Association, a toxicologist who contributed to the Salk polio vaccine, and a United States Navy Surgeon General. You have every right to be proud of your achievements and of your alma mater.

I will close now with an Invocation given by the Reverend Henry Channing, Chaplain of the U.S. House of Representatives, spoken over a hundred years ago:

WILLIAM E. VANDAMENT: COMMENCEMENT ADDRESS

To live content with small means;
To seek elegance rather than fashion;
And refinement rather than fashion;

To be worthy, not respectable,
And wealthy, not rich;

To study hard, think quietly,
Talk gently, act frankly;

To listen to the stars and birds,
To babes and sages, with open heart;

To bear all cheerfully,
Do all bravely,
Await occasions,
Hurry never,

In a word, to let the spiritual,
Unbidden and unconscious,
Grow up through the common.

Thank you, congratulations, and all good wishes in the years ahead.

A Sense of Place: Michigan's Upper Peninsula

William E. Vandament
The Wit and Wisdom

Education Policy and Faculty Governance

Nothing of significance should ever be done for the first time.

The academic goal of unlocking nature's secrets is incompatible with the task of designing the curriculum. Mother Nature wouldn't recognize a curriculum if it fell into her nest.

The Board and Other Constituencies

Gaining an education is among the five or six most important things in a student's life.

An important appointment or decision too easily gained will not endure. They'll eventually understand what you've done.

Life in the Bureaucratic Lane

As in Sergeant Preston's Yukon, only the lead dog and the stray get a change of scenery.

In the race between human folly and the development of procedures to control it, human folly is the easy favorite.

The Use and Abuse of Resources

During bountiful times, both the crows and the defenders of the corn crib become more aggressive.

Gift horses consume hay and usually leave exotic trails of their own.

The Administrator's Worst Enemy

The symbols of high office can be an addiction whose satisfaction requires increasingly higher dosages.

Sharing credit, like sharing toys, can make your teeth hurt but allows you to stay in the schoolyard.

Maintaining Perspective

Sic transit gloria mundi. The final test of fame is to have a crazy person imagine he is you.

In a college or university, all you have to work with are people.

A Sense of Place: Michigan's Upper Peninsula

William and Margery Vandament, 1964

William E. Vandament: A Chronology

Personal Data
Margery R. Lampe born	Quincy, Illinois	Feb 16, 1931
William E. Vandament born	Hannibal, Missouri	Sep 6, 1931
William & Margery married		Feb 2, 1952
daughter Jane Louise born		Dec 10, 1952
daughter Lisa Ann born		Apr 2, 1958

Experience

Northern Michigan University   1991–1997
    President and Professor of Psychology

The California State University (Fullerton)   1987–1992
    Trustee Professor and Professor of Psychology

    Project Director and Editor   1983–1987
    Registry of Higher Education Reform

    Provost and Vice Chancellor for Academic Affairs

New York University   1981–1983
    Senior Vice President for Administration

The Ohio State University   1979–1981
    Vice President for Finance and Planning

    Executive Assistant to the President   1976–1979
    Director of Budget and Resources Planning

State University of New York System   1975–1976
    Director of Studies, University Commission on Purposes and Priorities, State University

State University of New York at Binghamton   1969–1972
    Assistant Vice President, Planning/Institutional Research,
    Director, Institutional Research
    University Examiner
    Assistant Professor, Department of Psychology   1964–1969

Other

University of Massachusetts   1961–1964
    National Defense Education Act Fellow, Dept. of Psychology

Bacon Clinic, Racine, Wisconsin   1954–1961
    Psychologist,

Jacksonville State Hospital, Jacksonville, Illinois   1953–1954
    Psychologist

Education

Ph.D., University of Massachusetts (Psychology)   1964
Honors: Sigma Xi Associate (1963), Member (1964), Phi Kappa Phi (1964)

M.S., University of Masschusetts (Psychology)   1963

M.S., Southern Illinois University (Educational Psychology) 1953

B.A., Quincy College, Quincy, Illinois (Psychology)   1952

Recent Activities

Nat'l Center for Higher Education Management Systems
    Board   1985–1988
    Senior Consultant   1989–

Nat'l Assn of College and University Business Officers
    Financial Management Committee   1979–1983
    Chairman   1981-1983.

Middle States Association of Colleges and Universities
    Accreditation teams at Brooklyn College, SUNY-Genesee, Messiah College, University of Maryland, Medical College of Pennsylvania, Inter American University.

Selected Publications

Registry of Higher Education Reform, Volume I (1989). (Editor) Los Angeles: National Center for the Development of Education, 1989.

Managing Money in Higher Education: A Guide to the Financial Process and Effective Participation Within It. San Francisco: Jossey-Bass, 1989.

"Primer for Academic Administrators." *Change,* January/February 1989, 43, 58–59.

"Those Who Would Reform Undergraduate Education Must Recognize the Realities of Academic Governance." The *Chronicle of Higher Education,* November 30, 1988, A52.

"A State University Perspective on Student Outcomes Assessment." In D.F. Halpern (ed.), *Student Outcomes Assessment: What Institutions Stand to Gain.* San Francisco: Jossey-Bass, 1987.

"The Philosophical Imperatives for Educating Minorities." In *Serving the Changing Student Population.* Washington, D.C.: American Association of State Colleges and Universities, 1986.

"The Role of Financial Management in Institutional Administration." In Robert A. Wilson (ed.), *Administering and Managing the Finances of Colleges and Universities*. Tucson: Center for the Study of Higher Education, 1984.

"Generalization and the ISI in Human Eyelid Conditioning," *Psychological Reports*, 1970, 26, 717–718.

"Response Latency as a Function of Interstimulus Interval in Conditioned Eyelid Discrimination," *Journal of Experimental Psychology*, 1969, 82, 516–565.

"Differential Eyelid Conditioning as a Function of CS-UCS Interval and Distance Separating the CSs," *Psychological Reports*, 1969, 25, 407–411.

"Differential Eyelid Conditioning to Stimulus Compounds as a Function of Temporal Relations Between Stimuli," *Psychological Reports*, 1967, 21, 161–168.

---

with Jones, Dennis P. (Editors) *Financial Management: Progress and Challenges*. San Francisco: Jossey-Bass, 1993.

with Crawford, E.M. *Building Stable Support Systems—A Practical Guide*. Washington, D.C.: University Associates, Inc., 1978.

with Burright, R. G., Fessenden, R. R., & Barker, W. H. "Tables of Event Sequences for Sequential Analyses of Data in Psychological Experiments Containing Two Classes of Events," *Behavior Research Methods and Instrumentation*, 1970, 2, 290–296.

with Price, L. E. and Abbott, D. W. "Effects of CS and UCS Change on Extinction of the Conditioned Eyelid Response," *Journal of Experimental Psychology*, 1965, 69, 437–438.

_____. "Effects of Ready Signal Condition on Acquisition and Extinction of the Conditioned Eyelid Response," *Journal of Experimental Psychology*, 1964, 68, 516–518.

with Price, L. E. "Primary Stimulus Generalization Under Different Percentages of Reinforcement in Eyelid Conditioning," *Journal of Experimental Psychology*, 1964, 67, 162–167.

A Sense of Place: Michigan's Upper Peninsula

William and Margery Vandament with daughters Jane (l) and Lisa, 1962

Margery Vandament: A Peripatetic Life

Madonna Marsden

In the film "Groundhog Day," actor Bill Murray portrays a man doomed to live the same day over and over again until he finally gets it right. Agonized by the sheer boredom of repetition, Murray's character changes out of necessity. And by deciding to do things differently, he becomes a sensitive and caring human being.

Since marrying William E. Vandament in Quincy, Illinois on Groundhog Day of 1952, Margery Lampe Vandament has rarely experienced a boring day. She is a naturally caring and sensitive person who has always put the needs of others before her own. And as each anniversary passes, she never awakens to find it cold in Bill's shadow.

As wife of the President of Northern Michigan University, Margery Vandament is often referred to as "The First Lady." She'd rather just be Marge. The formal designation is "A bit grandiose," she says. "I'll leave the title to Hillary."

Is being the President's spouse a job? Is it a ceremonial function?

Marge creases her forehead. "I'm not sure how to define it. It's certainly not a position for which a university advertises. But there are definitely some important roles a President's wife can play."

"I was once asked if I thought the President's spouse should get paid," she continues. "It's an interesting question, and I did know a woman in the position who insisted that she should. She gave so much time to university social activities and fundraising that she did indeed feel she'd taken on a job there."

A knowing smile passes Marge's lips as she unfolds the rest of the story. "The university in question solved the problem by deducting a fair compensation from her husband's paycheck and issuing that amount in her name."

Though never an academic herself, Margery Vandament is savvy to the state politics of higher educational funding. She also knows that there are some jobs which simply require the labor of unselfish volunteers.

The Vandaments have moved eighteen times in the course of their forty-five year marriage. Marge's modesty prevents her from claiming to be an expert at anything except "packing boxes." Yet at each port of call during Bill's academic career voyage, Marge left a definite mark upon the community she inhabited.

While a faculty wife at the State University of New York at Binghamton, Marge busied herself with a number of volunteer activities centered around her two daughters, Jane and Lisa. She was a Girl Scout Leader and lunch mother and remembers that, "I was always the one the teachers counted on to drive on field trips. So many mothers had to work. I felt fortunate that I was able to give my time to my children and their classmates."

While the girls were at school, Marge worked with the League of Women Voters, frequently serving as a poll watcher. She also devoted one afternoon per week to continuing her musical interests. She played violin (an instrument she took up at age ten) with a group of other women each Wednesday. They were always on their way home by three o'clock, anxious to be there when the children returned from school.

Children have been an important part of Marge Vandament's life. But she has a great deal of empathy for women who feel burdened by motherhood. Her eldest sister gave birth to eight children in seventeen years; the other exhausted herself managing a brood of six.

When a Planned Parenthood was proposed in Binghamton, Marge was one of the leaders in making it a reality. She went door to door raising money, helped with the process of hiring staff, served on the Board as Assistant Treasurer, took charge of the volunteer program, and was Girl Friday in the office—answering phones, filing, billing, and doing bookkeeping. Her daughter Jane is currently vice president of that same organization.

When Bill served as Vice President at Ohio State in the late 1970s, Marge's compassion and life experiences once again assisted in filling a community need.

In the early 1950s, the Vandaments had lived in vacated army barracks in Carbondale, Illinois while Bill studied for his Ph.D. at Southern Illinois University. The provided furnishings were a small stove, an ice box (yes, an **ice box**), a space heater, a table and chairs and a cot. On a hundred ten dollars per month (forty-five of which paid the rent), Marge remembers that necessity drove them to invention. A sofa was constructed by commandeering an extra cot and rolling up an extra mattress to serve as a bolster. Stained boards nailed to matching orange crates made an inexpensive work station where Bill could study. Weekends were celebrated with popcorn and Kool-aid. A package of hot dogs was expected to last three meals.

"If we ran short of money, we had seven silver dollars we could use as collateral," Marge reminisces. "Bill and I won them one night when we were rich enough to go to the movies. The theatre played a game called 'WAHOO.' They'd spin a wheel and if it matched the number on your ticket, you won seven silver dollars.

"If the monthly budget came up short," she recalls, "we'd use the silver dollars as security against the next paycheck."

Realizing that quite a few students at Ohio State were also living from paycheck to paycheck and with make-do furnishings, Marge helped to enlarge the Buckeye Budget Store in Columbus. Those cleaning out households could find a market for superfluous items, and students in need could buy them at reasonable prices. Although the store was open only two days per week, Marge worked every day, taking in items and pricing them.

When they moved to Long Beach in 1983 after Bill accepted the position of Vice President and Provost at the California State University Systems Office, Marge took on a schedule that left little time free for herself. She worked full days at the Veterans' Administration Hospital in both a diabetes clinic and a cholesterol clinic. Each saw nearly thirty patients a day. She also worked as a volunteer in a program that distributed surplus government food.

The two most important days in the week, however, were the ones Marge spent delivering Meals on Wheels. Unable to be in Illinois with her mother (who by then was afflicted with Alzheimer's disease but remained in her own home thanks to the caregiving of a nearby daughter), Marge took on the care of California elderly who were in similar situations.

"We delivered sixteen to twenty meals a day to persons who were unable because of physical or mental impairments to cook for themselves. I really believe in Meals on Wheels, and I would never have missed a day doing that work. I knew how much it meant to those people when we would show up and bring them food and a bit of conversation," she recounts.

"One day I finished the last two stops on my route with a broken leg," Marge continues. "Although the song contends that 'It never rains in California,' it was raining on this particular day. The homes have tile steps, and I slipped on one, fell down three more, and landed on my right leg. It wasn't until quite a while after I got home that I was aware of enough pain to call a doctor."

Since moving to Marquette, Margery Vandament has volunteered her time at Marquette General Hospital's Hospitality House, involved herself in both a study group and University Women, and served on the advisory boards of the University Art Museum and the First Nighters Club, a support group of the theatre program. She is also on the city's board of Child and Family Services.

Marge is on the road almost every month attending NMU alumni functions. And she has been quite supportive of the accomplishments of current university students, attending events such as championship volleyball games and the performance of *Haywire* (NMU's original musical set in a U.P. lumber camp) at the Kennedy Center in Washington, D.C. In the summer of 1995, she traveled to Africa with students who were studying international business.

Africa was a study in contrasts, she notes. "I was astounded to find that Capetown was so much like Long Beach. It wasn't just the similarity in climate that took me by surprise," she says. "What really astonished me was that they had KFCs and Wimpies."

She ate ostrich and kudu. And learned first-hand the devastating effects of apartheid. "Most of the people live in thatched huts, or worse—with no water or electricity. They have no decent land which will help them become self-sufficient.

"I returned to Marquette wishing that I could do something about the greed which has caused so much poverty there. With so many people on the continent, life is often not valued." That discovery was an upset for Margery Vandament, whose deeds have been a testament to life's worth.

Husband Bill has plans to retire from the Presidency of NMU at the end of the 1997 academic year. They will return to their condominium in Long Beach, California. Marge hopes that they will also be able to have a part-time home in Binghamton, New York, where adopted grandson Austin lives. She would like to share in his care at least some of the time.

Marge met Bill when she was a ninth-grader at Quincy High School. She played the role of Calpurnia to Bill's Julius Caesar in an operetta during the school's Latin Festival. The script required them to sing to each other, and their mutual love of music formed a special bond between them.

It is likely that the Vandaments' retirement years will be just as busy as their working years. Marge is hopeful that they will allow her a bit more time to indulge in her two favorite pastimes—working crossword puzzles and reading mystery novels.

And when the last expertly-packed box is unloaded, perhaps Marge will volunteer some time to sing to Bill once again.

A Sense of Place

Contributors

Contributors

Robert "Buzz" Berube was appointed to the Northern Michigan University Board of Control in 1991 and became its chairperson in 1997. A graduate of the University of Michigan dentistry program, he has practiced in Marquette since 1975. Dr. Berube has served on the Marquette City Commission and twice been elected city mayor. He founded the Marquette Community Foundation and is a director of the First National Bank of Marquette

Marla M. Buckmaster has been a member of NMU's faculty for twenty-six years. She earned her B.A. from Western Michigan University and her M.A. and Ph.D. from Michigan State University in 1970 and 1979, respectively, where she became interested in the prehistory of the Upper Great Lakes region. The prehistory of the Menominee River Watershed was the subject of her dissertation. However, the discovery of Paleo-Indian projectile points at Deer Lake in Ishpeming, Michigan in 1987 changed the focus of her research to these first residents of Marquette County. Articles describing these finds, as well as those from another location, were published in the *Wisconsin Archeologist* in 1988 and 1989. A 1996 article in *Investigating the Archaeological Record of the Great Lakes State: Essays in Honor of Elizabeth Baldwin Garland* details the Paleo-Indians in the Upper Peninsula. Dr. Buckmaster also served as guest editor of the *Wisconsin Archeologist* in 1995; during this time the journal highlighted the prehistory of the Lake Superior region.

James L. Carter has been interested in Great Lakes area history for many years. A native of the Upper Peninsula, he has written numerous articles and several chapters in books on its history. He has been involved in publication of several books, as editor of *The Grand Island Story*, co-editor of *North to Lake Superior: The Journal of Charles W. Penney* and *American Voyager—The Journal of David Bates Douglass*, and author of *Voyageurs' Harbor* and *Superior—A State for the North Country*. He was a charter member of the Michigan Historical Preservation Review Board. He chaired the Marquette County Historical Society's John M. Longyear Research Library publications committee for many years, which published books on local and regional history. Carter holds a bachelor's degree from Aquinas College, Grand Rapids, and a master's from NMU, both in history. He has done additional graduate work at the University of Michigan. A former teacher and journalist, he recently retired from NMU where he was assistant director of Research and Development, news director, and director of the NMU Press. He continues to write and publish historical materials.

James M. Collins is a trustee emeritus of Northern Michigan University's Board of Control (1983–1991), a Judge of the 96th Judicial District, and a member of the Lake Superior Jobs Coalition.

A Sense of Place: Michigan's Upper Peninsula

Judith L. DeMark received a Masters of Arts in History from California State University at Hayward and the Ph.D. in American History from the University of New Mexico in 1984. She began teaching at Northern Michigan University in August of 1993 and is currently an Associate Professor of History. Her research interests are immigrant and family history. She served as editor of *Essays in 20th Century New Mexico* and co-editor (with Russell Magnaghi) of *World War II Memories,* a collection of student essays on Upper Peninsula veterans of World War II.

Harry Guenther is the Cohodas Chair of Banking and Finance, NMU's first endowed Chair and the Director of the NMU Bureau of Business and Economic Research. Dr. Guenther received degrees from Dartmouth College, the Amos Tuck School, and Indiana University. His primary teaching and research interests are financial institutions and markets, government regulation of business, especially financial institutions and environmental regulation, and regional economic development. He has travelled widely in the Middle East and North Africa as a consultant and continues an active interest in that region's economic and political developments. Recently completed research projects include *Opportunities for the Upper Peninsula Resulting from North American Economic Integration; A Study of the Need For and Feasibility and Purpose of An Upper Peninsula Venture Capital Firm;* and *Bank Credit Evaluation Procedures and Creating a Secondary Market for C&I Loans.*

Leonard G. Heldreth is Associate Dean of the College of Arts and Sciences and Professor and Head of the English Department at Northern Michigan University. He received his Ph.D. in 1973 from the University of Illinois, Urbana, with a dissertation on William Wordsworth. He joined the English Department at NMU in 1970 and in 1987 was appointed Acting Head of the English Department; a year later he became the Head of the Department, a position he has continued to hold, except for the 1991–92 academic year, when he was appointed Interim Dean of the College of Arts and Sciences. In 1994 he also assumed the position of Associate Dean of the College of Arts and Sciences.

He has presented over sixty papers at regional, national, and international meetings; he has also authored numerous critical articles, book chapters, book and theater reviews, and feature stories. From 1983 to 1989 he presented "Cinema Comment," a weekly film review on NMU's Public Radio station. Since 1987 he has written a film review column for the *Marquette Monthly.*

Lillian Marks Heldreth, an associate professor of English, teaches classes in English composition, mythology, popular culture, and Native American studies. She has published several articles in the areas of popular culture and the literature of the fantastic. She is a long-time Marquette resident with considerable experience in local journalism. For several years she researched, wrote, and edited *The Marquette Magazine,* published quarterly by Lake Superior Press. As her scholarly interests increased, she resigned from the editorship but has continued to write a column, "Living Farther North," for each issue of the magazine. Her contribution included here delineates a year's cycle from her essays, edited and arranged especially for the volume. The last essay in the cycle, hitherto unpublished, is chosen for its relevance to faculty life.

Earl Hilton was born in Wyoming and received degrees from the Universities of Wyoming, Wisconsin, and Minnesota. During World War II, he served as First Lieutenant, Field Artillery. He taught English at Northern Michigan University from 1950 to 1980. He also taught in a rural school and at the University of Wisconsin, Iowa State University, and Hacettepe University in Ankara.

In addition to a textbook entitled *Exposition,* co-authored with Darwin Shrell (Belmont, CA, 1967), Dr. Hilton has published essays on Twain, Anderson, Howells, Browning, Hawthorne, and the teaching of English.

Philip Legler completed an MFA at the University of Iowa and taught composition, literature, and poetry at Northern Michigan University. His poems appeared in publications ranging from *The New York Times* and *Mss* to well-known quarterlies and small literary magazines. He read on National Public Radio, and his poetry appeared in *A Change of View* (1964), *The Intruder* (1972), and *North Country Images* (1988). He co-edited with John VandeZande *Listen to Me* (1976), a collection of student writing. Following his death in 1992, the NMU English Department has awarded the annual Legler Prize for undergraduate poetry.

Michael M. Loukinen is a sociology professor and filmmaker at Northern Michigan University. His education includes a doctorate from Michigan State University (1976), National Institute for Aging Post-Doctoral Scholar, University of Michigan (1977), and a Fulbright Research Scholar, University of Turku, Finland (1982).

He produced, researched, wrote and directed four major documentary films—*Finnish American Lives* (1982), *Tradition Bearers* (1983), *Good Man in the Woods* (1987), and *Medicine Fiddle* (1992)—and has authored research articles about Finnish American migration, cultural change and identity. His documentaries have won top awards at national and international festivals at the American Film Festival, Council on International Non-Theatrical Events, Chicago International Film

Festival, Sinking Creek Film Festival, and the National Educational Film Festival.

He is completing a book focusing on cultural change across three and a half generations of Finnish Americans from a small, rural community in Baraga County in Michigan's Upper Peninsula.

Russell M. Magnaghi has been a history professor at Northern since 1969 and is the University Historian as well as Director of the Center of Upper Peninsula Studies. He has written extensively on Michigan and the Upper Peninsula.

Madonna Marsden taught English in the Chicago public schools and worked as a Head Start teacher in Minnesota before earning her doctorate from Ohio's Bowling Green State University and teaching English composition, literature, and education there for fifteen years. Since moving to Marquette, she has worked as a freelance writer and editor and contributes frequently to *Marquette Monthly*.

Michael T. Marsden is Dean of the College of Arts and Sciences and Professor of English at Northern Michigan University. The author and editor of numerous scholarly works, he co-edits the *Journal of Popular Film and Television* and also serves as Coordinator of the Northern Michigan University Press.

John F. Marshall is president and general manager of Lake Superior & Ishpeming Railroad Company, a member of numerous community action organizations in Marquette and the Co-Vice Chair of the Lake Superior Jobs Coalition.

Gayle Martinson was the University Archivist and Records Manager at Northern Michigan University from 1992 to 1996. She arrived as NMU's first professional archivist from the University of Wisconsin-Stout, where she had served in a similar capacity from 1978 to 1991. She is currently a manuscripts archivist at the State Historical Society of Wisconsin.

Eileen Roberts, an art historian in Northern Michigan University's Department of Art and Design, has been working with Native American material in the University Art Museum's permanent collection for several years. An article entitled "Compliance with Federal Law: The Losey Collection of Inuit and First Nations Art" will appear in the *1995–96 Proceedings of the Native American Studies Conference*, published by Lake Superior State University. Her endeavors have been coordinated with teaching a course on Native American Art and Architecture of the Great Lakes, which is supported by ongoing research in the field.

CONTRIBUTORS

Jon L. Saari was born in central Wisconsin in 1940 to a Finnish-American father (Montreal, Wisconsin) and a German-American mother (Wausau, Wisconsin). He grew up in a suburb outside Milwaukee and then spent ten years getting higher educated at Yale (B.A.) and Harvard (M.A., Ph.D.). Since 1971 he has been a professor of History at Northern Michigan University specializing in non-Western history, historiography, Finnish-American history, and most recently the ecological history of the Upper Peninsula. He was chair of the cultural and educational programs at FinnFest USA '96, where a version of this camp paper was first presented.

Glenn T. Seaborg, an Ishpeming native, has had a long, distinguished career in science, education, and public service. He is the only living person ever to have an element—No. 106, Seaborgium—named for him. He was co-winner of the 1951 Nobel Prize in Chemistry for his pioneering research in the chemistry of the transuranium elements, ten of which he and his colleagues discovered. He has been advisor to ten U. S. Presidents and served with distinction as the Chair of the Atomic Energy Commission and as Chancellor of the University of California at Berkeley. His continuing dedication to education is reflected in his work as chair of the Lawrence Hall of Science in Berkeley and his service on the National Commission on Excellence in Education.

Heather A. Sorensen was Processor of the John D. Voelker Papers in the Northern Michigan University Archives from 1993 to 1995. She received her undergraduate degree in history from Northern Michigan University in 1994. She is now the Records Manager at Caplan and Earnest, LLC., a law firm in Boulder, Colorado.

John VandeZande was born in Big Bay, Michigan and raised there and in Marquette. He is a graduate of Northern Michigan University and Michigan State University and taught in NMU's English department from 1964 until his retirement in 1996. In 1989 New York's Arbor House published his short story collection, *Night Driving*.

A Sense of Place: Michigan's Upper Peninsula

Production Staff

Stephen Hirst is a writer and computer specialist with NMU's Seaborg Center. A former Peace Corps Volunteer in West Africa, he has been a U. S. Government official and an editor in Washington and New York. He has written *Life in a Narrow Place* and *'Havsuw 'Baaja* about the Grand Canyon's Havasupai Tribe, with whom he and his wife worked for many years.

Sue Ann Salo has been the Secretarial Assistant to the Northern Michigan University Press since its revival in 1994 and handles all correspondence for the Press and maintains deadlines for publication, publicity of publications and budgets. Also Secretary to the Dean of Arts and Sciences, she has worked at NMU since 1985.

Melinda Stamp is a graphic designer who has worked for Northern Michigan University and Public TV 13 since 1987. She has participated in the design of many university publications and was instrumental in developing NMU's graphic identity. Melinda is a problem solver and a jack of all trades artist. She enjoys the challenge and variety of working in both academic and broadcast environments.

Karen Wallingford received her bachelor's degree in English from Colorado State University in 1992. She is currently a teaching assistant at Northern Michigan University, where she is working on her master's degree in English.

William and Margery Vandament, recipients of Doctor Honoris Causa at Northern Michigan University's 1997 Commencement

A Sense of Place: Michigan's Upper Peninsula

☙

The text is set in Bembo, modeled on typefaces cut by Francesco Griffo for Aldus Manutius's printing of *De Ætna* in 1495 in Venice, a book by classicist Pietro Bembo about his visit to Mount Etna. Griffo's design is considered one of the first of the old style typefaces that were used as staple text types in Europe for two hundred years. Stanley Morison supervised the design of Bembo for the Monotype Corporation in 1929 and modeled the italic on the handwriting of the Renaissance scribe Giovanni Tagliente.

Cover Melinda Stamp
Layout and Design Stephen Hirst
Editorial Assistance Karen Wallingford
Madonna Marsden
Production Sue Ann Salo

Printed and bound by BookCrafters
Chelsea, Michigan

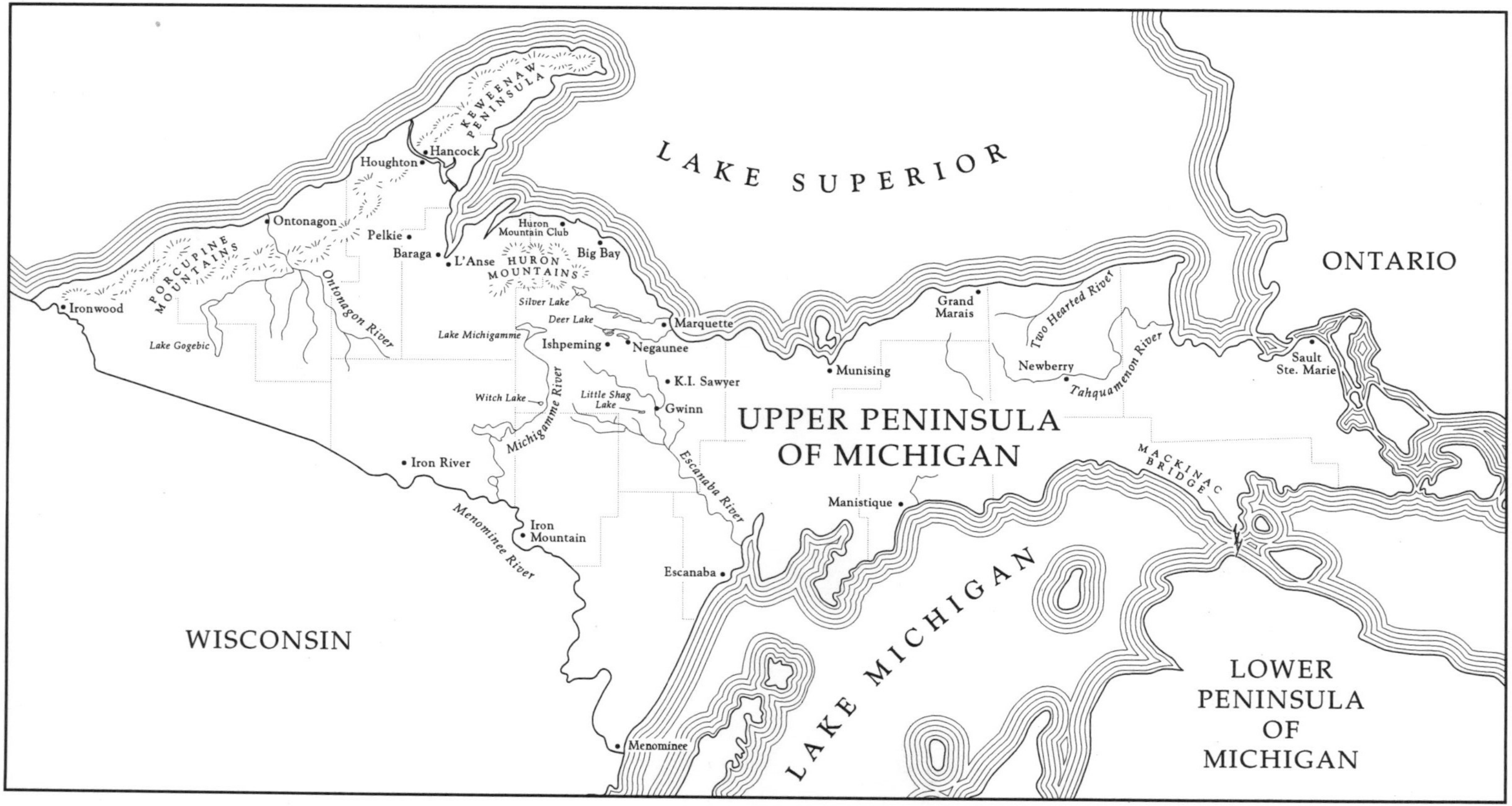
LAKE SUPERIOR
ONTARIO
KEWEENAW PENINSULA
Hancock
Houghton
Ontonagon
Pelkie
Baraga
L'Anse
Huron Mountain Club
HURON MOUNTAINS
Big Bay
PORCUPINE MOUNTAINS
Ironwood
Lake Gogebic
Ontonagon River
Silver Lake
Deer Lake
Lake Michigamme
Ishpeming
Negaunee
Marquette
K.I. Sawyer
Witch Lake
Little Shag Lake
Gwinn
Michigamme River
Munising
Grand Marais
Two Hearted River
Newberry
Tahquamenon River
Sault Ste. Marie
UPPER PENINSULA OF MICHIGAN
MACKINAC BRIDGE
Iron River
Escanaba River
Manistique
Iron Mountain
Menominee River
Escanaba
WISCONSIN
LAKE MICHIGAN
LOWER PENINSULA OF MICHIGAN
Menominee